ANATOMY OF THE AMAZON GOLD RUSH

Anatomy of the Amazon Gold Rush

David Cleary

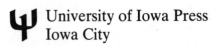 University of Iowa Press
Iowa City

Aos companheiros do garimpo, e à memória de Chico Mendes

Contents

List of Plates

List of Maps

List of Figures

List of Tables

Acknowledgements

My first thanks should go to Peter Riviere, of the Institute of Social Anthropology, Oxford University, who guided this project wisely from the beginning, and Alan Angell and Verena Stolcke, who made many useful suggestions on how to transform a thesis into a readable book. Research was financed by the Economic and Social Research Council in London from 1983 to 1986: I also received financial help from the Royal Anthropological Institute, in the form of a Radcliffe-Brown Memorial Award, and from my mother, Mrs Shan Duff-Smith, to whom I am more than grateful.

I could not have written this book without the friendship and help of many people in both Brazil and Britain. The Rector of the Universidade Federal do Maranhão, Professor José Maria Cabral, generously allowed me affiliation to the Departamento de Sociologia e Antropologia of the Universidade, which enabled me to stay for so long in Brazil. In São Luis I owe a great deal to Darrel Posey, Dan Linger, Lynn Simons, Sergio and Mundicarmo Ferretti and Carlos Augusto Ramos. I would also like to thank Deputado Gastão Dias Vieira, Deputado José Carlos Saboia, and Pedro Braga. In Belém, the Departamento Nacional de Produção Mineral, DOCEGEO and the Companhia do Vale do Rio Doce generously allowed me unrestricted access to their archives and technical personnel. I thank Luis Bandeira of DOCEGEO, Alberto Rogério da Silva, José Leal, Carlos Santos Neto, Otávio Blanco Rodrigues and Agildo Pina Neves, all of the DNPM, Davi Leal of the CVRD and Deputado Gabriel Guerreiro. In Brasilia: Jorge Carvalho, Rita Seguro, Alcida Ramos, Julio Melatti and Deputado Ademir Andrade. The Instituto Brasileiro da Mineração was generous with its records and patient in explaining its position. Marianne Schmink in Gainesville kindly shared her own work on the gold rush with me. In Oxford writing was made easier by the support of Melissa Parker, Charlie Davison, Steve Vertovec, Circe Monteiro, Anna Fernandez, Mary Vincent, Helen Lambert and Tom Cheesman.

Finally, I thank above all the villagers of 'Geraldo' and the garimpeiros of Cerqueiro, Nadi, Montes Aureos, Cedral, Trinta Cinco and Pica-Pau. I could not have begun to write this book without the help, interest and friendship of Santos Neto, Escuro, Antônio Garimpeiro, Paraíba, José Benedito, Chichico, Esídio, Edson, Geraldo Maciel, Pernambuco, Tarpona, Antônio Mineiro,

João da Mata and Zequinha. I dedicate it to them, and to the memory of Chico Mendes, assassinated 22 December 1988: *companheiros de verdade*.

DAVID CLEARY

A Glossary of the Gold Rush

Alvará de pesquisa	Mining permit
Azougue	Mercury
Balsa	Type of gold mining using chupadeira (see below) mounted on raft and a diver
Bamburrado	Someone who has struck it rich
Bamburro	A rich gold strike
Barranco	Digging, area of gold extraction, usually measuring 5 by 5 or 10 by 10 metres
Bateia	Gold pan
Blefado	Bankrupt
Blefar	To go bankrupt
Caixa	Narrow wooden sluice lined with blankets or sacking: essential part of all mining machinery used in garimpos
Caixão	Large caixa used with chupadeira (see below)
Cantina	Small store in garimpos
Cantineiro	Owner of cantina, trader and supplier
Chupadeira	Form of gold mining using motorised suction pumps, high pressure hoses and caixão
Cobra fumando	Simple wooden machine used for alluvium
Código de Mineração	Legal code governing Brazilian mining
Cuia	Small bowl, gold pan
Curimã	Material which has already been put through machinery at least once
Dalla	A series of sluices. Common in Tapajós garimpos, used in nineteenth-century gold rushes.
Desbravador	Pioneer prospector
Despescagem	Cleaning out of machinery and collection of gold
Diária	Work regime paying daily salary
Diarista	Garimpeiro working on diária
Dono	Owner of barranco and/or machinery
Fofoca	Literally 'rumour, gossip'. Initial phase of formation of garimpo, excitement provoked by gold strike.

Lontona	Type of sluice, dating from last century, especially common in Tapajós
Manso	Experienced garimpeiro
Meia-praça	Work regime where profit shared between dono and work crew
Meieiro	Garimpeiro working under meia-praça
Mergulhador	Diver on a balsa (see above)
Moínho	Small mechanical crusher
Ouro	Gold
Peão	Worker (can be derogatory)
Pepita	Nugget
Pesquisa	Prospecting
Porcentagem	Work regime where gold divided between dono and workers on a percentage basis
Porcentista	Worker under porcentagem
Rádio peão	Informal information networks in garimpos
Rebaixamento	Deepening of a barranco
Repassagem	The practice of passing material through machinery several times
Reque	Bonus payment (see Chapter 5)
Sacudia	Simple wooden machine; precursor of cobra fumando
Sociedade	Formal partnership in gold mining operation
Sócio	Somebody who enters into a 'sociedade'
Xeique-xeique	English: 'shake-shake' (Guyana): sacudia

Acronym Glossary

CEF	Caixa Econômica Federal. Federal savings bank in charge of state gold buying programme.
COLONE	Companhia da Colonização do Nordeste. Land colonisation company funded by World Bank and Brazilian government to regularise land occupation in western Maranhão.
CPRM	Companhia de Pesquisa de Recursos Minerais. State-owned prospecting and mining research company.
CVRD	Companhia do Vale do Rio Doce. Largest Brazilian mining company, federal government majority shareholder.
DNPM	Departamento Nacional de Produção Mineral. Federal agency supervising mining in Brazil.
DOCEGEO	Rio Doce Prospeção e Geologia. Prospecting subsidiary of CVRD.
IBRAM	Instituto Brasileiro da Mineração. Association of Brazilian formal sector mining companies.
MME	Ministério das Minas e Energia. Federal Ministry of Mines and Energy.
PDS	Partido Democrático Social. Governing party of military regime in power in Brazil from 1964 coup to 1985.
PEGB	Projeto de Estudo dos Garimpos Brasileiros. Research programme on garimpagem run by DNPM, CPRM and MME.
PMDB	Partido do Movimento Democrático Brasileiro. Main party opposing PDS from 1964 to 1985.
SNI	Serviço Nacional das Informações. Powerful military intelligence organisation used to oversee federal intervention in Serra Pelada.

Introduction

The research on which this book is based was carried out over almost two years in Brazil from April 1984 to March 1986. I did not originally intend to work on the Amazon gold rush. I arrived in Brazil with a research proposal about rural-urban migration in the state of Maranhão, in eastern Amazonia, and I had selected the city of Imperatriz in the south of the state as a likely place to do fieldwork. I knew from background research in Britain that Imperatriz was near to one of the largest goldfields, but as I had never been to Brazil I did not realise quite how important this fact was. When I arrived in Imperatriz the scale and the importance of the gold rush came as a revelation, and I decided I should not be bound by research proposals that had been formulated without direct knowledge of eastern Amazonia. I began to think that I should do research on the gold rush taking place around me instead, and confirmed this decision after casting around and realising that surprisingly little had been written about *garimpagem*, informal sector gold mining by social scientists.

The first stage of fieldwork was four months spent in the capital of Maranhão, São Luís, doing archive research on the history of gold mining in the state and improving my command of Portuguese to the point where I could start to do ethnography. From September 1984 three months were spent in the city of Belém interviewing politicians, staff of the state mineral agencies and companies and working in their archives. Two visits, one lasting five days and the other two weeks, were made to the city of Marabá during this time. Marabá, in southern Pará state, is the jumping off point for what was then the large and thriving mining camp of Serra Pelada, where I hoped to do fieldwork. Unfortunately, this proved impossible. Serra Pelada was at that time under the control of the federal government, and I was unfortunate enough to be trying to go there at a time when the bureaucratic situation was more than usually chaotic. After twice having to begin the process of application again after the body in charge of the mining camp changed, I gave up.

Fortunately, in January 1985 I got lucky. In São Luís I met a friend of a friend who had worked in a mining camp called Cerqueiro, part of the Gurupí goldfield in western Maranhão. For a fee, he agreed to take me there and introduce me to his colleagues. It was thus purely by chance that I ended up doing fieldwork in the Gurupí rather than anywhere else. I went there for five weeks in February, and paid two further visits from May to July and September to December, spending a total of five months, and it was during these visits that most of the ethnographic material presented in this book was collected. The second and third visits were unaccompanied.

I had been prepared for a certain amount of suspicion and hostility on the part of the *garimpeiros*, the gold miners. They are not warmly regarded by either the Brazilian government or mining companies, and initially at least there were rumours that I was a spy in the pay of one or the other. I took the view that there was no point in worrying about this, and that the only thing I could do was hope that over time my actions would bear out my explanations of who I was. These explanations varied according to the audience. Some garimpeiros with a middle class background knew what anthropologists are and what they do. To others for whom it would have been meaningless to introduce myself as a social researcher, I said that people outside the mining areas have strange ideas about what garimpeiros are like, and I was collecting material for a book which would explain things better. I felt this was one way of explaining myself in terms which did not patronise or distort. Although a few people were never convinced, the vast majority of garimpeiros with whom I came into contact accepted these explanations, and although I was always seen as eccentric I think I was only rarely perceived as an enemy.

Over time, as I had hoped, the initial barriers of suspicion fell away. I did what I could to hasten the process by bringing small gifts when I returned, giving people copies of photographs I had taken of them, and handing out postcards of Britain to satisfy people's constant curiosity about where I came from and what life was like there: many times I felt it was they who were doing anthropology on me rather than the other way around.

When I was in Cerqueiro I lived with a *dono*, a small entrepreneur, who became a close friend, and a succession of work crews. There were at least six *garimpos*, or mining camps, within a few hours walk from Cerqueiro, and at one time or another I visited them all, usually only for a few hours or a day with the exception of Montes Aureos, where I spent a total of two weeks. Everywhere I went people already knew who I was and what I said I was doing – a testimony to the ubiquity and importance of 'rádio peão', the information networks of the gold rush – and were remarkably generous and hospitable towards me. In Montes Aureos I had to shift my hammock every couple of days to satisfy the insistent offers of accommodation. I learnt to keep a low profile at meal times, because if I did not I had to eat several times over, frightened of giving offence by refusing. Many times I refused offers of small amounts of gold, explaining that I could not take them out of the country, but I was given (and accepted) several gold-veined stones 'to show the people in England'. Garimpeiros have a fearsome reputation in Brazil, and in the international media are often portrayed as desperadoes. All I can say is that the vast majority of garimpeiros I met showed me nothing but kindness, and I was often moved by their concern for my welfare.

From the ethnographic point of view, I found the gold camps an ideal research environment. The very fact that I was a foreigner, and perceived as a very strange kind of foreigner at that, worked in my favour. If nothing else, I was at least a welcome diversion from the routine of hard work that dominated daily life. I felt many garimpeiros were surprised and pleased to find a non-garimpeiro who took a genuine interest in their work and what they thought about it, and enjoyed talking and arguing with me. I found that people positively welcomed the taping of conversations, and derived great amusement from listening to their own voice when they played it back. I was also able to travel to São Luís with garimpeiro friends, and spend time with them during their breaks from gold mining.

To gather information I relied primarily on note taking, and the tape recording and transcribing of conversations and more structured interviews. In the Gurupí I recorded thirty-six C-60 tapes, and fourteen further tapes were recorded in interviews in Belém, Marabá, São Luís and Brasília with politicians, geologists, administrators, lobbyists and entrepreneurs. Field notes filled five large exercise books, and I also kept a diary when in gold camps. I applied a questionnaire to a hundred garimpeiros in the Gurupí.

Participant observation in the literal sense was minimal. I was not physically strong enough to work as most garimpeiros do, although I did learn to use a *bateia*, a gold pan, after a fashion. Apart from that, my sole direct contribution to any mining operation was twice working shovelling alluvium into a mechanical crusher. It was not simply a question of being physically incapable of working as garimpeiros do. I also felt that my position depended on not participating in gold mining myself. Had I worked more than very occasionally when one particular friend needed help, I would have lost the neutrality which made people feel they could talk to me frankly. I should also make it plain that all my informants were men. The garimpo is a largely masculine environment, but not exclusively so. Because of my position as a single male, and the machismo that is so much a part of male social life in Brazil, I did not feel that I could spend significant time talking to women in gold camps without giving rise to gossip and speculation.

The periods in between my visits to the garimpos were spent partly in Brasília and partly in São Luís, transcribing tapes, interviewing, and doing further archive research. I made one further visit of two weeks to Marabá and Imperatriz in August 1985 and returned to Britain in March 1986. In January 1988, after completing the thesis on which this book is based, I returned to Belém for a week, and was able to update much material in conversations with geologists and administrators I first met in 1984. I was also able to return to Cerqueiro, where my pleasure at seeing old friends once again was tempered with sadness, as I learnt of the deaths of two garimpeiro friends who had helped me during the first visits I made. I had thought I would stay only a few days, but should have known better than to try and make a fleeting visit. I fell ill and had to stay a couple of weeks, too weak for most of the time to leave my hammock, and during my convalescence old friends spent hours bringing me up to date on the many changes that had taken place in the two years I had been away, which threw valuable new light on the material collected in 1985.

I decided at an early stage that I did not want to write a community or even an area study about gold mining in a particular region, but to produce a book that dealt with the gold rush generally throughout the whole of the Brazilian Amazon. This was for three reasons. Firstly, it seemed to me that gold mining, while being extremely diverse, did have a common structure underlying its regional variations, and this had to be central to a book that purports to be about the Amazon gold rush. Secondly, there is no published source which deals at this level of analysis with gold mining in Amazonia, and therefore I felt there was a gap in the literature which I could reasonably hope to fill. Finally, although the ethnography on which much of the book is based was done in the Gurupí, and to a lesser extent in southern Pará, the information I gathered came from the experience of garimpeiros in all the areas of gold mining in the Brazilian Amazon. Many garimpeiros made sense of the Gurupí by comparing it with other goldfields they knew. I was operating under time and budgetary constraints which meant that I could never hope to visit the areas they talked about, like the Tapajós in Pará or the river Madeira in Rondônia, but in time I built up a fairly detailed knowledge of the gold rush in areas like these simply by repeatedly talking to garimpeiros who had worked there. I could cross check and follow up information with different garimpeiros to the point where I felt confident I could make useful points even about goldfields I never had the chance to visit.

The structure of this book reflects this concern with the wider picture. I have not restricted it to the Gurupí but tried to give some idea of the diversity of the gold rush by including facts and reminiscences from as many areas as I could, thus putting the Gurupí material into a wider context. I specifically use the contrast between the Gurupí and southern Pará, where I also did fieldwork, to show how gold mining varies from area to area and emphasise both the parallels and differences between regions of Amazonia. I have also been concerned to show that the history of gold extraction in Amazonia begins long before 1979, and make the point that the present gold rush can only be fully appreciated if one has a sense of historical perspective.

The book begins with an attempt to estimate the scale of gold garimpagem, and a description of the huge scale of the contemporary Amazon gold rush. This is followed by a survey of the technology used in gold camps, because the social organisation of gold extraction is incomprehensible without a knowledge of how gold is worked. The second chapter takes the Gurupí as an example of the long tradition of garimpagem in Amazonia, tracing its origins back to communities of escaped slaves in the early nineteenth century and following it through to the present day. It also serves as background material to the four chapters that follow based mainly on ethnography in Gurupí garimpos.

These deal successively with the formation of mining camps, their social and economic structure, and social relations within them. They show the great social diversity characteristic of the gold rush, with different types of garimpeiros being drawn from different strata of Brazilian society, and stress the importance of garimpagem to rural smallholders and the underemployed in urban areas. For them, and also for small and medium scale entrepreneurs, gold mining has become an attractive option that can easily be combined with other activities.

The final three chapters deal at length with the wider context of the Amazon gold rush, looking at the relationship between garimpagem, the Brazilian state, and mining companies. Chapter 7 examines the history of Serra Pelada, where the federal authorities intervened directly in a mining camp for the first time during the modern period. Chapter 8 looks more generally at the relationship between the formal and the informal mining sectors in Brazil, and the history of relations between garimpagem and the Brazilian state. Throughout this book a terminological distinction is made between garimpagem and 'the formal mining sector'. One could equally well call the formal mining sector 'capitalist mining', but it was felt that having to call garimpagem 'non-capitalist mining' would be too vague. The distinction between a formal and an informal mining sector seemed more accurate and useful. Finally, Chapter 9 is a general survey of the consequences and implications of the gold rush, which are seen as more positive than is generally assumed, despite misgivings and reservations about its implications for the environment and Indian land rights.

Some points should be made in conclusion. Firstly, I have not been consistent in giving the names of informants or placenames. After interviews, many people specifically said that they would like their real names mentioned, and where it was possible I have acceded to their wishes. In other cases, for reasons that will be obvious in context, I have changed names. Placenames pose a particular problem. In the part of the Gurupí where I worked, as elsewhere in Amazonia, people often give their names to places – garimpos, for example, are regularly called after prospectors who first found gold at the spot. Since much of my material about conflicts and rivalries involves people who gave their names to places, I have changed some placenames to protect their anonymity. As these fictitious placenames are mixed together with real ones, it would not be difficult to find them out. I therefore ask that convention is observed and that the fragile mask covering identities be left in place. All translations from interview transcripts and sources in Portuguese are my own. Words in Portuguese that are used in the text – of which there are many, given the impossibility of translating much of the technical vocabulary of garimpagem into English – are italicised on their first appearance only.

In conclusion, I think it important to make clear the limitations of this book. I am very conscious that it is not a comprehensive and detailed guide to the gold rush throughout the Brazilian Amazon. In many areas I have consciously sacrificed depth for breadth: my reasons for doing so are given above. This book only deals with garimpagem of gold, and takes no account of garimpagem of cassiterite, diamonds and other precious stones, rock crystal, wolfamite and sheelite, all of which are different.

I have made an effort to put garimpagem in the context of other extractive activities in Amazonia, like rubber and the Brazil nut trade, and also tried to show the connections between the gold rush and smallholder agriculture, the urban informal economy, entrepreneurs of various kinds, elite groups, mining companies and the Brazilian state. Several theses could be written on each of these topics without exhausting their research potential, and any treatment that attempts to deal with all of them simultaneously can only be general. I have tried to make sure that generality never slips over into superficiality, but some topics are not as thoroughly covered as I would have liked.

To me, writing about the gold rush has been both rewarding and frustrating. I found it to be a rich and diverse topic, but that very diversity forced harsh decisions about what to put in and what to leave out, what to develop at length and what to merely mention in passing. When I say that now, having spent four years researching and writing this book, it seems to me no more than a fairly detailed introduction to the Amazon gold rush, it is not false modesty. It is simply that I know very well how much I have left out, how few places I have been, and how much there is left for others to say.

Map 1   Principal goldfields in the Brazilian Amazon

❶ GURUPÍ, MARANHÃO   ❺ TAPAJÓS, PARÁ/AMAZONAS
❷ SERRA PELADA, PARÁ   ❻ RIVER MADEIRA, RONDÔNIA
❸ CUMARÚ, PARÁ   ❼ RORAIMA
❹ MATO GROSSO   ❽ AMAPÁ

Map 2   Gurupí goldfield, western Maranhão

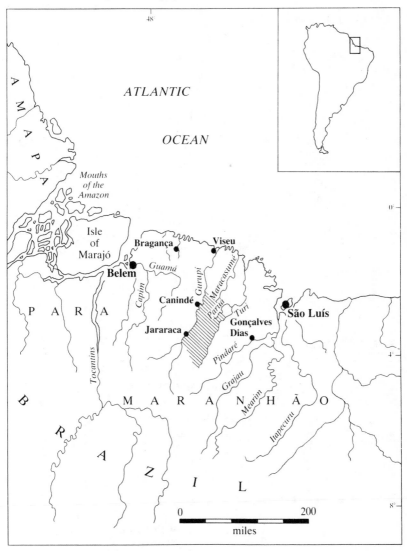

Map 3   Serra Pelada and southern Pará

1 An Introduction to the Amazon Gold Rush

This book is about what in Portuguese is called *garimpagem*. There is no exact English translation; it is best defined as small scale informal sector mining. In Brazil miners of this type are called *garimpeiros*: their diggings and the communities which form around them are known as *garimpos*. Garimpagem has traditionally been associated first and foremost with gold extraction, in Brazil and elsewhere. Brazil has a particularly rich tradition of gold mining: eighteenth-century gold rushes in Minas Gerais and Mato Grosso transformed the Brazilian interior during colonial times, and it was partly the search for gold which drove the frontiers of Brazil so deep into the South American land mass. This book is devoted to a contemporary heir to that long tradition of prospecting and mining in Brazil.

In 1979, for reasons which are still debated, the price of gold on the international market soared. World gold prices had in fact been steadily increasing since the early 1970s, but the price explosion that began in 1979 was unprecedented. In early 1980 gold reached a record peak of $850 per troy ounce, and though the price has fallen back and fluctuated violently since then, it has remained at what in historical terms is an extremely high level. This surge in prices on the London Metal Exchange touched off a gold rush in Amazonia that has affected Ecuador, Peru, Colombia, Guyana, Venezuela, Bolivia and French Guiana as well as Brazil, but it is only in Brazil that the rush has reached a level comparable to the great gold rushes of the last century. It shows no sign of abating: indeed, there is evidence that in Brazil the volume of gold production in garimpos has picked up during the 1980s, despite the falling back of the gold price from its 1980 peak. This book is an anatomy of that gold rush.

In order to grasp the social and economic implications of the post-1979 gold rush in Amazonia, one needs an idea of its scale. Unfortunately, garimpagem is an activity that could have been designed to make the statistician's task impossible, and all figures of the number of garimpeiros in Amazonia and the amount of gold that they mine are no more than rough estimates, and in many cases mere guesses. It is not difficult to see why. Most garimpos are rarely, if at all, visited by the technicians of the Departamento Nacional da Produção Mineral

1

(DNPM), the Brazilian state body charged with the regulation of mining, and only a fraction of all gold mined is sold to the state. Even if a thorough census of all garimpos in Amazonia were carried out, the figures would still be unreliable. The population of garimpos fluctuates considerably, as garimpeiros move to other regions of garimpagem or return to city and countryside as rainfall changes, the agricultural calendar shifts, and the urban economy waxes and wanes. Similar difficulties attend attempts to put a figure on the amount of gold – or other minerals – that garimpeiros produce. Even in the areas of federal intervention where selling gold to the state is compulsory, the DNPM estimates that at least a fifth of gold produced is smuggled out. Private gold buyers often do not record the gold they buy, in order to avoid tax, and much gold is illegally shipped out of the country. Every so often – from September 1982 to September 1983 for example – the Brazilian government mounts a gold buying drive. When the state price is competitive and an effort is made to buy gold in garimpos themselves rather than the nearest town, the much greater amount of gold sold to the state gives some idea of the scale of buying and selling that goes on invisibly at other times, in an enormous informal economy that cannot be quantified with any great degree of accuracy.

Nevertheless, we can say what units should be used to describe the scale of garimpagem in contemporary Amazonia. The number of garimpeiros in garimpos at any one time runs into the hundreds of thousands, and they produce scores of tons of gold worth, in the late 1980s, over a billion dollars annually. The DNPM estimated that in 1986 Brazil produced 89.4 tons of gold, over 90 per cent of which came from garimpos.[1] At August 1987 prices, that was worth about 1.1 billion dollars. From September 1982 to September 1983, when the gold price was higher, the federal savings bank running the state gold buying programme spent 1.9 billion dollars buying gold from garimpeiros. In 1988 DNPM geologists at the Belém residency, who have more regular and intensive contact with garimpos and garimpeiros than any other formal sector mining professionals, estimated 1987 garimpo production at around 120 metric tons of gold. If these figures are even approximately correct, they put Brazil in third place among world gold producers, above traditional gold exporting countries like Canada, Australia and the United States. It may well be the case that only South Africa and the Soviet Union mine more gold than the Brazilian garimpeiro.

Historically, this level of production matches and even surpasses the great nineteenth-century gold rushes. California from 1848 to 1856 produced an average of 80 tons of gold annually, while the Klondyke produced a total of 42 tons between 1896 and 1900. Only the South African gold rush, which averaged more than 100 tons annually, out-produced the contemporary gold rush in the Brazilian Amazon.[2] Despite being essentially an informal economic system, gold garimpagem in Amazonia is currently a billion dollar business.

Table 1.1 sets out official gold production figures, together with DNPM estimates when available, from 1975 to 1987. It repays close examination. The large disparity between the official figures and the more informed DNPM estimates only lessens in 1980, as a direct result of federal intervention in the large garimpo of Serra Pelada and the setting up of state gold buying posts inside the garimpo itself. The fact that a single garimpo, even one as rich as Serra Pelada, was able to more than triple the official production figure within the space of a year suggests that the pre-1980 figures are almost worthless, well under half of real gold production levels. The huge rise in official production from 1982 to 1983, which was due to a state buying offensive, makes the official 1982 figure look like a serious underestimate. The fact that in 1984 Uruguay, which is not a gold producing country, exported 29.4 tons of gold, most of which must have come from the Brazilian Amazon via Sao Paulo, suggests that the real 1984 figure was over 50 tons, while the figure of 24.1 tons in 1986 is a gross underestimate, as the DNPM figure makes clear.

There are other indications that the volume of production has been picking up during the 1980s: the large rise in the number of airstrip garimpos in the Tapajós goldfield in central Pará state, for example, noted in many official sources,[4] and the rapid increase in the amount of gold sold to the state in the Cumarú goldfield since 1981. The only areas of garimpagem for which even approximate figures of gold production exist are Serra Pelada, Cumarú, and to a lesser extent the Tapajós. These are given in Table 1.2, with the caveat that while they may be useful for ranking these three areas of gold production relative to each other, the actual figures are conceded by the DNPM to underestimate production by over half in the case of the Tapajós and between a quarter and a fifth for Serra Pelada and Cumarú.

The estimates for the number of gold garimpeiros are even more tenuous. For gold production figures the DNPM does at least have the amount of gold sold to the state and the figures of the largest gold buyers in Itaituba and Santarém, where most of the gold produced in the Amazon's largest goldfield is sold. For population estimates the only basis are rough estimates sent in by the DNPM posts in the most

Table 1.1 Official gold production figures and DNPM estimates of real gold production figures, Brazil 1975–87 (metric tons)

| | Official production | | DNPM estimates | |
	Total	Garimpo output	Total	% from garimpos
1975	5.1	–	12.5	65.5
1976	4.7	–	13.6	69.2
1977	5.1	–	15.9	76.3
1978	8.6	–	22.0	81.8
1979	4.3	–	25.0	86.7
1980	13.8	–	35.0	88.0
1981	17.3	12.9	35.0	–
1982	25.5	20.9	34.8	–
1983	55.0	47.5	–	–
1984	39.0	32.0	61.5	–
1985	30.5	23.0	72.3	–
1986	24.1	–	89.4	–
1987	83.8*	–	120**	–

Sources: 1975–80 Guimaraes *et al* (1982); 1981–82 Anuario Mineral MME-DNPM (1983); 1983–86 Anuario Mineral MME-DNPM (1987); 1987
 * Gold 1988 – Consolidated Gold Fields PLC
** Personal communication, DNPM geologists, Belém, January 1988

Table 1.2 Official figures for gold production in Serra Pelada, Tapajós and Cumarú garimpos, 1980–6 (metric tons)

	Tapajós	Cumarú	Serra Pelada
1980	3.4	–	6.836
1981	6.251	1.7	2.591
1982	8.648	1.9	6.82
1983	10.53	6.38	13.946
1984	–	–	4.48
1985	–	–	–
1986	–	9.5	3.5

Sources: DNPM–PEGB–CPRM 1980b–1984b (Serra Pelada); DNPM-PEGB-CPRM 1980c–1983c (Tapajos); DNPM–PEGB–CPRM 1982d–1983d (Cumarú); Anuario Mineral MME-DNPM (1987)

important areas of garimpagem – which means that smaller goldfields like the Gurupí, Amapá and Roraima are usually not included. The figures that result are really no more than guesses. For what they are worth, the Fundação de Assistência Aos Garimpeiros, a now defunct mining agency, put the total number of all types of garimpeiro in the early 1970s at between 200 000 and 284 000,[5] the DNPM estimated about 200 000 gold garimpeiros alone in 1980,[6] and Guimarães, Guimarães and Brandão put the number of gold garimpeiros at precisely 148 200 in 1982.[7] The FAG figures seem very high, as gold garimpagem was only beginning to recover from the postwar trough in the early 1970s, but the other estimates seem a little low.

This can be inferred from a variety of sources. The interesting thing about the levels of gold production discussed above is that they do not follow movements in the world market price of gold during the 1980s. The gold price reached a high point in early 1980, but quickly fell back and since then has fluctuated a great deal, well below the $850 per troy ounce it had touched at its peak. Gold production in Brazil, on the other hand, has since 1979 apparently increased steadily. This cannot be explained by increasing technological sophistication: modern garimpo technology was already well established by 1981, and has not changed significantly since. Moreover, the really big gold strikes are now several years old: Serra Pelada in 1979, Cumarú in 1980. Given these two factors, the implication is that this increasing volume of production must be due to an increasing number of people in garimpos. My own impression would be no less of a guesstimate than the figures cited above, but I think it likely that the number of gold garimpeiros in Amazonia fluctuates around the 300 000 mark. This figure includes only garimpeiros in garimpos at any one time: as we shall see, many more people depend wholly or in part on the gold rush for their living than are directly engaged in mining gold.

Imperfect though any statistical discussion of garimpagem is bound to be, one point remains clear: the sheer scale of the gold rush, even when lower estimates are used. The explosion of gold garimpagem in the Brazilian Amazon since 1979 has been by some way the greatest extractive boom Amazonia has seen since the heyday of the rubber boom. On the available figures, contemporary Amazonia far out-shines the Klondyke and stands comparison with California. The gold rush has changed the relationship between the formal and the informal economy within Amazonia as a whole, not just within the mining sector. It has had significant knock-on effects on smallholder agri-culture and the urban economy throughout the region. In many parts of Amazonia it has transformed the social, economic and political landscapes just as surely as it has the look of the lands it has touched.

THE TECHNOLOGY OF THE GOLD RUSH

The social organisation of garimpagem has always depended to a large degree on the technology used to extract gold. Although the Amazon jungle may appear monotonously uniform to the outsider, to the garimpeiro it is a collection of micro-environments from which gold can be extracted, each one presenting characteristic technical problems and solutions. The different production methods used on various types of gold deposits underpin the mosaic of social relations in the garimpo, and are where any analysis of the gold rush has to begin. The technology used in the garimpo often bears little relation to the complex and capital-intensive methods employed to mine large mineral deposits by state and private companies in Amazonia, but from the date that mineral extraction in Amazonia began down to the present far more gold has been discovered and mined by garimpeiros than by geologists and mining companies. Since 1979 this trend has if anything intensified.

It is possible to reconstruct from a variety of sources the way in which technology in the garimpo has evolved since the eighteenth century. There was never a hard barrier between garimpagem and formal sector mining: technological advances in the formal sector were and are often adapted for use in the garimpo. There are now increasing signs that garimpagem is contributing to change in methods in the formal mining sector in Amazonia. The more open-minded personnel of private companies and the state mineral bodies, suddenly thrown into intensive contact with garimpeiros since 1979, are acknowledging that there are advantages to be gained from seeing garimpagem as an alternative technical mining model, deeply rooted in Amazonia and with a respectable prospecting and production record as regards gold. But before exploring the details of this process, a little more formal geology is necessary.

Gold deposits fall into two main types that geologists call primary and secondary deposits. A primary deposit, also known as a lode or a colluvial deposit, is gold embedded in rock, usually quartzite. Over time these rocks erode and gold may be washed away and deposited along water courses: these are secondary deposits, also called alluvial deposits, or placers. As water courses shift and new geological features emerge, what was once alluvial gold can end up deep underground covered by more recent geological formations. There is no reliable way that the presence or absence of any other mineral can be used as an indicator of gold. The normal method of prospecting in the formal mining sector is to locate a promising area through a combination of geological precedent and the collection of samples, and then to proceed to core sampling, where drills are sunk to various depths and sections of the shaft are brought up for analysis, building up a cross-sectional map of the subsoil. Prospecting in garimpagem is much simpler, and, it can be argued, more effective.

Of all aspects of garimpagem, prospecting has changed the least in terms of technology used, the basic instruments, the *bateia* or gold pan, remaining essentially unchanged from the eighteenth century on, the only difference being that previously it was made of hard wood, and is now made from zinc. The bateia is a conical pan tapering to a point in the centre, with a radius of about forty centimetres and a diameter of around a metre. There is also a smaller pan called a *cuia*; it is nothing more than a round bowl that can be used just as well for eating as for prospecting (see Plate 1). Both rely on the fact that gold is a very heavy metal. Material in which gold is thought to be present is simply scooped into the bateia or cuia, water is added and the mixture stirred up a little. It is then rotated clockwise and anti-clockwise in rapid succession. Lighter material gravitates towards the rim of the bateia, where it is periodically washed away, while heavier material, including gold, moves towards the centre (see Plate 2). When the concentrate is thought to be sufficient, drops of water are gently added with the finger while the bateia is held at an angle, to wash away any heavier impurities that may have found their way to the centre. Once this is done, any gold can easily be seen glinting against the dark metallic background. The whole process takes between five and ten minutes, depending on how much care is taken.

If one had to choose a single instrument to symbolise garimpagem it would be the bateia; it is the most basic part of the serious garimpeiro's kit and is used many times daily. Its use is the first skill which newcomers to the garimpo must learn. It requires more dexterity to use properly than appears at first sight. Many garimpeiros will say that learning how to use a bateia takes only a few days, and it is true that the basic technique does not take long to master. But learning how to pan properly takes several months rather than days. The real skill comes when using the bateia in an area of fine grained gold. Fine grains present a problem because micro-bubbles attach themselves to the gold particles and keep them floating on the surface of the water used in the bateia. This water is almost always muddy, the particles are small and difficult to see, and the inexperienced can often flush gold away. It is possible to gauge how experienced garimpeiros are by seeing how skillfully they use the bateia. The cuia, being smaller, requires even more skill and dexterity, and only experienced garimpeiros use it. The advantage the cuia has over the bateia is its smallness; slung on the back, the bateia can be a hindrance in forest, becoming entangled with creepers and branches.

The bateia is also the most versatile instrument the garimpeiro uses. It is the basic prospecting instrument, but has many more applications. In the course of any mining operation the bateia is used constantly within the *barranco*, the area of gold extraction, to test material to decide where exactly to excavate and give a rough idea of the level of gold to be expected. No matter what machinery is being used, every so often a sample is taken of its reject to see if gold is escaping. It allows one to tell whether material being worked is exceptionally rich, in which case there are special procedures to be followed. It allows one to say whether the gold particles are fine or coarse, each of which demand certain adjustments in technique. At a pinch, the bateia can be used to work material in the absence of any other machinery, although the small volume of material it can process at any one time severely limits its usefulness. And finally, at the end of the working day when machines are cleared out and the gold recovered in the operation known as *despescagem*, it is the bateia which is used.

A garimpeiro who makes prospecting expeditions is called a *desbravador* and may be alone or with a small group. Only the most experienced go on serious prospecting expeditions, because apart from requiring a fair degree of both skill and luck if it is to succeed, one must also be able to live and move around in forest with only a bare minimum of equipment. Prospecting is called *pesquisa*:

Eduardo, when you go into an area to do pesquisa, what do you do?
I use a pickaxe, a bateia or a cuia, and a small spade. I sling a *jamanxim* [a wicker rucksack] on my back and put in what I need – rice, manioc flour, salt. I take a shotgun and cartridges and two or three hunting dogs. I look for a stream bed and test a sample in the bateia. Depending on the result you go up the stream to the headwaters, looking to see which side the gold branches off to, what outcrops it comes from, using the bateia all the time. When you get to a place where the gold changes direction you follow it until you get to rock.

Let's say you find a good spot. What do you do to work out how much gold there is?
Well, you use the bateia and pay attention. If the result is, let's say, two tenths of a gram, it'll yield about ten or twelve grams per day. You use the bateia here, there, over and again, and then you calculate. Gold comes down, you know. It's washed away. So we know that it comes from above, from rock, and we go after it. If it gets into a stream bed we take out the *cascalho* [alluvium] at the point where it enters the water course, until we hit a layer on the bottom that has no gold. You look at the depth of the layer where there is gold and using the bateia you can say whether it will give you three, five, or ten grams a day, or maybe more.
What about an area where the only gold present is in rock?
No, you don't understand. Look, gold in rock has to release grains. Let's say that going up a hill you see a rock formation, you bear it in mind and then at the foot of the hill you find gold in the bateia. Rock has to release grains of gold and at the foot of the hill you can find it just scraping the topsoil, taking out the leaves and twigs and putting the earth in the bateia. From there you follow it until you get to the foot of the rock formation. Then you know that that's the place, and you can start looking for gold-veined rock because it will be there. . . You keep an eye open for changes. While you walk you always look at the ground and where there is a change it could be because there is some mineral there and you use the cuia or the bateia to find out what mineral it is; gold, iron, cassiterite, or whatever. Let's say the soil is clayish and a little further on it gets sandy. You have a good look and sometimes you can see veins where the soil changes colour, one red, one whiter, another black. It must be mineral, so you get out the cuia to see what it is. Besides that, sometimes you can tell just by looking at rock if it has minerals, because often veins can be seen clearly.
Eduardo, how did you learn to do all this?
My son, through prayer and asking God to open my mind, because we don't have this knowledge, it comes from God. And experience as well.

Once a promising area has been located with the bateia and the cuia and a rough idea gained of the direction the gold has taken, in alluvial deposits prospecting enters a more detailed phase during which a methodical attempt is made to map the gold out more extensively. It works on a principle that garimpeiros put in the form of a dictum, *o ouro explode de baixo pra cima*, gold explodes from the bottom to the top. Gold on or near the surface is thought to be a sure indication of gold in greater quantities further down. It is therefore essential to have a good idea of the levels of gold in the topsoil. This is built up by means of *poços* or *pranchetas* laid out on a grid pattern. A poço is simply a hole scooped out of the topsoil with a bateia, about a foot in depth. The contents are examined in a bateia and poços dug at intervals of a metre or so in a straight line for as far as is thought necessary. The prancheta is a little more methodical; it is a shallow trench, again about a foot in depth, dug out in a straight line, which is sunk in an area where the level of gold found in the initial sampling was exceptionally high. The soil displaced is continually tested in a bateia to establish the area of high gold concentration. Several trenches are generally sunk parallel to each other.

With a primary rock deposit, prospecting is more difficult. The problem is not so much locating the deposit, because they can be traced by following an alluvial deposit as Eduardo explained, but in establishing the level of gold the rock contains and thus being able to decide whether it is worthwhile extracting it. Whether or not the rock will be tested depends on the richness or otherwise of the alluvial deposit, as it is a laborious process to be avoided while there is still alluvial gold easily available. Pieces of rock are simply chipped off and pounded into a fine sand in a hardwood or iron mortar and pestle called a *pilão*, and the result is then tested in a bateia. Rock in which gold is found is often hard quartz, and crushing it in a pilão to a powder sufficiently fine to test in the bateia takes at least two hours and often considerably longer. What usually happens as a result is that the prospector will first concentrate exclusively on alluvial deposits. In the garimpos which form around them, sooner or later *moínhos*, mechanical crushers, will arrive to work part of the alluvium. They are difficult to transport, as they have to be dismantled and put on the back of a mule, and it would be out of the question to take them on a prospecting expedition. But once they do arrive at an alluvial garimpo it becomes much easier to take rock samples: they are simply fed through the moínho with a bateia at one end to collect the crushed stone, and examined in the usual way. Thus over time a mixed garimpo exploiting both primary and secondary deposits evolves, although in their early stages almost all garimpos are exclusively alluvial. This means that since the 1930s, when mechanical crushers first began to be used in Amazonia, it is misleading to use the phrase 'placer miners' as a synonym for garimpeiros. Where a primary and a secondary deposit exist in close proximity garimpeiros work them both.

Once a deposit worth exploiting has been found, there is a wide variety of methods that the garimpeiro can employ to get the gold out of the ground, depending on the type of deposit and the capital, or lack of it, available to invest in machinery. Some machinery requires little or no capital: it is simply made up from wood easily found in the jungle with the addition of sacking, felt blankets and pieces of tin. Other machinery can be made to order in the industrial areas of the big cities and can cost thousands of dollars. In the garimpo, one can make an easy distinction between machinery that is motor powered and machinery that is not, and for convenience they will be called mechanical and manual technology respectively. But it is important to realise that there is no hard and fast distinction in garimpos between the manual and the mechanised. Even the most mechanised operations in the garimpo require a great deal of manual work as well, and constantly make use of manual techniques such as the bateia to determine how to employ machinery. Even at their mechanically most complex, mining operations in the garimpo are best thought of as semi-mechanised. There is a striking contrast between the garimpo and the formal mining sector in this respect. In its most developed and technologically complex form, such as the enormous bauxite and iron ore operations at the Serra do Carajás in southern Pará, formal sector mining in Amazonia operates on an altogether different plane of expertise and scale. Technology in the garimpo has limits; it is not capital-intensive compared to formal mining, and it cannot work at depths regularly exploited by the formal mining sector. Nevertheless, in the case of gold extraction it can be argued that there are advantages in relatively portable technology that is not capital intensive.

Manual technology for processing alluvium in garimpos consists of three instruments: the *lontona*, the *dalla*, and the *cobra fumando*. The lontona and dalla are portable wooden sluices made up of a series of wooden boxes lined with sacking or felt blankets, with the addition of a *caixa* at one end. A caixa is a narrow wooden plane covered with sacking, across which small wooden rods are jammed; they are called riffles by mining engineers and *taliscos* by garimpeiros (see Plate 5). Mercury is sprinkled behind the riffles and in a small box at the top of the caixa through which material enters. The mercury amalgamates with gold, making it heavier and thus more likely that it will be retained in the lining of the caixa. A lontona is one box with a caixa, a dalla is a stepped series of boxes with a caixa: both require a work crew of between six and ten. They are used mainly for *repassagem*, the reprocessing of material that has already been worked once. Neither the lontona nor the dalla is native to Brazil. None of the nineteenth or early twentieth century commentators mention them, not even the DNPM crews whose most important function during the 1930s and 1940s was often thought to be the assessment of technologies used in the garimpo.[8] But they had been used for a long time to work placer deposits elsewhere in the Americas. In the California gold rush of 1849 they were called the 'long tom' and the 'dollar', and seem to have been introduced by Mexican miners moving north; they were known by the same names in British Guiana.[9] In 1956 gold was discovered in the Tapajós region south of the city of Santarém. News of the discovery filtered through to the Guianas, and Guyanese garimpeiros travelled south bringing knowledge of how to build and operate lontonas and dallas with them, which they passed on to the more inexperienced Brazilians. One garimpeiro from Maranhão who was in the Tapajós in 1958 remembered them:

> There were blacks there at that time. I don't know where they came from, maybe the interior, or Africa. They spoke two languages; a bit of Portuguese and some other language they used to talk amongst themselves, but I don't know what it was. We used to call them *crioullos*. There were two things they were good at. One was prospecting, they were always doing that, always moving around in the forest and not staying in any one place for very long. And the other thing was the lontona. They knew how to build the lontona.

It seems likely, then, that the lontona and dalla were introduced to Brazil in the 1950s, and have since become established for reworking material already processed by a less efficient machine. A testament of the effectiveness of repassagem is the longevity of some of the Tapajós garimpos, the oldest of which have been in continuous production since 1956. The Tapajós is still the area where the lontona and the dalla are most used and where manual skills generally are most developed.

But for the majority of garimpeiros the lontona and the dalla have two disadvantages. One is that they are not very portable: once assembled they can be very bulky, as the more boxes that are used to extend the sluice, the more efficient they become at extracting gold. In addition to this, building a dalla or a lontona from scratch, using only wood from forest trees, is a skilled job that requires experience of both garimpagem and carpentry that not all garimpeiros have. There are smaller machines which do not require as much skill to assemble; the 'rocker', as it was known in California and the Yukon, which in Brazil was called either *xeique-xeique* or *sacudia*,[10] and the cobra fumando. The sacudia predates the cobra fumando but it is difficult to say when it was introduced into Brazil. That it was introduced is clear from the etymology of xeique-xeique, obviously an attempt to render the English 'shake-shake' into Portuguese. The English is Creole, which suggests that like the lontona and the dalla it was imported from British Guiana. During the 1930s it was one of the most common methods of working alluvial gold, and was still in use in the 1940s in some parts of Maranhão according to old garimpeiros, although by then it was rapidly giving way to the cobra fumando. By the time of the opening up of the Tapajós garimpos in the late 1950s it had disappeared completely.

From descriptions given by old garimpeiros and extant photographs,[11] the sacudia can be precisely reconstructed. It consisted of a sheet of tin with holes punched in it to act as a filter, set in a wooden box with a caixa attached. The whole assembly was mounted on cradle-like rockers which were moved by pulling a bamboo pole that was sunk through one corner of the machine. One person would shovel alluvium onto the tin, while another would take care of the water supply that passed through the machine. A third would vigorously rock the sacudia with the bamboo pole while a fourth person picked out stones, putting them aside to be examined later, and mixed the alluvium with water to help its passage through.

The sacudia was a definite improvement on the bateia as it could work something like three times the amount of alluvium in a working day. But in terms of recovery of gold it was nothing like as efficient as a skilfully wielded bateia, and keeping it in constant and vigorous motion was physically very tiring. In addition, apart from the caixa and the tin filter there was nothing to slow the flow of water through the machine: in any machine of this type water has to be slowed as much as possible or it will wash away the lighter, finer-grained gold particles. Consequently the sacudia could only be used to any effect on coarse-grained gold, and nuggets. These disadvantages led to the appearance of the cobra fumando in the 1940s, which seems to have been a Brazilian adaptation and improvement of the basic rocker design.

The cobra fumando is still the most common form of manual working of alluvial deposits in Brazilian garimpos. Its name can be used to date the time of its appearance, as it was a popular nickname for soldiers of the Brazilian Expeditionary Force to Italy in the second world war. It has two advantages over the sacudia. Firstly, a board was inserted at an angle under the tin sheet to slow the flow of water through the machine. Secondly, rather than rely on rocking and water flow alone to get the alluvium through the tin filter, it is simply scrubbed through with the hand or a piece of wood. This increases the volume of material that can be processed and makes it less tiring to operate (see Plates 3 and 4).

An assessment of the efficiency of manual technology in the garimpo is given at the end of this chapter, but there are some points that should be borne in mind if the bitter debates that currently surround the Amazon gold rush are to be put in perspective. Manual technology in the garimpo is not mechanically complex: this is not surprising given the small range of materials available to someone who cannot afford to buy industrially produced machinery. But the point is not so much that manual technology is inefficient (which is in any case arguable, as will be seen) as that it is practically free. All that is needed to build one is a certain amount of knowledge, some wood, and a minimum of mechanical competence. Lontonas and dallas are more difficult, but not impossibly so for an experienced garimpeiro. This means that people with little or no capital can construct a machine that raises the volume of material that they work to the point where, with reasonable levels of gold, good returns can be made and the purchase of more sophisticated industrially produced machinery becomes possible.

At the same time, manual technology in the garimpo has certain inherent limitations. There are important types of deposit that it cannot work. Primary deposits can only be worked manually with the bateia and pilão, a method so slow and inefficient that it is rarely used. The cobra fumando, despite its better performance when compared to the sacudia, is still not good at working fine grained gold – gold tends to get washed away even when experienced garimpeiros are using it,[12] and the very use of the lontona and the dalla to work material that has already been processed by the cobra is an indication of the limitations of the latter. Also, not all alluvial deposits can be worked using manual technology. It is restricted to small water courses which either run dry at certain times of the year or are small enough to be dammed. Secondary deposits on the beds of large rivers cannot be worked on any scale using manual technology, and some of the most important gold deposits in Amazonia, such as those along the river Tapajós and its tributaries in Pará, and the river Madeira in Rondônia, are of this type. Both primary deposits and secondary deposits in large water courses could only be worked on any scale by garimpeiros with the advent of more sophisticated machinery during the 1970s. By 1979, garimpeiros were technically capable of mining a far greater range of gold deposits than had ever been the case before, and this was an important contributory factor explaining the unprecedented scale of the post-79 explosion of garimpagem in Amazonia. It is worth looking in some detail at how this increased technological sophistication developed.

THE MECHANISATION OF GARIMPAGEM

The use of small engines, motor-driven pumps, mechanical pans, tractors and mechanical crushers in garimpagem dates from the 1930s. The machinery was filtering down from the United States, where it had been developed, and it was widely realised in Brazil that it could be advantageous to deploy it in Amazonia. In the early 1930s gold garimpagem in Amazonia was going through one of its more visible phases, and this happened to coincide with a popular revolution that brought Getúlio Vargas to power in 1930. One of the results of Vargas' accession to power was the creation in 1934 of the Departamento Nacional da Produção Mineral to oversee the mineral sector and intervene in it when necessary. One of its tasks was the enlightened idea of faithfully reporting on garimpagem as it existed at the time, and on the basis of this knowledge to provide technical aid. Although the DNPM would later degenerate into an inefficient and paternalistic organisation, from 1934 until about 1943 DNPM personnel, some of whom were exceptionally dedicated and intelligent, attempted to provide technical help and advice to garimpeiros. They produced a manual advising on different foreign makes of portable engines, mechanical panning machines and crushers,[13] and reported in detail what machinery was being used by garimpeiros.[14] Although the DNPM was too short of resources and too understaffed to have been solely responsible for it, it so happened that the years of this policy coincided with the evolution and consolidation of what was henceforth to be a mix of manual and motor-powered techniques in the garimpo. Garimpagem has been something of a hybrid in terms of its technology ever since. But at that time this machinery was not produced in Brazil and was very expensive to import. Mechanisation was an option that was only open to the very richest garimpeiros and this limited its application. In 1944 the Bretton Woods conference agreed to fix the price of gold at a level considerably lower than it had been traded in since the early 1930s, and when the Bretton Woods agreements came into effect in 1948 they made it uneconomic to use expensive imported machinery in garimpos. However, the opening up of the Tapajós to garimpagem from 1956 meant that Brazilian industry, beginning to be capable of meeting demands for machinery produced in Brazil, now had the Tapajós as a proving ground.

By the late 1970s the manufacturing sector in Brazil, now far more developed, had accumulated a great deal of knowledge and experience about small-scale machinery that could be used in garimpos, and was able to respond very quickly to the huge surge in demand that took place in 1979. Critically, unlike the 1930s the machinery produced could be afforded not only by rich entrepreneurs but by medium and small scale operators as well, to the point where even the poorest manual garimpeiros could aspire to accumulate enough capital through their endeavours to enable them to buy industrially produced machinery. It very soon became apparent that the garimpagem that emerged from the period of frantic activity while the gold price climbed to unprecedented levels would be a much more formidable competitor to the formal mining sector than had ever been the case before, and would survive the inevitable fall in the price of gold. This was partly because of extraneous social and political factors, but was also due to the rapid technical advances that had been made in garimpagem. Within a couple of years, approximately from 1979 to 1981, three distinctive mechanical modes of production spread outwards from long-established centres of garimpagem, and manual garimpagem received an important boost with the mechanisation of water supply that one now finds in varying degrees in almost every Amazonian garimpo.

The three forms of mechanised production that one finds in garimpos are known as the *balsa*, the *moínho*, and the *chupadeira*. All three were pioneered in the Tapajós but since 1979 have diffused throughout Amazonia, although, typically, given the chronic lack of an industrial base in northern Brazil, they are manufactured for the most part in the south, in the factories of São Paulo and Rio Grande do Sul. One particular innovation, the balsa, is still associated above all with the Tapajós, which even during the peak years of Serra Pelada has always produced more gold than any other region of garimpagem. The balsa certainly outstrips any other form of mining in garimpagem in terms of gold production, and enabled garimpeiros for the first time to extract gold on a large scale from rivers as opposed to streams.

Balsa is Portuguese for raft, and it consists of machinery mounted on a raft which is towed along rivers to deposits on the river bed, over which it is moored and supplied, in most cases, from an airstrip cleared in the forest nearby. The main element of the machinery is a large motor pump that can be thought of as a huge vacuum cleaner. From one end of it a wide diameter hose made of flexible plastic is led. On the end of the hose is a metal screen to prevent small stones clogging the pump. A diver, the *mergulhador*, in full diving gear, takes the hose down to the river bed and uses it to suck up alluvium, which is pumped up to the raft. One person is permanently stationed on the raft next to oxygen cylinders to ensure the diver receives a constant supply and to monitor the *cabo de socorro*, a cable which the diver takes down with him and through which he communicates to colleagues by means of a system of pulls, requesting more or less oxygen, more or less power on the hose, or asking for assistance. The alluvium is passed through pipes attached to the other end of the motor pump to a *caixão*, a very large cobra fumando (see Plate 6). There a third person works scrubbing the alluvium through the filter, as one would on a cobra, putting stones and gravel aside to be processed later.

Usually all three members of the work crew can dive and they replace each other on the river bed every three or four hours: a raft will often have two three-man work teams so that production is continuous, supported by a cook, and, if the owner of the raft is rich, a mechanic. The initial capital investment required to set up a raft is the highest of any form of garimpagem, running from a minimum of about $5000 for a threadbare operation with second-hand machinery to around $15 000 for a well-equipped new raft. This does not include running costs, which can be considerable, as supplies and fuel usually have to be freighted in by air at considerable expense.

The *mergulho*, as raft garimpagem is called by garimpeiros, is the most hazardous form of garimpagem. There is no safety regulation by outside bodies, diving equipment is often defective, and there is widespread ignorance about its proper use, especially amongst novices. On the river bed there is the possibility that walls of silt created by the removal of alluvium might collapse on top of an unwary diver. The river current has to be struggled against constantly and can increase very quickly because of rainfall upstream that the diver and his companions do not even see. During the rainy season, even garimpeiros recognise that the mergulho is too dangerous in some areas. They have to contend with stinging rays which are common on the river bed and can sting through a wetsuit; although usually not fatal to a young man, it is agonisingly painful. Visibility is invariably very bad, with the lamps divers carry mounted on their heads unable to penetrate more than a short distance through the silt disturbed by the operation. Decompression sickness, the bends, are a danger when working at depths of more than a few metres, and there are no facilities for treating it. Drifting logs can cut oxygen supply lines, which are also easily snagged and broken in the jumble of lines that are inevitable when several rafts work moored together. Although there are no statistics, accidents are common and often fatal:

This happened on the 1st of December 1984 when I was working in Porto Alegre on the Tapajós. The problem was that the diver I was working with was inexperienced. We went down together and after working for a while I saw that a part of the bank was ready to collapse on top of us. I went over and signalled to him to get out, that it was too dangerous. He took a grip with his hands to push himself on the very part of the bank that I had seen was going to collapse. When I saw him do that, I got out straight away. If he had come out with me at that instant he wouldn't have died. Well, he hesitated, and the bank collapsed. When I got to him he was still alive, although he was buried up to his chest. I couldn't free him, and two other divers came over to help me. But we could see that the rest of the bank was going to collapse at any time. So we had to leave him. A few seconds later the rest fell and covered him up. Although we tried to recover the body we never could. It is not a good death. Any diver could tell you about similar cases they've seen.

Despite this, the volume of alluvium that a raft can work is greater than any other form of garimpagem and the gold yields are correspondingly higher. As all rafts are worked on a percentage basis the potential rewards for those willing to run the risks are great. The areas where rafts operate, most notably the Tapajós and Madeira rivers, are where garimpeiros think it is easiest to get rich quick. Rafts first appeared in the Tapajós in either 1976 or 1977, according to DNPM personnel and garimpeiros who worked in the region in the 1970s, but they were already common there before 1979, as the increase in capacity the raft represented made it profitable to work deposits even at the prices before the 1979 surge. After 1979 the number of rafts increased rapidly, and although there are no reliable surveys they can be numbered in the thousands in the Brazilian Amazon as a whole. A crucial advantage of the raft that was instrumental in its rapid dissemination is its mobility; unlike other machinery in garimpagem it does not have to be dismantled and then transported when it has to be moved. It is simply towed by boat or canoe to new locations along navigable stretches of rivers.

The chupadeira, also known as the *draga*, is the land version of the raft. It also pumps material to a caixão from a hose operated by someone in a digging. It is used in conjunction with a high pressure water hose, which blasts away the material it is played onto to be sucked up by the powerful pump with attached hose, the chupadeira proper, operated by the second member of the crew (see Plates 7 and 8). This combination is most commonly used to work alluvial deposits, but can be used on the occasional primary deposit in friable rock. It is also very common as a rapid method of excavating or deepening a barranco, a process that is called *rebaixamento*. When the chupadeira is being used in this way, the caixão is dispensed with and the material simply pumped where it will run off. A rebaixamento that is done manually by a work crew equipped merely with spades and pickaxes (see Plate 9) can take days: a chupadeira and pressure hoses in the hands of experienced garimpeiros can accomplish the same in a few hours.

A complete chupadeira outfit, which consists of a caixão, the chupadeira proper, another pump for the high pressure hoses, at least two small motors, pipes, and hose, would cost around $5000 new but can be picked up for a fraction of that price second-hand in garimpos. The minimum crew necessary to operate one is four: one on the caixão, one operating the high pressure hoses, a third working the chupadeira itself and a fourth person sifting the area around the chupadeira to pick out stones that might get sucked in. In practice a chupadeira crew is generally at least six or seven people, two or three extra persons working on the vital task of keeping the chupadeira clear and available to help unblock pipes when blockages do occur.

Even moderately hard rock would block the pipes of a chupadeira at once, and this means that the application of the chupadeira to work primary deposits is extremely limited. The machine used to work primary deposits is the moínho, a small mechanical crusher using a pair of steel flails attached to an axis, driven by a large reinforced fanbelt attached to a small motor, with a caixa attached to the mouth of the moínho (see Plate 5). Rock has to be first broken to the size of small pebbles before it can be put through the moínho, as anything larger can break the steel flails and puncture the metal covering which encases the machinery. Large stones are cracked by piling them on a charcoal fire for one or two days, and are then crushed further by mallets if need be. Moínhos are commonly used on alluvial deposits. With alluvium a flail can last for a couple of weeks or more before breaking, but hard rock can wear out a flail within a day. A large supply of flails ready to replace those which break is thus a prerequisite of garimpagem with a moínho. It is the cheapest form of mechanised garimpagem, a unit of motor and crusher costing between $1500 and $2000 dollars new, and requires only one person to feed it with material, although several more will have to work excavating material and breaking it down before it is fed into the moínho.

While machinery, whether manual or mechanised, is in operation, the level of gold to be expected will be roughly known from the results of occasional testing of the material going through with the bateia. When operations cease at the end of the day a final process called *despescagem* takes place in order to recover the gold. Despescagem is the same no matter what machinery is being used, as the one element common to all of them is the presence of a caixa, or a caixão in the case of the raft and the chupadeira, where the gold extracted is deposited. At the bottom of the caixa a bucket is always placed while the machinery is in operation to catch any particles that escape lodging behind the riffles or in the lining of the caixa. When the machinery is stopped, water is passed through very gently, the riffles are taken out and rinsed, and the small mercury-filled box at the top of the caixa is emptied so that its contents run down the lining of sacking or felt. The caixa is then brushed with the hand and mercury, amalgamated with gold, flows down into the bucket. It is at this point that the garimpeiro begins to have an idea of whether or not it has been a good day: mercury that has not amalgamated with gold flows down to the bucket very rapidly, while mercury that has mixed with gold sidles reluctantly down the caixa because of its weight. Best of all is when one sees clumps of mercury that are too heavy to be dislodged by the water flow, a sure sign that they are heavily impregnated with gold (see Plate 10). Once this has been done the lining of the caixa is rinsed and beaten with a small stick to force out finer particles that may have lodged there, and finally the bare caixa is scrubbed with a brush to remove gold particles. Despite this, over time all caixas acquire a golden sheen from minute particles of gold lodged in the grain of the wood.

The bucket which contains the mercury amalgam is then taken to a pool, and the bateia is used to separate it from the other waste that the bucket contains. Once this has been done, excess mercury that has not amalgamated with gold is carefully run off into a cuia. What remains in the centre of the bateia is the gold that the day has yielded mixed with an equal mass of mercury (see Plate 11). This amalgam is then tipped into a piece of finely woven cloth, which is often merely the T-shirt the garimpeiro is wearing, and twisted around hard to expel any further excess mercury, which escapes through the weave of the cloth. The amalgam is then heated with a butane torch: the mercury evaporates away in a toxic white gas, the gold glows red-hot for a few seconds, and then as it cools acquires its familiar colour, to approving comments from the garimpeiros clustered around, watching intently (see Plates 12 and 13).

All forms of garimpagem, both manual and mechanised, require water. The most water-intensive are the chupadeira and the moínho. For these it is necessary to build a water tank, which is made from logs that are then lined with plastic sheeting and filled with water pumped in, often from considerable distances. Thus to be fully equipped the operators of a chupadeira or a moínho need, apart from the machinery that extracts the gold, a motor pump and a good deal of hose to ensure that their machinery can be kept working: this adds about $700 to capital costs if they are bought new. Water supply is often a problem during the dry season in northern Brazil, even though 'dry season' is a relative concept in much of Amazonia, where it is rare to have even a fortnight with no rain at all. Yet even this creates problems for operators of machinery. Streams and creeks run dry very quickly and owners of water-intensive machinery have to range over a large area to find a stream that still has enough water to pump in to the water tank. The problem is especially acute for those operating a chupadeira together with a pressure hose. Rain, when it does come, can often be a mixed blessing. It resolves difficulties of water supply but makes working conditions very much more difficult. It fills diggings very quickly, which then have to be pumped dry before work can begin in the morning, and this lops at least an hour off the working day. Once the water is pumped out it leaves behind it a slippery liquid mud that garimpeiros call *melechete*. It is unpleasant to work in melechete and also more difficult, because the bottom of diggings is turned into a morass where gold-bearing material is difficult to distinguish from simple overburden without intensive testing with the bateia. Heavy rainstorms erode the sides of barrancos and often cause them to collapse, wiping out in a few minutes weeks or even months of painstaking and backbreaking work.

Garimpagem is to a certain extent a seasonal activity because of rainfall. Every year has lean periods, at the height of the dry season for anyone not near a major river, and at the height of the rains for everybody. Nevertheless, it is rare for production to grind completely to a halt in any area, and those who are able stockpile material to process when conditions are too bad to work. In garimpagem rain is both necessary and dangerous: ideal weather for the garimpeiro is a fine balance that assures a constant water supply without disrupting working conditions or washing out an operation. On many occasions the weather is capricious and this balance is not reached. Despite the refinements and technical advances that have taken place in garimpagem, the garimpeiro is still fundamentally at the mercy of the elements – although Amazonian weather can severely handicap even the most technically sophisticated operations of the formal mining sector as well.

CONCLUSION

Understanding the techniques of gold extraction and gold prospecting that garimpeiros use is important not only because they underlie social and economic organisation in the garimpo. It is also helpful in separating ideology from fact in the often heated debates that surround the Amazon gold rush. Politicians, technocrats and formal mining sector interests have since 1979 generated a great deal of rhetoric on garimpagem, most of it critical. It will be argued in greater detail elsewhere that both the Brazilian state and the formal mining sector have invariably seen garimpagem in terms of a dyadic opposition between it and 'rational' and 'organised' mining, represented by the mineral extraction carried out by state and private capitalism. An element in this ideological attack is the denigration of garimpagem as technically rudimentary and inefficient. The Código de Mineração, the legal text that regulates all mineral activity in Brazil, defines garimpagem precisely in terms of a supposed technical backwardness, which is often taken to be *a priori* evidence of 'the low cultural level of garimpeiro communities':[15]

> Article 108. The worker who extracts useful mineral substances through rudimentary and individual mining techniques shall be called by the generic term of garimpeiro
> Article 109. Garimpagem is characterised by:
> i.   Its rudimentary nature as a mining activity.
> ii. The nature of the deposits worked. . .[16]

Those at the sharp end of this debate are the geologists and technicians of the DNPM, and more recently their colleagues in the state-owned prospecting companies, the Companhia de Pesquisas de Recursos Minerais (CPRM) and the Companhia Rio Doce Prospeção e Geologia, known as DOCEGEO. Since 1979 all three of these bodies have been thrown into intensive contact with garimpeiros. Their personnel have lived in, observed and occasionally administered garimpos, and they have been called upon to provide information for political decisions that affect garimpagem and mineral extraction in Brazil as a whole. Part of their task is to make assessments of the technical efficiency, or lack of it, of the garimpo.

Garimpagem as a form of mineral prospection has come out rather well from being put under the microscope in this way. A DNPM field geologist called the bateia 'still the most effective instrument in the prospecting of gold' and proceeded to use it in surveys of the Serra das Andorinhas and the Tapajós, commenting that 'the results showed yet again the simplicity and objectivity of the method, which besides its low cost conveniently gives an immediate result on the spot, avoiding the long delays involved in laboratory analysis'.[17] Similar conclusions had been reached seven years earlier by the British geologists of Riofinex Ltd, a subsidiary of Rio Tinto Zinc, who spent two years struggling with evident professionalism to find economic deposits in the Tapajós:

> It is still doubtful that trace-element mineralisation could be an effective pathfinder for gold. Even the proposed use of lead and zinc in stream sediment surveys to locate gold-bearing source rocks is superfluous: the garimpeiro with his pick, shovel and cuia has already done an excellent job of locating gold anomalies – they are called garimpos.[18]

Watching garimpeiros in action was an illuminating experience for many of these technicians, and seeing them prospect led to admiration on occasion, as an ex-head of the DNPM residency in Santarém explained:

> In the Tapajós you really have garimpagem, garimpagem of the old school. A garimpeiro arrives with a simple piece of hard wood, makes a hole, and calculates the location and volume of the alluvium by counting the grains of gold he takes from the hole with the cuia. Once we were on the river Crepurí testing a new prospecting method and a garimpeiro was there. Out of curiosity we asked him to use his cuia to find out the volume, to see if it agreed with our soundings. I

tried to memorise how he did it but it was very difficult; he was making lots of calculations in his head and he lost us. And then suddenly he says we'll get so many grams here, so many grams over there, up to a total of around 400 grams. We didn't believe him, it was difficult to believe at the time. But our calculations showed 320 grams and so he got very close to the real figure, an error of only eighty grams. I thought it spectacular.

The evidence is rather more ambiguous when it comes to assessing the techniques of gold extraction used by garimpeiros. Although no published tests have been carried out by geologists on material worked with a bateia, there is little doubt that in skilled hands it will recover all the gold present in a sample: the drawback is low capacity, not inefficiency of recovery. The few tests that have been made on material put through machinery in garimpos are apparently damning, but their usefulness is severely limited by a lack of awareness of normal work practices in garimpos. A DNPM study of rates of gold recovery from cobra fumandos in Roraima came to the conclusion that up to 40 per cent of the gold present before the alluvium was put through the cobra was lost.[19] But this followed only a single washing, not pointing out that reject is carefully saved by garimpeiros and put through machinery several times: what a test like this has to establish is the cumulative rate of gold recovery after reprocessing. These give a rather different picture. A study of material that had been reprocessed several times in Serra Pelada, for example, found a level of gold of only .4 to .7 grams per metric ton, and this in an area where the technical level of garimpagem is universally recognised as being lower than somewhere like the Tapajós.[20] Mining in the formal sector would find even this level of gold in its reject unacceptable, but in comparing the two one is talking of a difference of a few tenths of a gram per metric ton only.

The technical limitations of garimpagem have more to do with the depths at which it can work than with the inefficiency of its technology per se. Garimpagem cannot work at depths of more than a few tens of metres. The technology of galleries and shafts associated with deep mining is unknown to garimpeiros in Brazil, despite being practised by garimpeiros in countries like Bolivia and Guyana. The great depth of Serra Pelada, ironically, was only made possible because of the large scale application of mining technology normally associated with the formal mining sector, carried out by outside contractors brought in once the political decision had been made to keep garimpeiros working the site.

Another element in the propaganda drive against the garimpo is the allegation of lack of work safety. This has rather more foundation than accusations of technical inefficiency. The dangers of diving have already been described, and although other forms of garimpagem are not so precarious any garimpeiro would admit that safety conditions in garimpos are far from ideal. Rain erosion or unwise excavation can cause the collapse of barrancos, no protection is used by those operating machinery, and the almost complete absence of medical facilities in garimpos means that accident-related injuries are treated late, if at all. Greed or financial pressures sometimes result in gold being mined with a reckless disregard for the possible dangers. The only protection against the collapse of barrancos is the stopgap shoring up of the sides with logs. Cynical though accusations about the lack of work safety from the state and the formal mining sector may be, neither of which demand or apply rigorous standards of work safety in other spheres, it is true that as currently practised garimpagem is often a dangerous occupation. Whether it is statistically any more dangerous than the occupations from which garimpeiros come is a moot point: standards of work safety are not high in Brazil. Even more worrying are the health implications and environmental consequences of the intensive and almost completely unregulated use of mercury in Amazonian garimpos: these will be examined in Chapter 9.

Despite these reservations, garimpo technology has three cardinal virtues. The first is portability. All manual machinery can be dismantled and carried, or simply abandoned in the knowledge that material will be readily available to build more at the next site of gold extraction. Even the most complex industrially produced machinery used in garimpos can be taken apart and transported by mule. This is a crucial advantage in Amazonia, which despite the construction of a highway network and the improvement of air and river links since the 1960s is still a region which lags far behind the rest of Brazil in transport facilities.

As a result, overheads in garimpagem are minimal, and this means that garimpeiros can work deposits that would be uneconomic to the formal mining sector. The Tapajós is a good example of this. Besides the Riofinex survey, the 1970s also saw geological surveys by Anglo-American and the Brazilian multinational Andrade Gutierrez. All of them rejected the levels of gold they found as uneconomic. Andrade Gutierrez, for example, said that for it to be worthwhile to set up operations in the Tapajós they would require a secondary deposit of 20 million cubic metres at a minimum concentration of .1 grams per cubic metre and a minimum world market price of 600 dollars per troy ounce.[21] Yet all DNPM estimates for the true level of gold production in Tapajós garimpos in 1979 vary between ten and twenty metric tons. For the formal mining sector, Amazonia is a problematic area to make investments in. The costs of setting up a large mining operation are always high, but especially so in an area chronically underdeveloped in terms of the infrastructure necessary to such projects. The distances involved are enormous and the environment is notoriously difficult. Garimpeiros, on the other hand, can make a virtue out of necessity. While they appreciate access to facilities like roads and electricity, they are not essential to garimpagem and the capacity to do without them means that garimpagem is much more flexible and mobile than the formal mining sector when it comes to working gold in Amazonia.[22]

In addition, garimpo technology is extremely accessible. It is cheap and easy to operate. Its very simplicity means that in most cases the principles on which it operates are clear and newcomers to the garimpo can make a reasonable attempt at constructing at least a cobra fumando within a short time. The most complex piece of machinery the majority of garimpeiros ever have to deal with is a small internal combustion engine, and there is no shortage of competent mechanics in garimpos. When all these factors are combined, it is not difficult to see why garimpagem has emerged as a formidable competitor to the formal mining sector in Amazonia. It has very low overheads, it does not require more than minimal transport facilities, it is not reliant on a steady power supply, its basics are easily learnt by newcomers to the garimpo within a short time, it is an extremely effective form of gold prospecting, it has expanded both capacity and the range of deposits that it can work very significantly over the last decade, and it is more efficient at extracting gold than it is generally given credit for. Despite some limitations, in many ways it is far better at fine-tuning itself to the realities of Amazonian conditions than any other form of mineral extraction found in the region.

2 Garimpagem in Maranhão

At first sight garimpagem in Amazonia seems rather spasmodic, with frantic bursts of activity punctuating decades of silence. Gold extraction is obviously linked with fluctuations in the world market price, but this alone does not explain the patchiness that marks the appearance of garimpagem in the historical record. There is also a sense in which garimpagem, and garimpeiros, can be thought of as a hidden social formation. In western Maranhão, and in other parts of Brazil, garimpagem began as a clandestine activity, practised by communities of runaway slaves or by groups of miners evading Portuguese attempts to tax and regulate all mining in Brazil during the colonial period. Garimpagem has been illegal for most of its history, as it is still technically illegal today. It depended for its survival on remaining invisible to the authorities, flourishing most in areas where the political writ of the state did not run, and where as a rule historical documentation leaves something to be desired. Garimpeiros tend not to submit applications for mineral concessions, or leave written records of their activities, and the further back one attempts to trace their activities, the more one has to rely on fleeting references and oblique clues.

In Maranhão, as elsewhere, garimpagem appears to flare up every few decades. This apparent irregularity, and the consequent characterisation of garimpagem in terms of episodic and chaotic eruptions, lends itself well to the metaphor of disease: 'gold fever' in English, *febre de ouro* in Portuguese. The usual translation of 'gold rush' into Portuguese is *corrida de ouro*, literally 'gold race', and much of the historical work in both English and Portuguese on gold mining in colonial Brazil often seems little more than the recording of corridas which flare up and die down like recurring bouts of malarial fever.

As a counterbalance to this perspective, there is very little historical work which takes a single area of gold extraction and examines garimpagem closely for any length of time. The purpose of this chapter is to fulfil that need by looking at the history of garimpagem in the Gurupí goldfield in western Maranhão (see Map 2), relying on oral as well as written sources. It gives some idea of the historical roots of the gold rush that began in 1979, and serves as introductory background to the chapters that follow based on ethnography in garimpos in contemporary Maranhão.

27

The first mention of Maranhão as a gold bearing region was made by Estácio da Silveira Sá in a book published in Lisbon in 1624, *Uma Relação Sumária das Cousas do Maranhão*. At the time that it was written the Portuguese had only just managed to expel the French from the small hamlet of São Luis, the only European settlement in all of Maranhão, and virtually nothing was known about the interior. The first person to make the trip overland from São Luis to Belém was the explorer Pedro Teixeira, later to make himself famous as the leader of an epic journey from Belém to Quito. He crossed what would later become one of the two zones of gold production in Maranhão in 1624, but never made any mention of finding gold. Silveira's assertion that Maranhão was 'a region rich in gold and silver' can be dismissed as part of the hyperbole which generally accompanied the reporting of discoveries in the Americas.

In the 1620s the Jesuits entered Maranhão for the first time, and by the 1650s they were establishing missions and concentrating Indians in settlements along the Gurupí and Pindaré rivers (see Map 2). This is taken by all commentators who mention gold, including sources basic to the history of garimpagem in the state,[1] as the start of gold extraction in Maranhão. Yet no hard evidence was ever cited to back up the assertion. It is possible to trace the way that this was casually and vaguely mentioned by the earliest commentators, and then repeated and amplified by those who came after until it became established and unquestioned truth. The first historian to mention the link with the Jesuits was Gayozo, writing in the early part of the nineteenth century:

I have little information concerning the mines of the captaincy, but it is said with some certainty that there is gold in the area of the Pindaré. As that region is infested with hostile Indians it has never been discovered. Some Indians affirm that in the highlands of Tiracambú those same Indians use the pieces of gold that they find to make decorations for their women. It is said that another Indian found some traces suggesting that the fathers of the old Company of Jesus exported some of that most precious metal to this city [São Luís], which they did by means of a road from the river Pindaré that begins in a lake called Cajaramá, where some years ago the ruins of a house were found, along with the remains of a huge canoe almost rotted away by time . . . various explorers intended to follow this road to the Tiracambú, but fear of Indians made them return. The same thing happened with other expeditions that tried to enter the area.[2]

This is a tantalising quote. The Serra do Tiracambú does in fact form the southern limit of one of the two areas where gold is found in Maranhão. Later explorers in the nineteenth century were categorical in stating that Indians in the area did not know of gold, let alone how to work it, but they were seeing the Indian population at a time of rapid dislocation and change, and it cannot be absolutely denied that Indians there in the eighteenth century used gold in some form or another. But the main point is the indirect and anecdotal nature of the evidence that the Jesuits actually mined gold. To understand the possible reasons behind such an assertion one has to realise the troubled nature of the relationship between Jesuits and early settlers in Maranhão.

From the beginning Maranhão suffered from a severe labour shortage, aggravated by the much-remarked aversion of the Portuguese to anything remotely resembling manual work. The mortality of enslaved Indians was extremely high, and all historians of the region and period[3] have noted the severe tensions this generated between settlers and Jesuits. The retention of Indians in missions, rather than their release as slaves, caused great resentment. It resulted in charges that the Jesuits were deliberately hoarding Indian labour for their own nefarious projects, including gold mining. In Maranhão, where settlers were too poor to afford African slaves, the shortfall was not made up with the import of Africans until a boom in cotton and sugar production towards the end of the eighteenth century. Some idea of the depths to which settler-Jesuit relations sank can be gained from the frequency of anti-Jesuit riots and rebellions in São Luis. The first of these occurred in 1661, when the Jesuits were temporarily expelled from the city, and in 1684 the governor found it necessary to execute two ringleaders of a rebellion that used anti-Jesuit feeling as a rallying point. It seems more than likely the claim that the Jesuits were mining gold was a slander, designed to weaken the position of the Jesuits in the eyes of the Portuguese court and the governors sent out from Lisbon to administer the province. There is no record of any kind of gold reaching São Luis from the interior before the nineteenth century, and if, as Gayozo says, gold did come from the interior missions on the Pindaré to São Luis, it is remarkable it did not produce a *corrida*. This absence of a gold rush is all the more striking when it is clear that the interest was certainly there. The municipal government of São Luís sponsored two expeditions to the Pindaré river to find gold, one led by Marcos da Boa Vida which lasted from 1720 until 1722, and another led by Bartolomeu Franco in 1724. Both were expensive failures, and the settlers were sharply reprimanded in a royal proclamation dated

30 May 1730, where the King ordered them to 'cease making futile expeditions and stick to agriculture, which is more suitable for you'.

For a time the proclamation was respected. In the final quarter of the eighteenth century Maranhão experienced an economic boom, as cotton and sugar production expanded to take advantage of the disruption of supplies to Europe caused by the American War of Independence and the Anglo-French struggle for mercantile supremacy in the Caribbean. As a result, on the west coast of Maranhão there was a rapid growth in the number of plantations, which for the first time could be worked by imported African slaves, capital and credit now being easier to obtain. The western coastal towns, Cururupú, Turiaçú, Carutapera and Viana, grew quickly. This plantation development also moved inland, to a certain extent, along the many rivers that lead to the interior, especially the Gurupí, the Maracassumé and the Turiaçú (see Map 2). Nevertheless, away from the coastal and riverine plantations, the area between the three river systems was still, by the 1850s, dominated by the hostile Urubú Indians, and, it became plain, by communities of runaway slaves.

Conditions on the plantations were often harsh, and the jungle, over which the settlers had little authority and no control, must have seemed invitingly close. Most sources concur that from about 1810 runaway slave communities, known as *mocambos* or *quilombos*, began to form in what were generically termed 'the jungles of Turiaçú'. These settlements were clandestine and in an area which even today is fairly remote, so it is not surprising that written records of them are sparse. But they were known to be producing gold from somewhere in the interior, and they became strong enough to pose a physical threat to planters around the towns of Santa Helena, Turiaçú and Viana. Of the nineteenth-century commentators, Marquês is the most forth-coming, in his geographical almanac of the state published in 1870:

> Since 1811 quilombos began to form in the district of Turiaçú, which found itself threatened by an insurrection that would inevitably extend to the counties of Alcântara and Viana, thus putting at risk the property and personal safety of the inhabitants and preventing access to fertile and potentially rich territory . . . the slaves living in these settlements occasionally numbered more than 200 and *lived from the production of the mines of Maracassumé*, which they bartered in Santa Helena and other places for food, ammunition and other goods, maintaining relations with villagers and river traders. Some, those in Cruz Santo for example, lived exclusively from

agriculture in clearings in the jungle, carefully avoiding all contact with outsiders.[4]

This is expanded slightly in the later entry on Turiaçú:

More than 40 years ago this area was infested with quilombos of various size, and the combined efforts of the authorities of both Pará and Maranhão could not solve the problem, despite several military expeditions. However, during the governorship of Dr. Machado they were finally eradicated . . . unfortunately, they reappeared during the administration of Dr. Franklin Dôria [1867] and it cost the Province much effort, money and even lives to put an end to them.[5]

Malte Brum, a French traveller who passed through Maranhão in 1861, also mentions the 'minas do Maracassumé':

In the interior is the valley of the Maracassumé, between the rivers Gurupí and Turiaçú. Escaped slaves seek refuge from their persecutors in that region and exchange the gold which they find for objects for their personal use. It is said that the gold was found on the surface, and that there was much of it. The chiefs of the expeditions sent against them said that the richness of the area in gold was remarkable, and exceeded all that public opinion held it to be.[6]

The picture that emerges from these sources is bare but certain basic facts are clear. During the first decades of the nineteenth century quilombos established themselves in the interior, especially in the area between the Gurupí and the Maracassumé rivers, extracted gold, created trading networks along the rivers to the coast, and eventually assumed sufficient importance for the government in São Luís to attempt to crush them militarily. The records of those attempts are the main extant written records of the quilombos.

It was during the governorship of Eduardo Olímpio Machado, from 1851 to 1855, that the first serious attempts were made by the state to put down the quilombos. Machado himself was a conservative monarchist, who resolutely opposed the first stirrings of liberal republicanism which were making themselves felt in São Luís at the time. It is thus unfortunate for Machado's historical reputation that the only surviving newspaper from the period in the state archive, apart from the official gazette, is *O Estandarte*, a scurrilous liberal broadsheet that relentlessly pilloried both his character and the actions of his administration. The edition of *O Estandarte* dated 16 February 1854 seized on the quilombo issue to embarrass Machado and devotes almost all of its space to the question. It reproduces in full an alleged letter to Machado from the ex-head of police in Santa Helena, the nearest Brazilian settlement to the quilombos, which is a plea for military assistance from São Luís. It opens by reminding Machado that the first such plea from Santa Helena was in 1841, and continues:

> Your Excellency knows full well that at all times ill-intentioned people are ready to help outlaws, and for this reason the slaves have found themselves confirmed in their temerity when, in the middle of the jungle, certain individuals opened up communications with the quilombos in order to buy the products of the ranches and farms which they rob, and also more recently the gold that they mine, it being well-known that the *mocambeiros* [inhabitants of a quilombo] have come across a mine from which they extract a not inconsiderable amount of gold. This is offered to the speculators who have established trading links in the area, who in return supply them with arms, gunpowder, and all the necessities that enable them to continue their depredations. The quilombos grow day by day, day by day the number of slaves who are induced to flee by their cousins who know the jungle increases, and soon the plantations and farms will stand deserted. . .

In June of 1853 a military expedition was finally sent from São Luís, but not before local settlers had tried, and failed, to deal with the situation on their own. That failure, of which an extensive account was given in the same edition of *O Estandarte*, is a detailed example of the interrelationships between slaves, traders, planters and mocambeiros in the region. Everything began in January of 1853 at the plantation near Santa Helena of a landowner named Antônio Bernardo Marianno:

> Bernardo had eight slaves of his in the quilombo, one of whom, by name Epiphánio, had obtained from him the promise of liberty if he could persuade the other seven to return, holding out to them the promise that they would not be punished. A fortnight later Epiphánio appeared, apologising for not having brought the others but with high hopes that he would soon be able to do so. He then returned to the quilombo.

However, on the 14 February, unbeknownst to Epiphánio, the settlers of Santa Helena sent another plea for help to São Luís, which painted the dangers from the quilombos in lurid terms:

the mocambeiros occupy gold-bearing lands and mine gold which they exchange for arms, ammunition, cloth, tools, and alcoholic drink. They speak to the other slaves on the plantations, and they in their turn become surly and insubordinate, and we have to be timid and silent, not correcting their faults, for them not to flee into the jungle. Thus the black cloud of rebellion swells, and we beg that the government help us to cut out this evil at the root.

It seems that, unofficially or not, the settlers of Santa Helena were promised that something would be done soon, and this became widely known in the region. The rumours were to have unfortunate consequences for Epiphánio in the quilombo:

Twenty days later Epiphánio returned with thirteen slaves who had come to see how the tempers of their masters were: they wished to return and even to persuade others to return, but wanted to be certain that they would not be ill-treated. But when these slaves arrived the secret was out, and the place was alive with rumours that the government was going to send soldiers. The slaves found out about this and returned to the quilombo along the jungle trails at once. The result was that soon afterwards, on the 6th of May, the slave Epiphánio and one other man were murdered on Bernardo's plantation by mocambeiros who had realised that he was plotting against them.

Two weeks later Bernardo gave shelter to a slave called Manuel, who was fleeing from the quilombo, and was warned that he was about to be attacked. Bernardo just had time to arm those of his retainers that he trusted and to send a message for help to Turiaçu. The plantation was attacked, one of the mocambeiros and Bernardo's white foreman were killed, but help from his neighbours and the small police detachment from Turiaçú arrived before the attack could be pressed home and the mocambeiros fled. Flushed with this success, the local settlers decided to take advantage of the presence of the police detachment, pressed Manuel into service as a guide, and marched out to attempt to put an end to the quilombos themselves. But on the tracks they were ambushed, Manuel and two police troopers were killed, and without a guide the expedition had to return. It was probably this failure which led the ex-head of police to make his appeal on the 30 May and led Machado, finally, to send troops to Santa Helena. It was a decision that would have momentous consequences for the region, as for the first time, although it would prove to be only temporary, São Luís would bring the area under its control.

It is vividly obvious from this episode that by the 1850s the quilombos posed a serious threat to the settlers around Santa Helena, and that there was good reason for Machado to fear a thrust at the important town of Viana, as would happen in 1867. It is clear from the files of *O Estandarte* that 1853 was a year of marked quilombo activity. Besides the Maracassumé quilombos, there were other engagements with casualties reported on 6 October, 4 November and 24 November near the towns of Rosário and Icatú, both uncomfortably close to São Luís. It also seems clear that the gold mined at the 'minas do Maracassumé' was very important for the survival of the quilombos, allowing them to become a much more serious threat to public order than they might otherwise have been. It is obvious that gold enabled them to create trade networks, through selling gold to river traders on the Maracassumé and Turiaçú, and acquire trade goods in return, including arms. This divided the local Brazilian population. Plantation owners were deeply troubled by the growing importance of the quilombos, but the river traders and the suppliers of goods in Santa Helena and the coastal towns had come to a profitable accommodation with the mocambeiros. They must have resented military intervention, reasoning, correctly as it turned out, that it would interrupt their commercialisation of the gold coming from the interior.

It is also clear that the first people to take up garimpagem on any scale in the interior were runaway slaves. Maranhão is at roughly the same latitude as West Africa and both are areas of tropical rainforest similar in terms of climate and topography. The slaves who were imported into Maranhão in the last part of the eighteenth century came from West Africa, mainly from what today is Dahomey and Benin. It is significant that this was and is an area where gold is extracted on some scale. It seems more than likely that garimpagem in the interior of Maranhão began when Africans from this area fled from the coastal and riverine plantations and found themselves in surroundings not unlike West Africa. Some of these refugees would have had the knowledge to notice the presence of gold and mine it. In this way the 'minas do Maracassumé' came to the notice of Brazilians, but the gold production was not spectacular and Brazilian penetration into the area was still localised and weak. These two factors combined to ensure that it would be some time before effective moves were made to wrest control of the area from the quilombos.

The military expedition left São Luís by boat on 24 June 1853, under the command of an army captain named Leopoldo de Freitas. Apart from a brief record in the official gazette of Machado's orders,[7] no record remains of the composition of the force nor how it was guided to the quilombos. But it seems that in August two quilombos named as Cruz Santo and Maracassumé were attacked by Freitas. The modern Cruz Santo is a site about forty miles to the west of the Maracassumé, near Montes Aureos, where a British firm would set up operations in 1858. It was certainly a quilombo at one time, and it seems almost certain that these were the two places attacked. The casualties, if the figures are to be believed, were quite high: in *O Estandarte* they were given as twenty slaves killed, forty-six captured, and thirty returning to their masters of their own accord, for the cost of only six wounded on the part of the expedition.[8] Freitas was loud in his proclamations that the quilombos had been crushed, but *O Estandarte*, reasonably enough, pointed out that the slaves accounted for were only a small fraction of the slaves known to be there, that only two quilombos had been attacked when more were known to exist, and that it was more likely that the majority of the mocambeiros had simply withdrawn into the jungle on the approach of the force. Events were to prove that this reading of the situation was correct.

With the area now opened up, exaggerated rumours of the 'minas do Maracassumé' began to filter back to São Luís, and Machado sent a state commission to explore and evaluate the area in September 1853. It appears that it returned to São Luís in January 1854 and presented a report in March of the same year. It was published in a semi-official newspaper called *O Observador*, but unfortunately the files for that year of the newspaper are missing and it seems likely that what would have been a fundamental source for the history of garimpagem in the state is lost.[9] What is clear is that the Machado administration was now able to indulge a passion for the development of Maranhão by means of foreign colonisation and investment. In a situation where definite knowledge of the Gurupí was minimal, exaggerated rumours of the 'minas do Maracassumé' swept São Luís. It was clearly less of a risk to invest in western Maranhão with the quilombos out of the picture, for the time being at least, and private companies soon began to turn their attention to the region. 1854 saw the organisation of two schemes that envisaged the importation of colonists to work on projects that combined agriculture with gold extraction. In both the idea was that the state government would provide transport facilities and subsidise costs, besides guaranteeing the physical safety of the colonists.

The first scheme, the Companhia de Operários do Maracassumé, was hatched by a company that was formed in São Luís in 1854, with state government backing, called the Companhia Maranhense de

Mineração. It planned the importation of forty Chinese labourers from Rio de Janeiro to work the deposits at Montes Aureos, and they arrived in Maranhão in January 1855. The other was organised by Portuguese capitalists in Oporto, under the name Companhia de Prosperidade. It bought gold-bearing land on the western coast at a spot called Pirocauá, where reports of gold finds can be traced back to 1819, imported 112 Portuguese colonists, and set them to work clearing plots in the jungle for farming and gold diggings. Both enterprises were complete fiascos. The government of Maranhão, thrown into confusion by the death of Machado from fever in 1855, never fulfilled its commitments. There was widespread fraud and disorganisation in the management of the two schemes, and a high rate of desertion amongst the colonists. The schemes collapsed within a few months of each other in 1858.

Weakened by the failure of the Maracassumé colony, dispirited by the death of Machado and handicapped by the lack of investment capital in São Luís, from 1856 on the Companhia Maranhense de Mineração followed a strategy of attempting to interest third parties in its holdings at Montes Aureos, trying to sell or lease the mineral rights to the site which it had acquired in the first flush of enthusiasm in 1854. At this time, the first evidence of foreign interest in Montes Aureos appeared. It is unclear whether it was at the instigation of the British consul in São Luís (one of the most powerful figures in Maranhão at the time), or a separate manoeuvre by the Companhia Maranhense de Mineração, but in 1857 an English geologist called Thomas Martin took samples of material from Montes Aureos and sent them back to London. They were found to have a gold level of 47.2 grams per metric ton, which is extremely high, so high that the possibility of adulteration by parties from the Companhia Maranhense de Mineração interested in unloading the site cannot be discounted. Even so, as the total sample was only a cubic metre taken from one spot, it was not conclusive evidence of a large and very rich deposit, as was assumed at the time. Two German engineers were sent out from London the same year to carry out a feasibility study, and on the strength of their positive report a company called the Montes Aureos Gold Mining Company was formed on the London Stock Exchange in December 1857. It then paid £100 000 raised from stock flotation to the Companhia Maranhense de Mineração for a seven year lease of Montes Aureos.[10] By the end of 1858 the most prominent Brazilian capitalist of the period, the Barão de Mauá, had invested money in the venture, machinery had arrived from Britain and been floated down the Maracassumé to a landing, where it was dismantled and transported to Montes Aureos, work had started on the construction of two earth dams to form a reservoir to provide a water supply, and two more mining engineers were sent out from England. The mounting of the operation at Montes Aureos was a prodigious feat, and it was by far the most significant gold mining operation in Maranhão until the early 1980s, as the size of the abandoned machinery and the one dam still in existence attest (see Plates 14 and 15).

It was, however, short lived. In 1865 the lease ran out and for reasons that are not entirely clear, but which may have had something to do with Maranhense resentment of what was seen as British appropriation of Maranhão's mineral wealth, it was not renewed. The mining engineers left, and it was decided to abandon the machinery where it stood rather than incur the expense of returning it to Britain. There are traces of mining activity from this period in Cruz Santo but the principal remains are at Montes Aureos. There the English left spades, pickaxes and pieces of a large pump, together with a large steam boiler and a mechanical crusher for succeeding generations of garimpeiros to wonder over and debate how they could have been transported to the spot, where even today the only access is over narrow jungle paths which even a mule occasionally has problems negotiating. More machinery was left to rust at the landing on the Maracassumé, which as a result came to be known as Ferragem – Rust. Garimpeiros in Montes Aureos constantly come across what they call *ferro velho* – old iron – from the period, unearthing nuts, bolts, screws and even bottles in the course of their excavations. In 1985 one garimpeiro showed me a perfectly preserved mica crucible, into which molten gold would have been poured before being cast into bars, with the words 'Plumbago Company, Battersea Works' still clearly visible on the bottom. Record exists of the Barão de Mauá's reaction to the failure: he complained that he had been misled by over-optimistic geological reports and that 'the deposits were already exhausted'.[11] There are some suggestive reasons given in oral accounts as to why the British left, as will be seen.

The immediate result, however, was that the region returned to the control of the mocambeiros. Ironically, the result of the brief tenure of the Montes Aureos Gold Mining Company was to ensure that the area would be kept in trust for the mocambeiros, as their monopoly of the mineral rights together with the continuing hostility of the Urubú combined to make the area unattractive to others who might have wished to enter it. When the British pulled out no Brazilians were living in the area to fill the vacuum, and the mocambeiros simply moved out of their jungle retreats further to the west and took possession of their old haunts once more. Once again they posed a threat to Santa Helena and further afield to Turiaçú and Viana. This can be read from an examination of the by-laws of the coastal town of Turiaçú.[12] An edition of the by-laws drawn up in July 1859 makes no mention of quilombos or mocambeiros, which fits in with the lessening of the problem after the expedition of 1853 and the entry of the Montes Aureos Gold Mining Company, whose initial construction and transportation work would have been at its peak in 1859. But in a further edition in 1865 there is another article inserted:

> Every free person who negotiates with escaped slaves, or who supplies them with arms, lead, gunpowder, bullets, food, or any form of goods, shall, besides suffering the penalties applicable under Article 115 of the Criminal Code, be fined 30 mil-reis and double that amount should the offence be committed a second time. If the offender should be a slave, he or she shall be taken to a public prison to await the punishment that the law shall determine. However, if it is proven that the master either knew of or connived at the transaction of the slave, then he must pay the fine specified above.[13]

This is clear evidence of the division of interests within the Brazilian community, and a sign that the trading networks in existence since at least the 1840s sprang up again once the British left the area. That the problem had reached a new and dangerous level was demonstrated in 1867 when the mocambeiros attacked Viana. There is a source from the town of Pinheiro, to the east of Turiaçú, which gives a little detail:

> The quilombo of São Benedito do Céu,[14] in the jungles of Turiaçú, organised armed groups that attacked towns and villages. In 1867 they sacked three plantations and actually tried to besiege Viana. There they were driven off by troops of the line helped by backwoodsmen. On the 11th of June there was an engagement near the plantation called Santa Barbara and the mocambeiros retreated.[15]

The brief administration of Franklin Dôria that same year had to devote itself almost entirely to public order questions, in which the renascent Turiaçú quilombos loomed large. Circumstances further favoured the quilombos with the demands on the state government for men to be sent to the war with Paraguay, and the depletion of army and police detachments throughout the state.

Because the area once again became hostile, with fierce resistance on the part of both Indians and mocambeiros to Brazilian penetration, the area around Montes Aureos almost disappears from the written records until the twentieth century. The two fleeting references that do exist are interesting because they both suggest that garimpagem was still being practised by mocambeiros in the region. The German cartographer Gustav Dodt made a journey to the source of the Gurupí in 1872, and although he saw no quilombos he does mention that 'Montes Aureos has been known for a considerable time as a gold-bearing region' and records some contact he had with Urubú warriors:

> They use iron tips on their arrows, which surprised me, and told me that they were supplied with them by some quilombos of Negroes, which as is known exist in this parts. I surmised that these were in turn acquired from river traders by the Negroes in exchange for the gold which they mine at Montes Aureos.[16]

The other reference is a mention that in 1887 an army captain constructing the Belém-São Luís telegraph line came across a group of mocambeiros on the Gurupí river at Itamauary 'working as garimpeiros'. He engaged one of them, named Agostinho, to act as his guide, and this man would also be contracted by the geologist Lisboa for the same purpose in 1890. He told Lisboa that an attack had been made by Indians against a quilombo called Limão in 1878, but no written record of the attack exists.[17]

'A TIME OF KINGS': ORAL ACCOUNTS OF GARIMPAGEM IN NINETEENTH-CENTURY MARANHÃO

In addition to documentary sources there are oral accounts of the history of garimpagem in the Gurupí. The material presented here was collected in 1985 in and around Montes Aureos, and to be evaluated properly it should be placed in the context of the recent history of the region.

Only a small fraction of the present-day population of the part of the Gurupí that includes Montes Aureos and the other old quilombo sites were actually born in the area. They are concentrated in several small villages populated almost entirely by blacks, many of which are identifiably old quilombos whose names occur again and again in the written records: Limão, Itamauary, Camiranga and Jibóia, amongst others. Since the early 1970s a state land colonisation project called COLONE has attracted a large influx of smallholders into the Gurupí from all parts of Maranhão and occasionally from neighbouring states as well. In addition a large number of garimpeiros have been entering the region since 1982, with the result that those who have lived in the area for considerable lengths of time have been buried beneath intensive waves of in-migration for more than a decade.

During five months spent in Gurupí garimpos, only three people were encountered who could recount in some detail the accounts reproduced and discussed below. Of these three, one had been born in the area, worked off and on in garimpos since 1941, including Montes Aureos in the late 1940s, and had been told these oral histories since early childhood by family and friends. The other two came to the area in the early 1970s and began to work in garimpos soon afterwards. In this they were exceptional, as garimpagem was at a very low ebb in Maranhão in the early 1970s, and they were also unusual in that they had entered the area well before the later influx of smallholders and garimpeiros, who had transformed the region by the time fieldwork was carried out. Both of them had the chance to meet and talk with garimpeiros still in the Montes Aureos area who had worked there since the 1940s, although not necessarily always as garimpeiros, and it was named individuals with this background who were cited as the sources of these accounts. Most of these ageing garimpeiros have now died; those who remain are too old to support a life in the jungle and have returned to their families in various villages of the region. Difficulties of time and transport meant that none of them could be located and interviewed, which means that this material must be regarded as merely a small sample of the oral accounts of the past in the Gurupí, no more than a taste of an oral history of garimpagem in the region that remains to be written.

The question 'Who were the first people to find gold in this region?' never provoked a uniform response amongst garimpeiros in the Gurupí, most of whom, having either seen or heard of the machinery rusting in Montes Aureos, answered that it had been the English. The three informants with more experience of Montes Aureos replied that it had been the 'mocambeiros'. But this same question put to garimpeiros on the coast in 1933 by the historian Rubem Almeida evoked an altogether more detailed answer:

The blacks who we heard, descendants of the old mocambos of Camiranga and Itamauary, all agreed on the incredible amounts of gold extracted by the foreign companies. Today these blacks are the keepers of the secrets of the goldfields. When asked to whom we owe the discovery of the deposits the name of a mocambeiro was mentioned again and again. The celebrated Agostinho Mafra, they say, was the one who had the gift of finding gold. Estevão, his successor, transmitted the secret to Tito, Valério, Alexandre, Tibério and Pedro, and thus it came down to the living, to Amâncio, Daniel and Raimunda from Camiranga . . . (there follows a list of 10 names) . . . all of them from Itamauary, Caribe from Pirocauá, and many others from Turiaçú, Santa Helena, Viana, Pinheiro, and Carutapera.[18]

Nothing approaching this level of detail is contained in the accounts collected in 1985. Only two names are mentioned, both described as *reis* [kings], who are identified as quilombo leaders during the *tempo dos reis*, the time of the kings:

They say that when the English left here, they left because the police wanted to expel them and were going to send a column of troops to get rid of them. They didn't want to go, but they didn't have any choice. When they left, Rei Serafim was living in a garimpo called Cipoeiro, about six kilometers along the track to Limão from here [Montes Aureos]. With the departure of the English he captured the blacks who had to stay, who came from Angola, imported by the English. So a lot of blacks stayed here, and Rei Serafim was a black too. He managed to subject them because he was the strongest. Time went on. His black subjects increased in number, he had a lot of gold. But then he began to kill the new babies who were born, as if he wanted to be alone in the end, almost alone. When this started to happen two blacks fled and went to São Luís, where they denounced him. And so the police came, but it took a year for them to arrive. When they fled, Rei Serafim hid some gold that he had, but there was a little girl living with him who he thought might have seen where he had hidden it. So he went and put her eyes out and tried to kill her, but she escaped. The police caught him and took him to São Luís, and he died in prison there two years later. And everything that he had, all the places that he founded, everything was abandoned. He was the first to plant cocoa here, in Limão you can still see things that he planted, lots of things, mango trees, lime trees, orange trees. And that's all I know about Rei Serafim.

The other accounts make no mention of Rei Serafim, but give rather more detail about another figure called Rei Estevão:

It was after the English that what I'm going to tell you happened. It was after them that Rei Estevão was here. He lived in Limão, Limão was founded by him. This Rei Estevão was a slave, a black, from Africa, from that time when Brazil and many other places were being exploited by the foreigners. He worked around here, and then fled to the jungle and became an outlaw. He started to take blacks away from the plantations of the region. He put them there [Limão], a remote place, and formed his own plantations. And so they called him King. His power and influence grew and he communicated with Turiaçú, Pinheiro, and other places.

Why did he do that?

He had to leave to buy things. He lived from the garimpo and used to leave to get things that they ordered. This, that and the other. He sold gold. He had gold and he sold it. He got hold of machinery too. A geologist in Pinheiro made a lontona for him. They thought he could work better with it so they made it for him.

The combination of garimpagem with agriculture is also mentioned:

Estevão had one mocambo called Limão and another called Cacual. Cipoeiro was also a mocambo. They worked in agriculture as well. You can see why: all those people there, in the middle of the jungle, they had to live from what they could grow. But they didn't export it the way they did with gold. It was only for their own consumption. And another things is that they planted various sites around here. For example, in Cacual there is a huge cocoa tree that they planted in the middle of the jungle: it used to be his. There are quite a few cocoa and mango trees around if you know where to look for them, and you don't find them around here unless somebody plants them. When I arrived here for the first time in 1968, I even found orange trees, very old, scattered in the forests.

Rei Estevão came to grief in a similar manner: power unbalanced him:

There were a lot of people in the mocambo, I don't know exactly how many but it was a lot. Rei Estevão lived together with them and the Indians in the forest. But later he became perverse and ordered the execution of several people, because he was the king and could do whatever he wanted. They were beaten to death. He also forced all the women to sleep with him. And so it went on, until there arrived an adopted son of his who he had brought up, who fell in love with a young woman. Rei Estevão saw this and was jealous, so he forced the young girl to sleep with him. His son was furious and went to Turiaçú to denounce him. That's when they began the hunt for him, which ended when he was arrested and died.

The police came from Turiaçú?

Yes. Through the jungle by way of Pinheiro and from there they were guided through the forest. Rei Estevão knew the jungle and saw that they were coming after him, and fled along the back trails. But his son knew the jungle too and they went after him. In the end they caught him. They thought he was a bandit, and the adopted son complained that there was no woman there that Rei Estevão didn't sleep with. So they tied him up and took him to Pinheiro. But he didn't arrive there, he died angry, because he had been a great king and when they arrested him and took him away he saddened, and refused food and water until he died.

And what happened afterwards? Who took his place?

The Indians tried. They attacked and took over, killing many people. They respected Rei Estevão, you see, and when he died they invaded and burnt everything. The problem was that in the time of Rei Estevão the blacks were united. But it seems that after Rei Estevão was taken away there was a dispute between the blacks and the Indians, and the Indians surrounded the quilombo and attacked them. There was one black who fought very bravely and killed several Indians before the Indians could kill him. At this the Indians got really angry and drove them out, right up to the river Gurupí. The blacks took refuge on an island in the middle of the river called Chatão, but even there the Indians attacked them using canoes and they had to leave and live on the far bank of the river in Pará. His descendants still live there, in two settlements called Jibóia and Itamuari. So the Indians took over the area, until the manual garimpeiros I told you about. Indians don't know how to work the garimpo. Later on the garimpeiros came up the Maracassumé and the Gurupí from the coast, but that was afterwards, in the 1930s.

All the placenames mentioned in these accounts still exist; most of them are settled. On a map it is possible to identify the places that are said to be old quilombo settlements, include the evidence from documentary sources, and tentatively plot the population movements that are said to have taken place. These accounts are especially interesting in that they refer to the period during which the written record gives us almost no information. Two places in particular, Jibóia and Itamauari, the two enclaves on the Gurupí away from the Urubú attacks, can be regarded with a fair degree of certainty as quilombos that have been continuously inhabited by escaped slaves and their descendants from before the abolition of slavery in Brazil in 1888 until the present. The fact that Dodt, a meticulous observer, travelled the entire length of the Gurupí in 1872 and made no mention of their existence dates their establishment between that date and the arrival of the army telegraph team in Itamauari in 1887. Of the other placenames mentioned, Cipoeiro, Montes Aureos and Jibóia are still garimpos, although they have not been producing gold continuously since the last century. Until they were driven out by the Urubú it is clear that gold was being extracted by the mocambeiros at a variety of sites.

Thus in the area between the Gurupí and the Maracassumé rivers, a black population, in the face of great difficulties and frequent attacks, managed to survive, if at times by only the skin of its teeth, reproduce, and maintain a presence in the area down to the present day. The oral accounts of the past of these 'Maroon' groups are to a large extent oral accounts of the past of garimpagem. They can be used, in conjunction with the written record, as evidence of certain general facts that are important in the reconstruction of the sequence of events between 1865 and the 1890s.

They indicate the resurgence of garimpagem and the reconstruction of trading networks with the surrounding area and the coast after the departure of the British, which can be confirmed from other sources. They suggest that economic life in the quilombos was based on a combination of gold extraction and agriculture, which seems logical and is supported by the groves of fruit trees one finds scattered across the forests and in garimpos. They also indicate troubled relations between Indians and inhabitants of the quilombos, more than plausible given the evidence of open warfare between Indians and Brazilians during this period, the dislodging of the mocambeiros from the Montes Aureos area, probably during the late 1870s, and the subsequent discovery of other gold deposits at sites nearer the Gurupí, which were probably the first gold garimpos in the state of Pará.

THE TWENTIETH CENTURY

The twentieth century saw the gradual but inexorable encroachment of wider Brazilian society into the Gurupí, and the end of the period when it could be described as an area unknown to all except Indians and mocambeiros. It is not surprising that one of the side effects of this process was a marked improvement in both written and oral records. There were garimpeiros on the coast in the early years of the century, and the 1930s saw an acceleration of garimpagem both on the coast and in the interior. It was to become the best-documented rush in Brazil during that period, thanks to the work of a team of geologists and engineers sent to the Gurupí in 1934 by the Belém residency of the infant Departamento Nacional da Produção Mineral (DNPM). They proved to be more than competent scientists: many times they exceeded their narrow geological brief to provide accounts of the social and economic organisation of garimpagem in the 1930s and 1940s that are without equal.[19] After a pause during the 1950s that lasted through the 1970s, garimpagem in Maranhão entered a period of rapid growth that would eventually dwarf the 1930s and 1940s. At the time of writing, it can safely be said that the numbers of people engaged in garimpagem and the amount of gold being produced in garimpos in Maranhão are higher than they have ever been. Nevertheless, in the context of the explosion of garimpagem that has taken place in Amazonia since 1979, the garimpos of Maranhão do not bear comparison in terms of numbers and level of gold production with other regions of garimpagem in the states of Pará, Mato Grosso and Rondônia.

Before the 1930s, the long tradition of European adventurer–entrepreneurs in the region, which began with the Montes Aureos Gold Mining Company, reached its fullest expression in the person of a Belgian, Wilhelm Lind. In 1905, fresh from a futile attempt to interest the government of Pará in a railway construction scheme, he obtained official permission from the governor in São Luís to explore a tract of land between the Gurupí and Maracassumé rivers that included Montes Aureos and the old quilombo sites. DNPM sources say that he extracted gold from a place called Tira-Couro, near to where the mocambeiros were found in 1887, and that he made several expeditions to Montes Aureos and surrounding parts, facing constant hostility and occasional attacks from the Urubú and finally being forced, as the mocambeiros before him had been, to retire to the island of Chatão in the middle of the river Gurupí. This fits in with some comments made in an oral account in 1985:

There was a German, I think a German, a gringo in any case; his name was Guilherme. They say that he was a real character and that he extracted a lot of gold from around here. They even say that he turned up once in Carutapera alone with six kilos of gold, but I don't know if that's true or not. He explored this area a lot. He used to have a house on Chatão. They say that he lived there with three Englishmen and one night they had an argument and he killed them all, but again nobody knows if that's really right. He asked for a permit to come to Brazil for two years to look for gold. It was a law or something. But there's no record that he left, so it seems that he fled, taking the gold with him.

Lind is a shadowy figure. The DNPM geologists who worked in the Gurupí during the 1930s, Paiva, Souza and Abreu, say that he dominated the area 'more or less violently' until the 1920s,[20] but it is hard to see how one man could violently dominate an area for more than two decades where military expeditions had previously failed, and Lind must have come to some form of accommodation with the ex-mocambeiros and the Urubú, the exact nature of which remains to be clarified. The Maranhense press of the period carries no information about him, and the only thing that can be said with confidence is that in 1920 at the land registry office in Viseu, Pará, he lodged a claim for an enormous stretch of land between the Gurupí and the Maracassumé and beyond, reaching up to the Puruá river (see Map 2), at the same time claiming mineral rights for an astonishing thirty-three named placer deposits within this area. It proved to be his undoing: an army captain was sent with an Indian pacification team to investigate, refused its validity, and the state of Pará rejected the claim in 1924. The case went to the courts but foundered in legal delays and procedural quibbles. What happened to Lind afterwards is not clear. He certainly left the region: some say that he went to live in the northeast of Brazil, others that he died, so his departure and eventual fate are as elusive as the time that he spent in the Gurupí. Nevertheless, it seems that somehow he was able to tap local knowledge not only of the deposits that had been worked intermittently by the mocambeiros and their successors in the area around Chatão, but also of the old deposits around Montes Aureos now dominated by the Urubú, it being inconceivable that Lind, neither a geologist nor a garimpeiro, could have found thirty-three placer deposits unaided.

One consequence of the eventual pacification of the Urubú Indians during the 1920s was a growing interest in the Gurupí. From both oral and written sources it is clear that the 1920s saw a cautious movement of garimpeiros from the coast down the Gurupí and Maracassumé river systems. The Urubú, although still giving cause for concern, no longer posed the serious threat to life and limb that they had done in previous decades, and the process of *pacificação* was to formally end in 1931, when they were induced to move to a reserve to the south of Montes Aureos. There were garimpeiros once again in Montes Aureos during the 1920s, and when the DNPM team arrived there in 1934 they found small nuclei of garimpeiros at Guarimanzal, Montes Aureos and Cipoeiro.[21] They were the advance guard for what would become a garimpo of several hundreds at Montes Aureos in the 1940s, including some entrepreneurs who brought in the most complex machinery to be used in the area since the departure of the British. Paiva, Souza and the Abreu include some remarkable photographs (which may well be the first photographs of gold garimpeiros in the Brazilian Amazon) of a complex system of sluices that were installed by 1934 in a garimpo near Montes Aureos called Macacos,[22] and in 1942 a DNPM geologist gave an inventory of the machinery being used by one Moacyr Pinheiro in Chega-Tudo: a mechanical crusher, five petrol motors, a compressor, an alternator, a small generator, an electric pump and explosives.[23]

There was also an upturn during the 1920s in gold garimpagem on the coast, in the area around Pirocauá, where the Portuguese Companhia de Prosperidade had come to grief in the 1850s, but where several sources confirm the local population had divided their energies between fishing and gold extraction since the early nineteenth century.[24] Much activity was centred around an island near the mouth of the Gurupí called Ilha do Inglês: it should by rights have been called Ilha do Francês after a French gold mining company operated there in the 1870s, but the earlier activities of the British in the interior had forever marked all foreigners as English in the eyes of the Gurupí's inhabitants, to the chagrin, one imagines, of the French mining engineers. In 1932 the state government sent a São Luís historian, Rubem Almeida, on a fact-finding tour of the region, and he left a memorable description of Inglês in 1933, which equalled in tone, though far surpassing in quality, much of the journalism that would come to be written about the modern Amazon gold rush:

In no time at all hotels, restaurants and cafes sprang up together with dozens of bars and saloons, even a small fairground, where artists of the worst quality presented shows. Next to the diggings stalls offered the most diverse goods and services in the midst of a continuous dust-cloud: clothes, dresses, barbers and cooks. Gambling ran riot, unchecked by the authorities. Syphilis and tuberculosis were rampant. Boats full of families arrived daily from Viseu, Bragança and Belém. They disgorged their human cargoes on the beaches of Maranhão, where shelters were improvised in hours. The area, with the constant coming and going of people of both sexes and all ages, carrying on their heads the bateias full of alluvium to be washed in the salty waters of the nearby creek, made me feel as if I were in another China whose inhabitants used the traditional cone-shaped hats upside down.[25]

All this activity on the coast and in the interior was drastically affected by a collapse in the price of gold after the end of the Second World War. This was remembered in 1985 by an old garimpeiro who had been working in Inglês at the time:

> I remember that sometime towards the end of the 1940s the price fell a good deal and I began to look for something else to work in besides the garimpo. Many people were leaving Inglês. Some went back to fishing, others went into the forest and started to clear plots to grow food, and there were many others that I never heard about. I had got to know a boat owner who ran along the coast delivering letters and supplies to the towns and villages. He took me on and in time I became a pilot, although I never owned my own boat. Then when the price got better a few years ago I went back to the garimpo, but this time to Montes Aureos, to be nearer my family.

During the 1950s and the 1960s, with the gold price still in the doldrums, garimpagem was at a very low ebb in Maranhão. Some indication of this was that in 1970 the Superintendência do Desenvolvimento do Maranhão sent a team to make a short survey of garimpagem along the coast and found that in the município of Turiaçú there was no longer a single garimpo, although further to the west around Luis Domingues and Godofredo Viana they did record thirty-eight garimpos: the great majority of these appear to have been old garimpo sites rather than garimpos actually producing gold.[26] By this time garimpagem in the interior was in a similarly parlous state, with only a few dozen people working irregularly at garimpagem around Montes Aureos, according to the testimony of those living in the region at the time. But an examination of applications made for the concession of mineral rights in the Gurupí shows that although garimpagem may have been falling off, some interest in the interior was being shown by mineral firms. Working through a Brazilian subsidiary, Mineração Arapiranga, a French company called Badin made five separate applications between 1974 and 1980 for exploration and mineral rights to areas of land around Montes Aureos, including Limão, where in 1979 there was a conflict involving an alleged invasion of company lands by a small group of garimpeiros.[27] One indication that garimpagem had by the end of the 1970s picked itself up a little from the trough was an estimation of the garimpeiro population of the interior at around 600 in 1979 by a geologist who worked there during the period.[28] But this situation was to be transformed very shortly.

The steep rise in world gold prices in 1979, the discovery of the huge gold deposits at Serra Pelada at the end of the same year, and the subsequent heavy media coverage given to what rapidly became the largest garimpo in the history of Brazil, combined to produce a massive upsurge of interest in garimpagem throughout eastern Amazonia. Western Maranhão had by then been opened up by the Belém-São Luís highway, completed in 1970, and for some time small farmers had been moving into the region, either spontaneously or under the COLONE land colonisation projects. In 1981, literally just over the border in Pará, a large gold strike was made at a garimpo called Cachoeira. It rapidly drew a large number of garimpeiros attracted by the prospect of working on a garimpo that straddled a major road, rather than accessible only by air or after difficult land and river journeys. Cachoeira proved to be a jumping-off point for many garimpeiros who either heard about or already knew something of the long history of gold extraction in the region. Within a year garimpos began to spring up again along the coast and in the interior, the largest being the old site of Chega-Tudo (where Moacyr Pinheiro had worked in the 1940s and which was probably once a quilombo), and a new discovery on the Maranhense side of the Gurupí river that came to be known as Serrinha. It was in this area that fieldwork was carried out in 1985.

This historical overview of garimpagem demonstrates several things. It is interesting to see how conflicts between garimpeiros and mining companies have such a long pedigree, and to see the equally long pedigree of the association of garimpagem with marginality, both social and geographical, which was also a feature of the history of garimpagem elsewhere in Brazil. There are examples of the collapses and fiascos that marked ventures into Amazonia by formal sector mining and colonisation companies during the nineteenth century, as they would in the twentieth, demonstrating that capital and mechanisation were not in themselves sufficient to ensure success: both had to rest on a knowledge of local conditions, and this pre-condition was met as rarely in the last century as it is in this. It illustrates the crucial role played by Africans and their descendants in the implantation and later development of gold garimpagem (and, one could add, Brazilian mining in general). Finally, it is interesting that one of the most important features of modern garimpagem, its role as an option for those at the bottom of the social hierarchy, can be shown to have been as central for refugee slaves during the nineteenth century as it is for smallholders and the urban poor during the twentieth.

To return to the point at which this chapter began, it also shows that in Maranhão at least garimpagem has not been as irregular nor as spasmodic as one might suppose. It constitutes an important thread running through the economic and social history of western Maranhão since the first half of the nineteenth century. It should be remembered that Maranhão has always been a minor area of garimpagem, and could never hope to rival, in terms of size and importance, parts of the states of Minas Gerais, Pará, Rondônia and Mato Grosso. If this degree of continuity can be shown to exist in Maranhão, one of the more difficult areas to establish it, then it is likely that if suf-ficient research attention were paid to other better-known areas of garimpagem, then the old stereotype of a gold rush as an outbreak of *febre de ouro* could finally be laid to rest.

3 Fofoca: The Formation of Garimpos

The formation of a garimpo is a complicated process. It begins with an individual, or a small group of prospectors, and ends with scores, hundreds, thousands and occasionally tens of thousands of garimpeiros working around the area of the original strike. Social relations have to be defined, and space has to be apportioned for people to work. The sequence of events that begins with successful prospecting and ends with the birth of a mature garimpo is usually compressed into a few months, and rarely lasts for more than a year. It is a period of frantic activity, with radical changes following upon one another with bewildering speed. At first glance, all this activity appears chaotic, an expression of the proverbial anarchy and lawlessness of gold mining communities, but beneath the blur of events lie highly structured processes common to the formation of all garimpos, large and small.

Garimpeiros call this time of garimpo formation *fofoca*. Their definition of a fofoca is mercifully straightforward. It is when a garimpo is producing a lot of gold and people flock to the spot; it ends when production dips and people start leaving. Outside garimpagem, fofoca means rumour, or gossip, and this accurately reflects how garimpeiros come to hear of gold strikes, through what is nicknamed *rádio peão*, word of mouth reports that are embellished as they are passed on. Although all garimpos begin life as fofocas, the fofoca is by its nature temporary, a distinct and easily identifiable phase in the life-cycle of a garimpo.

It does not begin with the initial discovery of gold and sinking of a barranco by pioneer prospectors, but with the object of every garimpeiro's dreams, the *bamburro*, the discovery of an exceptionally rich patch of material. News of a strike is difficult to contain and rumours begin to fly, attracting garimpeiros from the vicinity. When they arrive, according to convention they must seek out the *dono da fofoca* and ask him to assign an area for them to work. The dono da fofoca is the pioneer prospector who first discovered gold at that site. He is often, but not necessarily, the discoverer of the bamburro as well.

One bamburro is not usually enough to maintain the momentum of a

51

fofoca: there are many cases of a bamburro petering out and the dispersal of the garimpeiros attracted by the initial excitement. But it is also possible that, with the expansion of the area being worked, other strikes are made. Once this happens, the fofoca really takes off. Garimpeiros from near and far flock to the site in an astonishingly short time. In a case witnessed during fieldwork, one day a barranco suddenly improved its daily production from less than ten to thirty-seven grams. Two days later, a neighbouring barranco also improved production. On the third day rumours that there had been a bamburro of 200 grams or more were being passed around as fact. Less than a week later the hillside where the two barrancos were located had been cleared of vegetation and at least 200 garimpeiros were demarcating barrancos. Nothing provokes the interest and curiosity of a garimpeiro so much as news of a bamburro in the area, and stories about bamburros are lovingly recounted:

> This happened five days after the fofoca began, in Jibóia, over on the other side of the Gurupí. A man found a nugget weighing two kilos and 752 grams, a real bamburro, at around eight in the morning. He showed it to everyone, because the garimpeiro is an idiot sometimes: when he finds gold he has to go around stoking up the fofoca, showing it around, drinking beer, drinking rum, living it up. Well, he wanted to weigh it but there weren't any precision scales; the only pair around was a crude scale they used to weigh meat. So the only thing to do was weigh it as if it were meat. They got hold of the nugget, scrubbed it with acid to get rid of some of the impurities, and weighed it in the meat scales; two kilos and 752 grams. So he called his two partners, and said to them 'Let's get out of here and sell it'. They loaded their guns, one went in front with a revolver and the other covered his back with a shotgun. They left at the run, in spite of the mud. That was the last anyone saw of them, although we know they sold the gold. This was two months ago, and we heard about it when we went there the week after it happened.

As this recollection suggests, fofoca can be a dangerous time. In the early stages of the formation of a garimpo a large number of people attempt to get hold of a barranco within the small area surrounding bamburros. This invariably generates problems because, as will be seen, there are many cases when the authority of the dono da fofoca is weak, and disputes over barranco boundaries occur as a result. At the same time, as garimpeiros say, *ninguém conhece ninguém porque todo mundo é de fora*, nobody knows anyone because everybody is from the outside. The friendships and other social links that help to regulate social relations in a mature garimpo have not yet had time to form, there is severe pressure on land, and in the midst of all this there are bamburros, a tempting target for the unscrupulous. Nevertheless, a fofoca in full flow can be an extraordinary sight (see Plate 16). It is difficult not to be affected by the atmosphere of frantic activity and excitement. As the physical and social landscapes undergo intensely concentrated upheavals, it is as if culture and social structure are thrown into a pressure cooker, and usually remote concepts like property regimes and structures of authority become much more tangible as one sees them taking shape, bending and cracking under the strain, and being replaced by others. The best way to illustrate this 'cooking', to convey the peculiar atmosphere of the culturally ordered chaos of the fofoca, is to present some concrete examples.

CERQUEIRO

Cerqueiro was founded in 1982 by Eduardo, an exceptional garimpeiro. In 1985 he was in his sixties, and had been in the interior of the Gurupí since 1968, years before smallholders and garimpeiros began to trickle into the forest in the 1970s. He worked for a time as a hunter, killing jaguars and selling their pelts, living either alone or with one or two equally hardy backwoodsmen. When the trade in jaguar pelts became illegal in 1972 he turned to farming, and also worked at a variety of extractive activities. During his years in the forest he had built up an encyclopaedic knowledge of the region and its history, which he combined with a gentleness of manner and peaceable temperament that made him a popular and respected figure. He and a companion were probably the first people since the 1940s to extract gold in the area between Montes Aureos and the Belém–São Luis highway; he is a seasoned and highly skilled prospector capable of living alone in forest for months at a stretch, immensely knowledgeable about the environment in which he works. It might have been expected that a person of his skills would have been very well placed to take advantage of the rebirth of garimpagem in the Gurupí that he, along with a select band of half a dozen individuals with a similar background, was jointly responsible for starting. But things turned out rather differently.

In 1982, Eduardo returned to some sites that he had known for years were gold-bearing, and began to prospect them seriously. After casting around a little, he sank a small barranco on the bank of a creek, working alone, at the same time that another backwoodsman was beginning work at a place ten kilometers to the north, which came to be called Nadí. In the summer of 1982 there was a large bamburro in Nadí, and shortly afterwards an even larger one on the plot of a woman smallholder called Maria, about six kilometers away from Eduardo. Both Nadí and Maria went into fofoca, but Eduardo, being deeper in the forest, was relatively little troubled by the influx of garimpeiros; the newcomers tended to stick to the fofocas at Nadí and Maria. Eduardo's gold production was low, barely covering his costs, and not attractive to garimpeiros seeing barrancos in Nadí and Maria producing kilo after kilo of gold.

Then, in October 1982, just as the fofocas at Nadí and Maria were dying down (although they would later re-ignite with a vengeance), Eduardo's production improved, though not spectacularly. It was enough to provoke a fofoca, although initially it was of modest dimensions. Eduardo fulfilled all the garimpeiro norms about how a dono da fofoca should act to the letter. He made no difficulties for the newcomers, assigned and demarcated barrancos on request, turned nobody away, and only demanded the traditional ten per cent of production in return. One of the people who entered Cerqueiro at this stage was a rich businessman, holder of the Coca-Cola franchise in São Luís. He persuaded Eduardo to sell his barranco for a moínho and engine to replace the manual technology Eduardo was accustomed to using. Eduardo then moved to another barranco he had cleared about 200 metres away. At this point he ceased to assign barrancos to newcomers in the area of his first barranco, although he continued to do so at his new site. That first barranco turned out to be by far the richest in the garimpo and produced more than ten kilos of gold. Remarkably, Eduardo accepted this with equanimity (he is an evangelical Protestant and thought it the will of God), feeling no bitterness and maintaining that the transaction had been fair, although more streetwise garimpeiros were not convinced. The main part of the fofoca was concentrated around Eduardo's first barranco, although Eduardo attracted some garimpeiros to the area of his second barranco when that too began to show reasonable levels of production.

In June of 1983 the fofoca was at its height, with around a thousand garimpeiros scattered in the general area of Eduardo's first barranco. Machinery was beginning to arrive in force. Eduardo, however, was unable to keep pace with the mechanisation of the garimpo. He is an excellent prospector and knows everything there is to know about manual technology, but he is hopelessly bad at dealing with industrially produced machinery, about which he knows nothing. His production dropped and became increasingly sporadic, as the moínho he had been bought off with turned out to be chronically unreliable. To make matters worse, in September 1983 a garimpeiro called Amorim arrived with a moínho and engine, and was assigned a barranco by Eduardo in the usual way. Amorim is an experienced garimpeiro, and was soon producing ten grams of gold a day. Eduardo, meanwhile, was becalmed, with a large pile of material he was unable to put through his own moínho, and reluctant to lose half of the gold by arranging for it to be processed by another moínho owner, which would have involved dividing the proceeds. Amorim saw the vulnerability of Eduardo's position, knew that he was too old and pacific to retaliate, and cynically began to put Eduardo's material through his own moínho without asking permission. This was a grave breach of norms, which with a younger man would certainly have provoked violent retaliation, but Eduardo could do little more than make complaints, which were ignored. Amorim also began to lie about his gold production to evade payment of Eduardo's percentage. Eduardo realised this but, fearful of losing the little he did receive, could do nothing. In February 1984 Amorim refused to pay any percentage at all, and this was the cue for all the others who owed their barrancos to Eduardo to stop payments as well. Eduardo was left with a barranco, a moínho that kept breaking down, and some residual prestige for being the founder of the garimpo in which he had become, to all intents and purposes, a marginalised and rather forlorn figure.

TRINTA CINCO

Carlos is a *colono*, a smallholder settled on a plot of land by COLONE, the state agency that runs a land colonisation project in western Maranhão. Before entering the COLONE scheme in 1981, Carlos had worked as a labourer in garimpos in southern Pará for a few months, where he picked up the rudiments of garimpagem, including how to use a bateia. In June 1985 Carlos found some gold in a stream bed on his plot, and began to work it with a cobra fumando. The gold production was low, but it happened to be a slack period in the agricultural calendar, and by August there were about a dozen people, all colonos and the majority members of Carlos's extended family, working with cobras but not paying Carlos a percentage if they had a kinship link with him. From the prospecting he did, Carlos thought the area had potential, especially if he could get hold of a moínho. He himself was far too poor to buy one, and he was reluctant to bring in a garimpeiro because he knew that if he did the news of any strikes would break quickly, and he was worried about invasions of his lot. He therefore quietly approached Zé, a community leader in the village of Geraldo, who besides being the local COLONE agent and head of the rural trade union was also the owner of a moínho and barranco a couple of kilometres away from Carlos's lot. Zé went there, did a little prospecting of his own, and agreed that the area showed promise. He proposed that he and Carlos should become partners; Carlos would provide the barranco and labour, Zé the machinery, and they would split the proceeds. Together they marked out a large barranco, ten metres by ten metres, in the most promising spot.

However, Zé did not want to shift his machinery from his other barranco immediately, and instructed Carlos to wait for a few weeks while he finished up in his other site. Carlos had to temporise; for a month he successfully put off arriving garimpeiros by saying that Zé was responsible for the area and they should deal with him. However, it caused resentment amongst the garimpeiros that at the same time Carlos allowed several colonos in. Then, on 20 August, the barranco of Soares, a colono unrelated to Carlos, produced a small bamburro of twenty grams of gold. Soares left Trinta Cinco and sold the gold to a buyer in Geraldo; as invariably happens in such cases the gold buyer passed on the news, Carlos could no longer conceal the area's promise, and the fofoca began.

Still Carlos played for time, trying to put off the now much more frequent requests for barrancos, which for the first time included several full-time garimpeiros with machinery. This quickly generated a great deal of tension, as it was generally assumed that the reason Carlos was being so recalcitrant was to conceal an exceptionally rich deposit. Complaints were made to Luisão, a prominent garimpeiro and gold buyer in Nadí. Finally, on 22 September, Luisão coordinated an invasion of Trinta Cinco. About fifty men, all armed, set out at dawn from Nadí and later that morning arrived at Trinta Cinco to find Carlos working in his barranco. Castro, an associate of Luisão re-nowned for his boorishness, stepped forward and asked Carlos if he was prepared to open the area to them. Carlos said that he was willing, but they should clear it with Zé first. Castro swore at him, shouted that Zé had nothing to do with it, the land belonged to Carlos, and since he didn't mind, they were going to move in. With this the invaders moved into the area, respecting the demarcated barrancos of Zé and the colonos, but marking out others next to them. Two brothers of Carlos, alerted by other colonos as to what was happening, snatched up their shotguns and rushed to the scene, but in the face of so many people armed resistance was out of the question. Shortly afterwards Zé, who had had previous disagreements with Luisão and disliked him, arrived to be faced with the fait accompli, although he must have noted immediately that his own barranco had not been touched. Luisão called him aside and the two had a private conversation out of earshot. The upshot was that Zé accepted the invasion, with the proviso that existing barrancos should be respected; in the circumstances, there was little else he could do. The newcomers paid no percentage to Carlos, and after the invasion those already there stopped paying the percentage as well.

In the event, it turned out to be a crucial episode in the embittering of relations between Zé and Luisão, which three months later would result in open warfare between the two as Zé took a carefully plotted revenge for his public humiliation. But for the time being Trinta Cinco was open to all comers, who simply marked out unoccupied areas on arrival after consulting with those already there (see Plate 17). In Nadí Luisão's stock climbed to new heights. Ironically, it turned out to be much ado about nothing in the end; there were no further strikes and difficulties of water supply for the newly entered moínhos led to Trinta Cinco being almost completely abandoned by December.

MONTES AUREOS

Gold has been mined off and on in Montes Aureos since the beginning of the nineteenth century. It still contains monuments to an earlier mining era in the form of abandoned mechanical crushers and a steam boiler shipped over from Britain in 1859. In 1981 it had been effectively abandoned for about thirty-five years, although some garimpagem took place sporadically in its vicinity.

José is a northeasterner, who fled the droughts and the feudal land tenure systems of the interior of the state of Ceará to come, like many thousands of others, to the open spaces of Maranhão in the 1960s. He was taken on by a cattle ranch near Montes Aureos, and rose to become foreman. In 1981, attracted by the high price of gold and influenced by the publicity about Serra Pelada, he decided he would finally like to be his own master. He left his job at the ranch and with his savings bought a pump, a moínho and an engine. He began by working the tailings the English had left behind, and by 1985 he had become a prosperous garimpeiro well equipped with machinery, and the owner of a *cantina*, a small store, a herd of pigs and a banana field. But when he began to work on the tailings, he had been surprised by a visit from a young man of Japanese descent who told him he could not enter Montes Aureos because it was included in a mineral concession owned by a mining company based in Belém, of which he was an agent. José demanded documentary proof and was shown a photocopy of the concession. Unfortunately for the Japonês, as he was nicknamed, José had experience of legal documents from his time on the ranch, and saw immediately that the document was invalid; it had been made to the DNPM residency in Belém and not to the sub-residency in São Luís responsible for all mineral concessions in Maranhão. José refused to move, saying that since the document was invalid, and the Japonês had no obvious claim to the area as discoverer of the deposit or owner of a barranco, he had every right to stay. The Japonês blustered, but José in some ways is a formidable character and there was little he could do.

Until the arrival of José the Japonês had managed to retain control of an extremely large area, taking in not only all of the present garimpo of Montes Aureos but also the hillside of Monte Cristo behind it. But this was because the influx of garimpeiros into the area did not take off until 1982, and very few people apart from José wanted to mine gold in Montes Aureos. The situation changed in 1982; fofocas in Maria and Nadí to the north and Serrinha and Chega Tudo to the west attracted thousands of garimpeiros to the region. The Japonês was simply swamped. He quickly realised that alone he could do nothing to prevent people entering Montes Aureos, and fell back on using his photocopy to impress the newcomers into regarding him as the dono da fofoca and paying him a percentage. This worked with the first manual garimpeiros, but the fragility of his legal claim soon became notorious, mainly through diligent dissemination on the part of José, who was anxious to see as many customers as possible in his cantina, which he had shrewdly set up to take advantage of the many garimpeiros who passed through Montes Aureos on their way to Serrinha and Chega Tudo. Thus the Japonês was rapidly discredited, becoming just another owner of a barranco.

Montes Aureos spent a few months in fofoca in 1982 and 1983, but never anything to compare with the larger garimpos nearby. Newcomers marked out barrancos in unoccupied areas after consulting with those already working in the site; there was no dono da fofoca and no percentages were paid. One of the newcomers was Diadorim, who together with three companions worked a barranco that bordered the Japonês. Diadorim and his friends were violent and generally disliked; they drank a lot, and were chronically short of labour because of their habit of beating up those who worked for them when dissatisfied with their performance. The Japonês, a short tempered man at the best of times, had several disagreements with them. One day, while the Japonês was temporarily absent, Diadorim and his friends entered his barranco and began to work in it, the most heinous sin, short of outright murder, that a garimpeiro can commit. When the Japonês returned, Diadorim and his companions pistolwhipped him in full view of the garimpeiros in the vicinity, and told him they would kill him if he was not out of the garimpo by nightfall. The Japonês left and was not seen in Montes Aureos again. Soon afterwards, in August 1983, Diadorim and his companions left, to general relief. Diadorim himself was later killed in a knife fight in Pernambuco. By that time the fofoca was well and truly over. Gold production was falling, and many people moved on. By 1985 Montes Aureos was half the size it had been, but gold production was levelling out and it had evolved into a stable and peaceful mature garimpo.

In theory at least, the role of the dono da fofoca is fairly clear. He (or, exceptionally, she) is the person who marks out the boundaries of a barranco and allocates it to a newcomer. The exact size of a barranco varies according to the technology being used; a manual barranco using a cobra fumando would at the most measure five by five metres, and a barranco for a moínho twice that. Convention dictates that the dono ought not to refuse any request for an area, nor may the dono sell or rent an area which he himself is not working; once given, a barranco may not be repossessed for any reason, although it does happen that newcomers allocated a barranco who later decide to leave will, if they have no relatives or friends with them, return the barranco to the dono with thanks, for the dono to re-allocate as he sees fit. In return for all this, the dono is entitled to a percentage of the gold produced in any barranco he has demarcated and allocated. The exact percentage varies, but is usually around ten per cent.

It is also clear from these cases that the fofoca itself has different stages. It begins after initial prospecting, or is triggered by a bamburro in a garimpo that has already experienced a fofoca that subsided. In the case of a fofoca in an already existing garimpo the strike may be in a primary deposit; otherwise it is invariably alluvial. In a fofoca provoked by successful prospecting, there is an influx of garimpeiros using manual techniques, who are assigned barrancos by the dono da fofoca. If the strike proves to be a one-off, the fofoca may be abandoned. If not, the initial influx of garimpeiros quickens, this time including garimpeiros with more sophisticated machinery. At first the dono da fofoca continues to allocate barrancos and receive a percentage, but the more a fofoca becomes established, the more likely it is that he will lose his authority, either through gradual decomposition or a sudden crisis. The dono then becomes a garimpeiro like any other, with no authority over anything save his own barranco. Once this happens, newcomers simply mark out barrancos in unoccupied spots after consultation with those working in the vicinity, and do not pay a percentage. A grid of clearly marked barrancos comes into being. Sooner or later gold production will dip from the heady days of the initial strikes, and people start to leave. Sometimes a site may be completely abandoned, but it is more usual for a leaner but more mature garimpo to emerge, stabler than a fofoca both in terms of population numbers and the definition of social and property relations within that population.

When a prospector enters an area that bears no obvious signs of human occupation, it is regarded as common land which can be freely entered, belonging to those who work it. This is the same ideology that infuses spontaneous agricultural migration in Amazonia. What differentiates garimpeiros from smallholders is that the property regime they must set up is far more complicated; a productive piece of land is measured in metres rather than hectares, and many people have to be crammed into an area that is often a fraction of the size of a field of rice or manioc. Thus a great deal is happening on several different levels during a fofoca. Space is allocated to individuals, a property regime crystallises, authority over the area of gold extraction is asserted and comes under challenge, and at each stage of the fofoca different conceptions of legitimate rights and demands are in conflict.

When a prospector discovers gold in a particular spot, that fact confers certain prerogatives. He marks out a barranco, which can be no larger than the area he can realistically exploit, around ten metres by ten metres being the upper limit in most cases. All barrancos are the private property of their owners, exclusive and inviolate, and no other person has any authority over them. At the same time, it is deeply believed by garimpeiros that *o garimpo é para todo mundo, para quem quiser*, the garimpo is open to all, to whoever wishes to enter. In other words, being a dono da fofoca is an existentially uncomfortable role: the person who has to regulate and apply a central moral principle, which, in its assertion of universal access independent of means, is not only logically antagonistic to the idea of external regulation, but also somewhat doctrinaire in that it does not address the central question of exactly where people are to go once access is given.

The dono da fofoca is the only type of garimpeiro whose prerogatives stretch beyond the boundaries of his barranco. But, critically, while the exact nature of these prerogatives is vague, they certainly do not constitute *ownership* of anything beyond the barranco, and the exact boundaries of the area to which these rights extend cannot be defined. That the dono da fofoca has some form of jurisdiction over the immediate vicinity of his barranco is clearly shown by the convention that it is he who allocates barrancos to newcomers, and materially expressed in the percentage of gold production which he receives. But these percentage payments are not regarded as in any sense rent, nor can the dono sell an area: he does not own the vicinity of his barranco because he is not working in it, and 'the garimpo is open to all'.

In effect, the convention which bestows these prerogatives also undermines them, because, as requests for areas cannot legitimately be refused, the dono da fofoca must acquiesce in the surrendering of the area to which they apply to others. Once newcomers sink barrancos, that space becomes theirs and the dono da fofoca cannot take it away. In the early stages of a fofoca, when all attention is concentrated on an area never more than a few metres away from the spot where gold was first discovered, the nebulousness of the area over which the dono da fofoca has jurisdiction is not relevant. But sooner or later (and in the case of a large gold strike it can happen very quickly) the lack of defined boundaries of his authority becomes a problem. The space around the original barranco is filled by others, then others cluster around this nucleus, and still more people arrive who have to move further and further away from the initial strike. They will recognise the authority of the dono da fofoca less and less, in pro-portion to the distance that separates them from the original barranco. How long the dono da fofoca's authority takes to collapse varies according to circumstances, but, except in some special cases to be examined later, collapse it will.

It is tempting to think that the role of the dono da fofoca is a recipe for instability, institutionalising as it does an inherently contradictory bundle of social and economic relationships fated to break down in the short or medium term. But it would be a mistake to focus only on the tenuous nature of this authority without considering the nature of the property regime that it creates; thus, in contrast, is surprisingly stable.

Once demarcated, a barranco has fixed and inviolate boundaries, becoming privately owned space that may be sold or rented. The existence of the dono da fofoca as an institution means that the crucial early period, when coveted and potentially gold-bearing space has to be divided and allocated to specific individuals, is regulated. An individual with no economic stake in the barranco in question allocates it and marks its boundaries (usually by stringing a creeper or rope between wooden pegs) in full view of all garimpeiros working in the vicinity. It is done openly and unambiguously, and although the boundaries may not be respected and conflicts occur, lines drawn by the dono da fofoca have a moral force; they are a marker in more ways than one. They represent an important aspect of the internal regulation of the garimpo, and command a broad consensus because of the universal recognition that the alternative, a Darwinian survival of the fittest, would lead to anarchy. By the time his authority breaks down, there is at least a nucleus of barrancos clustered around the original barranco which have defined boundaries and owners. What was once common land, public space open to all, has crystallised into a grid of private and separate spaces in a way which still makes it possible to say that 'the garimpo is open to all'.

This is not to say that disputes over barranco boundaries in a fofoca do not occur; in fact, they are very common. It has to be remembered that the focus of a fofoca changes over time in accordance with the pattern of gold strikes, and this results in a great deal of variation in the way that a dono da fofoca regulates, or fails to regulate, barranco allocation. The initial bamburro that triggers a fofoca is always either in or very near the barranco of the dono da fofoca, the central point from which his authority radiates. This is not necessarily true of later strikes, which may occur in one of the more peripheral barrancos grouped around the initial strike.

The situation in this case is especially complicated, because it will lead to a movement of garimpeiros away from the barranco of the dono da fofoca to sites where his authority is less well defined. Movements of garimpeiros within the fofoca tend to be self-reinforcing; the more people working in an area, the more likely it is further strikes will be made, which will encourage more people to move there, and so on. It is common for there to be a marked redirection of garimpeiros over time away from the first strike, and when this happens the dono da fofoca can only lose. His authority in the new focus of the fofoca will rapidly be challenged; those who feel any grievance about the size or location of their barranco are much more likely to refuse to accept that somebody without a barranco in the immediate vicinity should decide where they should work. At best they will refuse to pay ten per cent of their production, and often refuse to pay anything at all. Once they do, it automatically means the end of all payments; even those working barrancos close to the dono da fofoca will stop paying, not seeing why they should have to do so while newcomers are exempt. A natural consequence of this breakdown of the moral consensus that leaves the regulation of barranco distribution in the hands of the dono da fofoca is a marked increase in disputes over barranco boundaries. They will be most common in a fofoca where the focus (or foci) of gold production shifts away from the initial strike, and the further away it shifts, the more frequent boundary disputes will be.

But even in a situation where the authority of the dono da fofoca breaks down very early, life is still not as Darwinian as might be supposed. Provided that a barranco is in use, it is very rare for it to be forcibly taken away from its owner, even by a rich and unscrupulous garimpeiro. Anyone contemplating such a move would have to be prepared to kill the owner of it, with all the dangers of police persecution, and, more to the point, a lethal feud with the owner's relatives, that murder would entail. Even should he do so, he would find that no labourers would be prepared to work for him, he would be unable to get credit at the cantina, and nobody would be prepared to lend him spare parts and fuel for his machinery. These are powerful sanctions; few people who were the target of them would be able to continue living and working in the fofoca. There may well be disputes over the boundaries of a barranco, but disputes over the ownership of barrancos themselves are very rare, because, partly thanks to the dono da fofoca, ownership of a barranco is never in doubt. Even in a fofoca where the dono da fofoca loses authority very quickly, violence measured in terms of death or injury, although present, is proverbial rather than real, and the ubiquitous violence in descriptions of garimpos by journalists and others is usually no more than a cultural construct that comes from people with no direct experience of garimpos.

Finally, it should be noted that there are important differences between a fofoca that starts where no garimpo previously exists, and fofocas in a garimpo which has already been a fofoca at least once before. This is reflected in the semantic distinction garimpeiros make between *uma fofoca*, using the indefinite article, and *estar em fofoca*, literally 'to be in fofoca'. When a mature garimpo enters fofoca once more, it is 'in fofoca' (*está em fofoca*); otherwise one talks simply of *uma fofoca* or *fofoca de X*, it not yet being clear whether the fofoca will be abandoned or whether it will mature into a garimpo proper.

Where a fofoca occurs in a previously existing garimpo, except in certain cases described below there is no dono da fofoca. Newcomers clustering around the new bamburro mark out barrancos in unoccupied spots after consulting with those already working there. The first fofoca a garimpo experiences is invariably the most problematic; ones that follow it are less so, even though later fofocas tend to be triggered by larger bamburros, because by then the level of mechanisation will be higher. Firstly, it is common for the area surrounding a strike in an established garimpo to be already covered by a grid of barrancos, which limits the influx of newcomers. Many of the garimpeiros who do make their way to the new site and can mark barrancos in the vicinity will be from other parts of the same garimpo, and share the body of communal knowledge about who owns what barranco and where, which tends to minimise disputes. There are already social networks and defined social relations both within these arrivistes as a group and between them and those garimpeiros fortunate enough to be the owners of the barranco that triggered the fofoca. Finally, newcomers from beyond the garimpo are not entering an area only very recently given over to garimpagem. It is in their interests not to alienate those already there, who can act as a bloc against them precisely when they are at their most vulnerable, only recently established and less well informed about local social networks and personalities. They therefore tend to be scrupulous in consulting those already working in the vicinity, who can tell them *onde não há dono*, where there is no owner.

TYPES OF FOFOCA

The principles that the garimpo is open to all, and that requests for a barranco cannot legitimately be refused, have already been mentioned. Nevertheless, in two of the three case studies used, attempts were made to restrict access to the fofoca. What happens when restricted access can be enforced? So far, only fofocas that occur in unoccupied lands have been dealt with. What happens when the land where gold is discovered already has an owner? And what happens in an area like the Tapajós, where garimpeiros cannot arrive shortly after a strike is reported because the overland journey is long and difficult, and there are often no garimpeiros within hundreds of kilometres? What about

Serra Pelada, the largest fofoca in the history of Brazilian garimpagem, where federal intervention took place? Or Cumarú, also the scene of federal intervention?

Although so far fofocas have been treated as if they were uniform, and there are in fact important similarities between all fofocas, it also has to be stressed that fofocas vary according to the physical and social context in which they occur. A fofoca in the Tapajós may be similar to a fofoca in the Gurupí, but there are important differences as well. A broad guide to the most important types of fofoca to be found in the Amazon gold rush is therefore necessary.

The fofoca of Serra Pelada, and later that of Cumarú, both of which were so large that they had explosive social and political implications for Amazonia and provoked forceful intervention by the federal authorities in Brasília, are clearly special cases and will be considered separately in Chapter 7. This leaves what can be called a 'closed fofoca', where access is restricted, fofocas that are not closed but which take place on land that has an owner, and fofocas characteristic of areas like the Tapajós, where entry is only possible by air because of the difficulties and distances involved.

Technically, in that much of Amazonia is covered by mineral concessions and land claims of various types, several of which often apply to a single tract of land, only a small proportion of fofocas take place in free land. However, as claimants to land are not necessarily physically present on it, and expelling armed garimpeiros is no easy task at the best of times, in practice most fofocas take place on land that is effectively free. But not infrequently gold is discovered on part of a cattle ranch, rubber or Brazil nut estate, or a mining concession, where the owners of the land are present; when this happens they have an important impact on the development of the fofoca. This is a situation anticipated in the Brazilian mining law, which states that owners of land on which mineral strikes are made are obliged to allow extraction to go ahead but are entitled to ten per cent of the proceeds.[1] However, the relevant legislation does not specify what mechanisms are to be used to collect this levy, and in effect landowners have two choices; to come to an accommodation with the fofoca and collect this levy as best they can, by whatever means they can improvise, or to attempt to dominate the fofoca by force, either expelling the garimpeiros or restricting access and controlling and manipulating the garimpeiros already there. Expulsion tends only to occur if the 'owner' of the land in question is a mineral company, anxious to retain exclusive rights over mineral deposits in a concession. The most notorious case of this type occurred in 1970 in Rondônia, when something over 20 000 garimpeiros of cassiterite were forcibly removed by the Brazilian army. A more recent case was the Serra das Andorinhas, near to the area of the Carajás iron and bauxite complex in southern Pará, when federal police removed around 2000 gold garimpeiros at the behest of the Companhia do Vale do Rio Doce in 1979. But where the landowner is not a mining concern, garimpeiros tend not to be expelled; gold on one's estate is a major asset, after all, and somebody has to extract it.

In the case of a fofoca on land with a recognised owner who decides not to restrict access, it is the landowner and not the garimpeiro who first discovers gold at a particular spot who becomes the dono da fofoca and takes over his functions. But donos da fofoca who are also owners of the land where the fofoca is situated are in a much stronger position than donos da fofoca in unoccupied land. They are usually far richer than the initial manual garimpeiros, and they can call on family and people already in their employment to reinforce their position within the fofoca. The usual sequence of events is for landowners to try and make themselves the dominant economic force within the fofoca. There are various ways of doing this. The prerogative of distributing barrancos can be used to give barrancos to relatives and to trusted members of the estate workforce. In addition, through percentage deals it is possible to contract incoming garimpeiros to work barrancos, dividing the proceeds according to a variety of methods. Thus the dono da fofoca can own large numbers of barrancos without generating resentment, provided that newcomers are accommodated at the same time and all the landowner's barrancos are seen to be in use.

They can also set up a cantina, where necessities bought in bulk or produced elsewhere on the estate can be sold to garimpeiros at a handsome profit, and through which they can control the granting or withholding of credit, a strategically vital element in the economic life of the garimpo. If access to the fofoca is difficult by land, they can build an airstrip, for which they can command landing fees, and through which they can control access. On top of all this, they are also entitled to a percentage from all barrancos, and, unlike less privileged donos, barring disaster or unusual circumstances they will collect it for a long time to come. Market forces appear to have kept the percentage down to five per cent in most fofocas of this type, probably because a higher level would discourage garimpeiros from entering, and the more garimpeiros who can be attracted to the fofoca, the more money the landowner is likely to make.

But despite all these advantages, they also operate under the same constraints as a garimpeiro dono da fofoca. They ignore requests for a barranco at their peril; too many refusals and they run the risk of a violent invasion, the consequent loss of a part of the estate, and the end of a very profitable state of affairs. The same thing is likely to happen if the landowner marks off for private use land that is not seen to be in production. Once a barranco is marked out and allocated, the landowner, like any other dono da fofoca, cannot take it away or have any say in its operation.

Taking all these factors into account, a fofoca on the land of a person who deals wisely with it is the most stable and trouble-free of all fofocas. There is no such thing as a problem caused by the vague boundaries of the area to which the prerogatives of the dono da fofoca applies. Landowner donos da fofoca have undisputed jurisdiction up to the boundaries of their estates. They can therefore regulate the allocation of barrancos far more effectively than a dono da fofoca in common land. Disputes are minimised as a result, and even when they do occur the greater authority of a landowner dono da fofoca means that they can take on an arbitrating role which garimpeiro donos da fofoca rarely have the prestige to assume.

A fofoca accessible only by air also tends to lead to a situation in which economic control and social authority are much more centralised than is the case in a fofoca on common land. On an open-closed spectrum an airstrip fofoca is an intermediate case; they are usually open to whoever wishes to enter them, but difficulties of access mean that only a few can enter at any one time. Airstrip fofocas are found throughout Amazonia, but are most common in the Tapajós. The Tapajós is an enormous area of about 100 000 square kilometres of forest and rivers, only very thinly populated. Roads are almost non-existent, and rapids make even river transport problematic in many places. In these conditions, the formation of garimpos and the structure of fofocas are rather different. In the Tapajós gold is usually discovered by a small prospecting team of garimpeiros, who are often relatives. Once a deposit is found, one garimpeiro returns to the nearest airstrip and from there flies to the towns of Itaituba or Santarém, where he strikes an agreement with a wholesale supplier and a pilot to freight in supplies. In the meantime, his companions are clearing an airstrip to serve the deposit. At first supplies have to be packed into sacks and pushed out over the fofoca, but once the airstrip is ready supplies and garimpeiros can begin to be brought in regularly.

What happens next depends on whether the initial prospectors were hired or working on their own account. If hired, they are paid off and the backer sets up a cantina to sell supplies and provide credit to newcomers, as well as, in most cases, running a transport monopoly with a fleet of private planes. If they are working on their own account, the founders of a garimpo set up a cantina and come to an arrangement with pilots and merchants in Itaituba or Santarém about transport and supplies. As time goes on, and some of the founders wish to move on and are bought out, strategic areas of economic life in the garimpo are concentrated in the hands of one or two individuals, although there are odd cases of a founding syndicate holding together for over a decade. The cantina, several barrancos, the planes that serve the airstrip, and a brothel, may all be owned by a single individual, who within the garimpo does not admit competition from anybody. If there is a bamburro, and a fofoca develops, the founders are the dono(s) da fofoca, but also enjoy the privilege of being able to control, via the airstrip, the rate at which people enter the fofoca. It is not that a dono in an airstrip fofoca would want to restrict access; it makes no economic sense to do so. Each additional garimpeiro is another customer who has to buy supplies at the cantina, or pay air freight charges if he buys wholesale in a town instead, another landing fee each time they enter or leave the fofoca, another seller of gold, and another customer for any other facilities that might have been installed by the dono, like an oficina, a machine repair shop.

Those wishing to enter an airstrip fofoca have to go and see the dono or his representative in Santarém or Itaituba, are assigned barrancos in the usual way once they arrive, and must agree in advance to pay a percentage of the gold they produce to the dono. The fact that access is mainly or exclusively by air means that donos can regulate the rate at which people enter in such a way as not to deny access, but at the same time keep it at a less frantic level which can more easily be controlled. Within the fofoca, the authority of the dono da fofoca is potentially as absolute as that of a landowner dono da fofoca: more so in many cases, because airstrip donos are almost always experienced garimpeiros, likely to be more adept at achieving economic domination of the garimpo than a landowner who is merely rich, ignorant of garimpagem and likely to make mistakes in handling garimpeiros. In these circumstances, an airstrip dono da fofoca often manages to retain control and authority almost indefinitely, for over two decades in some cases, long after the fofoca itself has subsided. This is recognised in the existence of a social category characteristic of the Tapajós, the *dono do garimpo*, who began as a dono da fofoca but who made the grade to dono do garimpo as the fofoca successfully accomplished the transition from fofoca to garimpo.

Obviously, the concentration of ownership in an airstrip fofoca can, and does, lead to abuses. In many cases it is a fine line indeed between monopoly regulation of entry and exit and what could be called a 'closed fofoca' or 'closed garimpo', where access is restricted, by force if need be.[2] Those that do exist are more usually cases of non-garimpeiro landowners who decide to seal off a fofoca than airstrip donos overstepping themselves; sealing off a fofoca involves policing the area, and it tends to be easier for landowners than donos da fofoca to put people into the field to enforce restricted access. In addition, a garimpeiro dono da fofoca will at least be aware of the ideal that 'the garimpo is open to all'. While this may not prevent them trying to create a closed fofoca in some cases, it makes them more aware of the hatred that doing so will provoke and the consequent difficulties of maintaining long-term control. They therefore feel certain constraints that ranchers especially ignore.

A closed fofoca is the most violent and unstable of all fofocas. They have certain features in common. Firstly, they tend to occur in thinly populated areas in which state control, in the form of police and state bureaucracies, is weak. Secondly, in order to close a fofoca the owner of the land on which it occurs has to have sufficient manpower to enforce restricted access; they therefore tend to be economically and politically powerful figures in the area. Finally, access to the fofoca has to be restricted at a very early stage, as soon as possible after the first manual bamburro. If intervention is not almost immediate, the influx of garimpeiros will rapidly make it impossible to bring the area under control. Even worse, if the attempt to restrict access is contested by garimpeiros and the landowner loses, then he loses all legitimacy in the eyes of the garimpeiros and may even be killed by them. If, however, the attempt is successful, even if only temporarily, control of the fofoca is absolute and the luckless garimpeiros within it are squeezed to levels unprecedented in any other form of garimpagem, with lucrative results for the landowner. The mechanisms through which this is accomplished go far beyond the confiscation of a high percentage of gold produced in barrancos, as Antônio, a garimpeiro who underwent the experience in southern Pará, explains;

For about eighteen months in 1980 and 1981 garimpeiros were humiliated in the ranch of Doctor Soares, in the district of Macedônia, part of the area that we call Cumarú these days. This was before the federal intervention there, when this particular area was dominated by Dr Soares and his gunmen. I knew the situation was bad, but rumour had it that it was a rich garimpo, so I went all the same. You could only get to the ranch by a small track. The gunmen set up a post on it, and you could only enter or leave on their say-so. If anybody tried to leave with gold, they took it off them. They searched everyone. Once you got in, if you needed supplies the only cantina was operated by Dr Soares. You went in and said what you wanted, but you didn't have the right to ask the price; you had to pay whatever they decided. Same thing with selling gold. You had to sell to them at their price and using their scales. If you brought along twenty grams they would weigh it and say it was fifteen and there was nothing you could do about it. And even for that fifteen the price was very low, so we lost out both ways . . . we did what we could to resist, not violently, you understand, there were too many of them. Some left through the jungle, taking their gold with them, avoiding the paths. I didn't do that, I smuggled my gold out. I had a hat with a cloth lining, so what I did was pick out the stitching inside the brim, put my gold inside, and sew it up again. I put the hat on my head and the gunmen didn't notice anything different. That's how I managed to pass. But you couldn't smuggle out more than 100 grams of gold a time that way. It wasn't like other garimpos around there, Redenção, Rio Maria, Xinguará. There might not have been much gold there, but you could work as you wanted, sell gold to whoever you wanted for a fair price, and buy things where you pleased.

Didn't you complain to the authorities?

Well, yes, people did, but not en masse. Denunciations by individual garimpeiros are useless, because everyone looks on the garimpeiro as if he were some kind of savage beast. If anybody did complain to the police Soares would go there [Redenção] and one lie of his would be worth ten truths told by a garimpeiro. Garimpeiros couldn't complain in his presence, only behind his back, because the man was a doctor [i.e. upper class; doctor is an honorific]. With him being the dono, what garimpeiro would say to his face 'You're doing us wrong'? So most people didn't complain, they were afraid. If you complained, your life would be in danger.

Even so, although Antônio could not know it at the time, the position of Soares was becoming increasingly tenuous. The federal authorities, who had only brought Serra Pelada under their control the year before, were nervous at the large numbers of garimpeiros moving into the Cumarú area. At the same time, complaints about closed fofocas and garimpos in the region (Soares was only one of several culprits) were filtering through to opposition politicians, church leaders and unionists in Redenção and Conceição do Araguaia, who through the PMDB (Partido do Movimento Democrático Brasileiro) were engaged in intense political struggle with the rural oligarchy. The oligarchy was PDS (Partido Democrático Social), as was the military government in Brasília. Once the opposition began to pass on these complaints to the state capital, Belém, the opposition parties had a field day. With elections imminent, the federal government decided to act to recover the initiative. Partly to defuse these criticisms, partly to take the heat out of the social tensions in Cumarú, and partly to bring the gold production under control so that it could be duly taxed, in 1981 the government took control of the area away from the oligarchs and sent in the relatively competent federal police to bring the region to heel. Antônio had the satisfaction of seeing what happened as a result:

> Things got better at the end of 1981 when the *federais* went in. It's funny, but the very roadblock which the gunmen set up in 1980 became the headquarters of the federal police. They put in a proper road and everything. After the intervention, there was justice in the region. Anything that came up, they would go and sort it out. They went into the estate of Soares to call the wrongdoers to reason and to declare what is right. From then on there was order and justice.

A closed fofoca or garimpo, then, is one in which violence, or, more exactly, the threat of violence, becomes an integral part of the relations of production. Lucrative though this is while it lasts, it is difficult to keep a fofoca closed. One factor is that the volume of complaints and denunciations that builds up in such cases makes it likely that state or federal authorities will intervene sooner or later. It should be remembered that although localised state power may be weak in some parts of Amazonia, the federal authorities are always capable of intervening with decisive force anywhere in Brazil if need be. Local weakness is a result of neglect, and not a general lack of power or capacity on the part of the Brazilian state. It simply has to be prodded into flexing its muscle, and a sufficient volume of complaints, combined with strategic self-interest, is usually enough to persuade it to do so. Once federal intervention takes place, it does so with an authoritarian disregard for local sensibilities, and figures like Dr Soares tend to find that the consequences of keeping a fofoca closed are horrendous; not only do they lose their position within it, but they are also politically sidelined by the federal authorities and lose political (although not necessarily economic) hegemony within the region. Large but temporary profits from a closed garimpo are little compensation for the disastrous long term consequences of keeping it closed.

Furthermore, closing a fofoca to garimpeiros is inherently self-defeating. It is like showing a red rag to a bull; it will immediately be assumed that the only reason for doing so is to hide an exceptionally rich deposit. This attracts even more garimpeiros to the area, making control of it only possible by the wider exercise of the very violence that is likely to draw the attention of the authorities. This is not to say that closed fofocas and garimpos do not exist in Amazonia, nor that more will not be created. But they are increasingly rare, and likely to become rarer in the future. Those that do come into being will be small and confined to the most remote areas of Amazonia. The development of transport links and the quantum leap in the depth of state penetration in Amazonia over the last two decades has meant not only that the interval between the committing of abuses and their coming to the notice of the authorities is shorter, but also that the state has the capacity to act decisively if it wishes. Where social tensions threaten to explode, or where the federal authorities believe there is political advantage to be gained, they have little hesitation in intervening, even at the expense of traditional allies. The higher the gold production in a closed fofoca, therefore, the more impossible it becomes for those keeping the fofoca closed to control the tensions inherent in the situation. Ultimately, only the Brazilian state has the power to close a fofoca and keep it closed. Serra Pelada, Cumarú, and the Carajás project are examples of such state-inspired closed fofocas, but they are so important they deserve separate consideration elsewhere.

4 The Social Structure of the Gold Rush

At first sight a garimpo appears to be a place where the social stratification that is so much a feature of Brazilian society is largely absent. People mix without apparent distinction in work and at play, and from a distance it is impossible to tell the doctor or the business-man from the smallholder or the building worker. It is not unusual to see a middle or upper class man cooking a meal for illiterate small-holders and ex-shop assistants. But appearances are deceptive, for within a few hours of arrival in a garimpo it becomes obvious that there are social hierarchies; some garimpeiros give instructions, others carry them out.

The garimpo is a place where people from a great variety of social and geographical backgrounds mix, but it is also a place which is fundamentally structured in terms of an occupational hierarchy. The single most important factor governing the place garimpeiros occupy, at least initially, in that hierarchy is the social background from which they come, and to which the majority return at regular intervals. This chapter is a description and analysis of these social and economic hierarchies, with the aim of producing some kind of model of the social structure of the post-1979 gold rush in Amazonia.

But first the question of to what extent one can speak in such general terms about 'the social structure of the garimpo' needs to be addressed. Rural Amazonia is a mosaic of various agricultural and extractive activities, some or all of which may be found in one area of garimpagem and be completely absent in another. One garimpo may be accessible by road and surrounded by smallholder colonists, while another might only be accessible by air and have no other people living anywhere in the vicinity. One garimpo may only mine gold with manual technology, while in another one finds tractors, bulldozers, and the widespread use of explosives. Some garimpos may be inhabited only by people from the immediate area, while in others, like Serra Pelada, one comes across garimpeiros from every state in Brazil. Nevertheless, even bearing in mind the regional variations in garimpagem that have been repeatedly stressed, a good case can be made out for saying that the common factors that cut across regional boundaries are such that, with certain reservations, one can talk of 'the social structure of garimpagem' and come up with general models which may not be comprehensive in any one case but do at least have the virtue of explaining something wherever they are applied.

Garimpeiros themselves are the first to recognise the essential homogeneity of their profession. Although there are various techniques of gold extraction, no single method is unique to one region and practised nowhere else. Many garimpeiros are remarkably mobile, criss-crossing Amazonia according to where the latest whisperings on the grapevine suggest that the pickings are rich, yet those with experience of one region have no difficulty in slotting into garimpos outside it. In every garimpo one finds a division between *donos*, owners of barrancos, and workers receiving either a fixed daily wage or a percentage of the gold produced. In every garimpo one also finds *sócios*, people who may or may not be resident in the garimpo who provide supplies, machinery, or financial backing to donos in return for a share of the gold produced. Save for the very beginning of a fofoca, every garimpo will have at least one *cantineiro*, a retailer who sells supplies to garimpeiros and may also provide credit. In addition, every region of garimpagem also contains many people who may not be permanently resident in any one garimpo, but who nevertheless depend, wholly or in part, upon garimpos for their living; cooks, itinerant gold buyers, prostitutes, pilots, mule drivers, hunters, travelling photographers, smallholders, bar owners and many others. There are, then, many similarities as well as differences between garimpos and regions of garimpagem, and a real sense in which one can talk about a generalised social structure of the gold rush.

The most important social division in the garimpo is between donos and workers. Much less numerous, but with strategically important roles, are sócios and cantineiros. Donos vary a great deal, ranging from the smallholder with a cobra fumando which he works occasionally at slack periods of the agricultural calendar, to the rich entrepreneur with sophisticated machinery and interests in related activities like gold buying and air transport. There are different kinds of worker as well. Some only work in the garimpo for a few weeks and then return to other rural and urban occupations. Less numerous, but structurally very important, are workers who regard themselves as full-time garimpeiros and spend most of the year in garimpos, often making long journeys between different regions of garimpagem. Before going on to look more closely at these different social types, some initial idea of the similarities and differences between donos and workers can be gained from the analysis of survey material collected in the Gurupí garimpos of Nadí, Cerqueiro, Cedral, Trinta Cinco, Montes Aureos and Pica-Pau. Although the sample sizes are small, fifty donos and fifty workers, they do contain certain indications which it is my impression would be confirmed in larger surveys in other areas of garimpagem.

The most striking contrasts between donos and workers in the survey were in age (see Figure 4.1), experience of garimpagem (see Tables 4.1 and 4.2) and geographical origin (see Figures 4.2 and 4.3). In terms of social background (see Tables 4.3, 4.4, 4.5 and 4.6) the differences, perhaps surprisingly, are not as striking as the similarities. The greatest contrast was in age. No less than 34 of the 50 workers interviewed were aged between 15 and 25 (27 were between 18 and 22 alone), whereas the age spread of donos was much more even, with exactly half of the sample aged between 25 and 35. This reflects one important difference between the two; workers tend to be single young males, only 13 of the 50 being married, separated or widowed, whereas thirty-four of the donos were or had been married. In length of experience of garimpagem, and experience of other areas of garimpagem, donos were markedly ahead of workers. Workers were also much less likely to be permanently resident in the garimpo; only 8 workers, against 36 donos, said that they spent more than half the year in garimpos. Thirty of those 36 donos gave the garimpo they were working in as their permanent place of residence, and 9 of them were living there with wife/partner and children.

It is the similarities of background rather than the differences which strike one looking at Tables 4.3, 4.4, 4.5 and 4.6; this seems to be an indication, as will be argued below, of the high rates of social mobility in garimpagem, which mean that a significant proportion of donos begin life as workers and move up. The importance of smallholder agriculture is very clear, but it is also obvious, in Tables 4.5 and 4.6, that urban occupations like construction work and shop assistants are common backgrounds for garimpeiros. Most of the urban occupations cited are clearly either informal or at the bottom end of the formal sector. This suggests that many garimpeiros, especially workers, are turning to garimpagem for at least part of the year after being squeezed in or dislodged from the precarious position in the urban and rural economies that they occupy.

A rough classification of background into urban and rural was also carried out, based on place of origin, place of residence, father's occupation, and work before garimpagem. Thirty donos were classed as rural and twenty as urban on this basis, against twenty-seven workers with a rural background and twenty-three with an urban one.[1]

Figure 4.1   Age distribution of Gurupí donos and workers

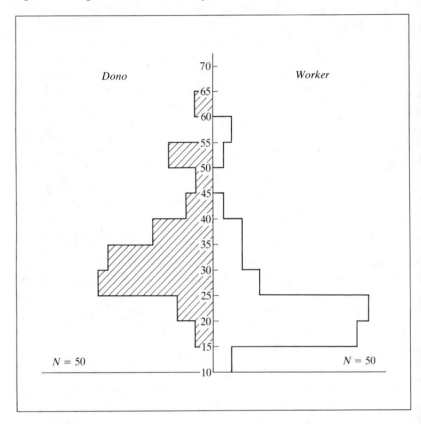

Figure 4.2   Origins of Gurupí workers

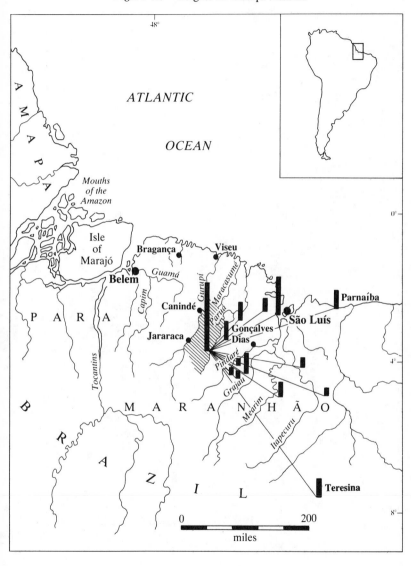

Figure 4.3   Origins of Gurupí donos

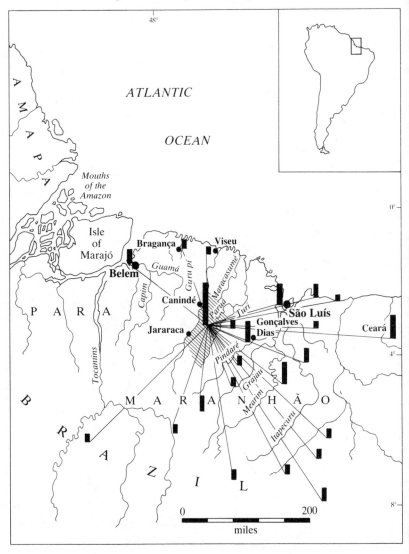

Table 4.1   When entered garimpagem? Gurupí donos and workers

Donos	Workers
1940 – 1	
1958 – 1	
1969 – 1	
1972 – 1	
1975 – 4	
1976 – 1	1976 – 1
1977 – 1	1977 – 1
1978 – 3	1978 – 1
1979 – 7	
1980 – 3	
1981 – 1	1981 – 4
1982 – 11	1982 – 6
1983 – 8	1983 – 4
1984 – 4	1984 – 15
1985 – 3	1985 – 18

Table 4.2   Worked in other goldfields? Gurupí donos and workers

	Donos	Workers
YES	36	19
NO	14	31

Even on such a limited sample, then, the importance of garimpagem for both the rural and the urban populations of eastern Amazonia is evident, as is a strong bias towards the lower rungs of the occupational hierarchy in both the city and the countryside. Only two out of fifty workers and eight out of fifty donos came from an unambiguously middle or upper class background. This implies, as will be argued in detail below, that garimpagem is a significant avenue of upward mobility for people who have very few options or prospects outside the garimpo. Once the eleven donos who used manual machinery alone are excluded from the total, thirty-nine donos using industrially produced machinery remain. Of these thirty-nine, no less than twenty-five began to work in garimpos as workers with no capital, and managed to

Table 4.3   Father's occupation: Gurupí donos

Smallholder	– 33
Businessman	– 7
Garimpeiro	– 4
Clerk	– 2
Carpenter	– 2
Butcher	– 2
Mechanic	– 1
Rancher	– 1
Soldier	– 1
Fisherman	– 1
Rural trader	– 1

$N = 50$. Some fathers had more than one occupation at various times

Table 4.4   Father's occupation: Gurupí workers

Smallholder	– 34
Garimpeiro	– 9
Rural trader	– 6
Carpenter	– 2
Truck driver	– 2
Mason	– 1
Fisherman	– 1
Doctor	– 1

$N = 50$. Some fathers had more than one occupation at various times

rise up through the occupational hierarchy of the garimpo by buying machinery with their earnings and setting up operations on their own account.

In addition, an attempt was made to find out how many of the workers could be thought of as upwardly mobile potential donos. After some consideration, it was decided that the best criteria for identifying this group were that to qualify for inclusion a worker should spend more than half the year in garimpos, have experience of at least two regions of garimpagem, have first entered garimpagem at least two years previous to the date of the interview, and prefer to work on a percentage basis – the latter being a sure sign of a full-time garimpeiro, as will be seen. These criteria were intentionally rigorous, but nevertheless eight out of the fifty qualified.

Table 4.5   Work before garimpo: Gurupí donos

Smallholder	– 27
Construction work	– 4
Businessman	– 3
Urban informal	– 2
Rural trader	– 2
Clerical	– 2
Cowboy	– 2
Timber	– 2
Taxi driver	– 2
Brazil nut worker	– 1
Carpenter	– 1
Politician	– 1
Student	– 1
Sailor	– 1
Rancher	– 1
Ranch foreman	– 1
Hammock weaver	– 1
Mechanic	– 1
Bus driver	– 1
Plumber	– 1
Soldier	– 1

$N = 50$. Some respondents had more than one occupation at various times

Table 4.6   Work before garimpo: Gurupí workers

Smallholder	– 26
Construction work	– 6
Shop assistant	– 6
Clerk	– 4
Rural trader	– 3
Mechanic	– 2
Timber	– 2
Hammock weaver	– 1
Student	– 1
Fisherman	– 1
Bus driver	– 1
Petty theft	– 1
Brazil nut worker	– 1
Trainee pilot	– 1

$N = 50$. Some respondents had more than one occupation at various times

Both donos and workers were also asked where they lived when they were not in a garimpo, or, in the case of those who gave a garimpo as place of permanent residence, the last place they lived which was not a garimpo. When the responses are mapped out (Figures 4.2 and 4.3), the contrast is clear. In the Gurupí, the workforce comes almost exclusively from the area of the goldfield itself, São Luís, and the heavily populated hinterland and river valleys of central and western Maranhão. Some workers do come from beyond the state, but only just; the cities of Parnaíba and Teresina in neighbouring Piauí state are right on the border with Maranhão. Donos, on the other hand, tend to come from much further afield. Even such a small sample contained donos from every sub-region of Maranhão as well as twelve from beyond the state, ranging from Goiás to the south, Belém to the west, and Ceará to the east. It should be borne in mind that in terms of Brazilian garimpagem the Gurupí is a minor goldfield which does not attract anything like the numbers of people who migrate to the Tapajós or Cumarú. In cities like Imperatriz or Marabá, which are jumping off points for the most important goldfields, one regularly comes across people from all parts of Brazil. The diverse geographical origins of donos in even such a small and relatively unimportant area of garimpagem like the Gurupí is a graphic indication of two factors which are basic to the understanding of the contemporary Amazon gold rush: the extreme mobility of some garimpeiros, and the way that many people from outside Amazonia itself are attracted to the garimpos.

With this general introduction to donos and workers in the Gurupí to set the scene, we can now proceed to a more detailed examination of the different social categories that one finds in the garimpo. Figure 4.4 represents a rather complex social and economic hierarchy in general terms, defining two types of worker, five types of dono, two types of sócio, and the cantineiro in an intermediate position between the dono and the worker. Each of the social categories which make up the model have different levels of economic resources, ranging from none at all to millions of dollars, different patterns of entry into and exit from garimpagem, different objectives and motives for working in garimpos, and different residential patterns, with some permanently resident in garimpos, others temporarily, and still others who may not be resident at all. Underlying everything are the differences and parallels in age, geographical origin, occupational background and experience of garimpagem that the survey data from the Gurupí hinted at.

Figure 4.4   Social structure in the garimpo

```
                                    REGIONAL ENTREPRENEUR

SYNDICATE————————— INTERNAL ENTREPRENEUR
MEMBER
                                    EXTERNAL ENTREPRENEUR


MINOR——————————— MECHANISED DONO
SOCIO
                                    MANUAL DONO

DONO
————————————————— CANTINEIRO————————
WORKER
                                    PORCENTISTA


                                    DIARISTA
```

1 The Diarista

Workers fall into one of two main types; the diarista, who is paid a daily wage, or the porcentista, who receives a percentage of the gold produced. Which of these work regimes is likely to be used in a given situation will be dealt with in the next chapter. The daily wage in 1985, and, if memories are correct, since 1979, fluctuated between 75 cents and U.S.$1.25 throughout Amazonia. This may seem low, but diaristas also receive food and accommodation as part of their agreement with a dono, the cost of which is not deducted from their wages. Furthermore, they will be owed a daily wage even if no gold is produced; the garimpo is thus unique amongst Amazonian extractive systems in that the dono may go into debt to his workforce but the reverse does not occur. In most garimpos, unless the diarista chooses to spend his money on alcohol or prostitutes there are few things available to buy, so the diarista arrangement is ideal for those who do not wish to make any long term commitment to garimpagem, and want a guaranteed sum, which they can calculate in advance, in their pockets when they leave. It is well suited to the needs of people who wish to spend no more than a few weeks in the garimpo. For them, coming as they do from families of smallholders or from the bottom rungs of the occupational ladder in urban areas, the sums that they bring home from the garimpo may be small in absolute terms but are often important to poor households that in many cases are not fully part of the cash economy. A typical case would be a smallholder family that produces crops mainly for subsistence. For these people, the money a single adolescent son can earn in a month in the garimpo is strategically very useful, especially if, as is often the case, more than one family member can be spared. This explains the importance, amongst workers as a whole, of single males in the 15–24 age bracket.

In villages and towns throughout Maranhão it is common for large groups of diaristas to leave in a bloc and travel together to areas like Serra Pelada and Cumarú where the demand for labour is intense and work can be guaranteed. Diaristas tend to avoid air-supplied garimpos, because the airfare they would have to pay makes them uneconomic. They are thus rare in the Tapajós and wherever raft garimpagem, with its percentage work regime, is to be found – the garimpos on the river Madeira in Rondônia, for example. In all other regions of garimpagem, and especially in Serra Pelada and Cumarú, the diarista holds sway. At any one time an absolute majority of all people working in Amazonian garimpos will be diaristas, and it is as a diarista that most newcomers to the gold rush have their first taste of garimpagem. But despite their numerical dominance, diaristas are firmly on the bottom of the social and economic hierarchy of any garimpo. Almost by definition they have the least experience, least skill and least status of any category of garimpeiro, and it is they who perform the most arduous tasks involving hard manual labour that donos and porcentistas avoid unless they have no choice; carrying sacks of earth out of barrancos in Serra Pelada, carrying sacks of rocks and gravel out of barrancos to mechanical crushers (a truly backbreaking job), and chiselling out hard rock with pickaxes. On the other hand, diaristas do not leave the garimpo because they have been bankrupted. For the most part, they leave with money in their pockets as they intended, exiting seasonally to return to agriculture or city-based activities. For the dono who can afford it, diarista labour has the advantage of allowing the exact calculation of labour costs in advance.

2 The Porcentista

Those who work for a percentage of the gold extracted are less numerous than diaristas but are in some ways more important. They tend to distinguish themselves from diaristas and specifically reject the term *peão* (peon), commonly used by donos to describe workers, arguing with some justification that it is an offensive and inaccurate word to apply to porcentistas, although they feel no qualms about applying it to diaristas. Percentage work regimes vary, but in most cases a porcentista will receive around five per cent. This makes the attraction of the percentage immediately obvious; in a barranco with a good level of gold production, perhaps even a bamburro, a porcentista can strike it rich as well as the dono. It is by no means unheard of for a lucky or skilful porcentista to make enough in a matter of weeks to buy a moínho or a chupadeira and set up as an independent dono. Thus some people who originally entered the garimpo as diaristas decide that they are more likely to go up in the world in the garimpo than anywhere else, and make a conscious effort to develop their knowledge and skills in order to increase their chances of striking it rich. Obviously, there are drawbacks to this strategy. Although the porcentista, like the diarista, receives food and accommodation and incurs no debt if no gold is extracted, five per cent of nothing is still nothing and almost all porcentistas have had to endure the bitter experience of working for several weeks or months and then having nothing to show for their efforts. Nevertheless, many porcentistas regard the daily wage with contempt, and would only work as a diarista when in extreme need. It is this type of porcentista who can be thought of as a full-time professional garimpeiro, a reservoir of potential donos with good chances of upward mobility. They spend most of the year in one garimpo or another and travel a great deal from area to area, with a special liking for the raft garimpagem of the Tapajós, where both the dangers and rewards are high. But not all porcentistas are professionals. Poor donos will often not be able to afford to pay a daily wage, and use percentage work regimes instead.

3   The Cantineiro

A cantineiro is the owner of a cantina, a small store. Most cantinas are unprepossessing; a wattle and daub hut indistinguishable, from the outside at least, from the crude dwellings in which a poor smallholding family might live. Nor is the range of goods the average cantineiro has to offer very impressive; a few basic foodstuffs like rice, beans and *farinha* (dried manioc flour), cigarettes, batteries, soap, perhaps some tinned goods, and, importantly, beer and *cachaça* (rum). Cantineiros will usually have arrangements with local food producers or with merchants in nearby towns or villages, if there are any, to be supplied with large amounts of staple foodstuffs wholesale, together with the oil and petrol essential to mechanised garimpagem. Often these supplies are obtained on credit, and the cantineiro uses his own discretion to release them on credit to garimpeiros; they are thus the final link in a series of debt/credit relationships that see a constant circulation of goods into the garimpo being paid for by gold coming out.

Every cantina has as standard equipment a pair of precision scales for weighing gold, and every cantineiro will try to have enough cash on hand to buy gold, at a price that will be fixed slightly below the latest market price paid by the state, which is relayed several times a day over the regional and national radio stations aimed at garimpeiros. The gold bought is used to pay off any debts the cantineiro may have run up with suppliers outside the garimpos. When gold is bought from a garimpeiro who in turn owes the cantineiro, interest may be charged on the original loan, but it is calculated on an ad hoc basis. It depends on how long the debt has been outstanding, how valued a customer the debtor is, what the gold price has been doing since the debt was contracted, and to what extent inflation has been raising the cost of goods that have to be bought outside and then resold in the garimpo.

A cantineiro's income comes from several sources. Firstly there is the profit from goods sold for cash or gold in the cantina; prices are at least twice the cost of the goods outside the garimpo, several times more in remoter garimpos, to compensate for high transport costs. Then there is the gold the cantineiro buys, which will be resold for a small profit to large gold buyers or the state gold buyers of the Caixa Econômica Federal, the federal savings bank which runs the Brazilian government's gold buying programme. There is the interest paid on credit extended by the cantineiro. In addition to income from the cantina many cantineiros also own barrancos and run their own gold operation. Some have the capital and imagination to branch into anything in which they can see a profit margin, whether or not it is directly related to gold extraction. In the Gurupí garimpos where fieldwork was carried out, other activities cantineiros undertook included pig farming, the gathering and shipping to São Luís of *titica*, a creeper that is used in making chic cane furniture for middle class homes, mule driving, owning (wholly or in part) hotels, bars and brothels that catered for garimpeiros both inside and outside garimpos, a machine repair service, renting out pumps and motors for short periods, the cultivation of fruit and vegetables, and speculating with rice.

The cantina is a focal point of social life in the garimpo. After work garimpeiros congregate there to chat and listen to the radio, and at weekends there are often mammoth drinking parties. The cantineiro is thus an important figure in the garimpo. Through extending credit, the cantineiro allows the large majority of donos who could not operate if they had to pay for everything in advance to get on with extracting gold. By advancing credit on a smaller scale to workers, who often have to wait to be paid until at least some gold is extracted from a barranco, or by advancing the money a dono needs to pay off workers, the cantineiro often heads off potentially violent disputes between donos and workers. Although garimpeiros are often loud in their complaints that interest charged is exorbitant and prices in a cantina outrageous, cantineiros respond that their costs and risks are high; people who know they cannot pay a debt often skip the garimpo, and there is little that the cantineiro can do about it. It was my impression that cantineiros were often harshly dealt with, especially by outside observers who merely noted the large disparity between prices inside the garimpo and prices outside it, without going into the reasons for the difference. Although some abuses undoubtedly occur, cantineiros operate under important restraints because they have to compete with each other. In a garimpo that is not closed, it is surprising how many cantineiros there are in even small garimpos. A concentration of even a small number of garimpeiros needing credit can only be served by several cantineiros, given the small amount of capital the average cantineiro has to play with. Cerqueiro, which at times would have been hard pushed to muster 200 garimpeiros, had three cantinas, with another two within easy walking distance at a neighbouring garimpo. Cantineiros whose prices are too high, or whose interest charges are too rapacious, will find themselves without customers as they are undercut by competitors. This competition between cantineiros tends to keep the prices of goods and credit down to a level which garimpeiros may grumble about but which ultimately they are prepared to accept.

4　The Manual Dono

Manual donos own barrancos but rely on exclusively manual technology to work them, most frequently the cobra fumando. A manual barranco is small, five metres by five metres being the upper limit, and is rarely worked by more than two people besides the dono. Usually the work unit for a barranco of this type is a small family group, a father and sons or a group of brothers. Manual donos are numerically the most common type of dono, although they are the poorest and firmly located at the bottom of the economic and social hierarchy that the different types of dono make up. Most are only part time garimpeiros who spend more time as smallholder farmers, working in garimpos as and when they can. One also finds a few manual donos who once owned more sophisticated machinery but were bankrupted, and are working with cheaper manual technology in the hope of producing enough to buy machinery once again. Outside the Tapajós, where manual garimpagem using the lontona and the dalla has evolved almost into an art, manual donos are overwhelmingly poor, part time, and come from a rural background. Nevertheless, they rarely leave the garimpo *blefado* (bankrupted)[2] because their costs are negligible compared to more mechanised forms of garimpagem; they return to agriculture and only work in garimpos as and when their agricultural commitments permit. Very exceptionally one comes across a manual dono who is an ex-porcentista working full time in the garimpo, who prefers working independently to submitting to the orders of a dono.

5 The Mechanised Dono

The next most numerous type of dono is the mechanised dono. Obviously, all donos who do not use manual technology can be thought of as mechanised, but there is a great deal of difference between a dono who uses tractors and bulldozers and a dono who has to rely on a single, often unreliable, moínho and motor. It is the latter kind of dono, a person who has some machinery and capital but not, relative to donos higher up in the hierarchy, a great deal, who is called a mechanised dono here. In terms of background and experience of garimpagem, mechanised donos are the most diverse group in the garimpo. Some will be experienced ex-porcentistas who invested their earnings in machinery and are now looking to do still better. Others are young men from middle or upper class families in the towns or big cities who have bought machinery and set themselves up as donos using money put up by their families. Some come from less exalted urban backgrounds, like taxi driving or road haulage, where they have managed to accumulate enough capital to buy cheap second-hand machinery and try their luck in the garimpo, where they see the possibility of much higher earnings than they could otherwise expect. Others come from rural backgrounds, investing the returns from a good harvest or a land sale in machinery; others started out as manual donos, never intending to go into garimpagem full time, and were pulled into it by a minor strike.

But mechanised donos do have some things in common. Firstly, they do not have a great deal of machinery. Very few of them could raise the capital necessary to equip a raft. As a rule, they live in a state of constant liquidity crisis, have little or no cash on hand and depend almost entirely on credit to keep going. They get credit either from a cantineiro, or, if they have the acumen and the contacts, directly from suppliers in villages and towns, where this is possible. For spare parts they limp along as best they can, trying to avoid the inconvenience and expense of sending something outside the garimpo for repairs, improvising, cannibalising abandoned machinery, and borrowing parts from friends. They pay off their commitments as best they can as they go along with gold extracted. They tend not to move around a great deal, partly because it is often difficult and always laborious to dismantle and transport machinery, but also partly because only novices are sufficiently credulous to run after the wild stories of new strikes, a process disparagingly known as 'chasing fofocas'. Those with any experience tend to think that the best strategy is to find a barranco that seems promising and stick to it.

As is to be expected, given the essential precariousness of their position, the rate of attrition amongst mechanised donos is high. Many are forced to give up the struggle and leave *blefado*. But despite everything many mechanised donos take pride in their independence, autonomy and skills, even if this independence is to a certain extent illusory, given their reliance on credit. If they manage to survive for any length of time in garimpagem, most mechanised donos become sufficiently skilled to more or less cover their costs in a barranco, and the typical mechanised dono is one who works hard to stay in the same place, taking a small loss on one operation and making a small profit on another, keeping going in the hope that sooner or later his perseverance will be rewarded with a bamburro. Along with some porcentistas, many mechanised donos are fiercely proud of their work, turning garimpagem into the keystone of the construction of their social identity, calling themselves garimpeiros and thinking of themselves as garimpeiros both inside and outside the garimpo.

6   The External Entrepreneur

Ever since the dramatic rise in the gold price in 1979, garimpagem has been an attractive investment option for those with capital to spread around, promising potentially large rewards for what to many investors seemed a relatively small outlay of capital. With the external entrepreneur, one enters the upper reaches of the dono hierarchy. External entrepreneurs are what the name suggests; businessmen from both urban and rural backgrounds who set themselves up as donos by buying machinery and barrancos, spending an initial period and regular intervals thereafter in the garimpo setting up and supervising operations. Usually the demands on their time and their other commitments outside the garimpo mean that they can only spend limited periods in garimpos, and they will appoint a *gerente*, a manager, to take charge of operations in their absence. However, in rich garimpos like Serra Pelada, or some garimpos in Cumarú or the Tapajós, gold extraction proves to be so lucrative for external entrepreneurs that it comes to overshadow their other interests. This is especially so since they tend to operate on a higher plane of technological sophistication, having the capital to afford tractors, several moínhos, or even a bulldozer. In this case, the external entrepreneur

may dispense with the gerente and spend more time in the garimpo himself.

It is a truth universally acknowledged by garimpeiros that unless an operation is personally supervised by the dono, others will enrich themselves at the dono's expense; this was certainly the case in the barrancos of the two external entrepreneurs only sporadically present in the garimpo where I was able to observe what happened when the owner was away. Thus despite their apparent advantages in the form of better machinery and more capital, external entrepreneurs more often than not end up losing money in the medium term and pull out of garimpagem, concentrating on their other activities. They do not leave *blefado*, as they can cover their losses from other sources. Also, they tend not to use credit at the local level, as they have the capital to buy supplies wholesale directly from producers and retailers and ship them to the garimpo using their own resources.

7 The Internal Entrepreneur

In garimpagem, unlike other extractive activities native to Amazon there is not necessarily a constant relationship between the time sp on extraction and the amount extracted, as there is, for example rubber tapping or Brazil nut gathering. Ever since the rise in the p of gold it has been possible for a dono who is lucky and/or skilf make a great deal of money in a short period of time. It is possibility which drives the mechanised dono to undergo conside privations and incur heavy debts. The way that a garimpeiro ca from being a worker to becoming a mechanised dono has alread shown; with the internal entrepreneur we come to the highest r the social and economic hierarchy of the garimpo at the local le is most commonly a mechanised dono who has managed to *ban* and chosen to reinvest the proceeds in garimpagem. There ar few who began as external entrepreneurs but whose success pe them to switch the focus of their interests to the garimpo. H they become internal entrepreneurs less frequently; their in of experience of garimpagem and the time they spend ou garimpo handicaps them.

Not all mechanised donos who strike it rich becom entrepreneurs. More often than not the proceeds of a ban frittered away in conspicuous consumption, or used to bu life outside the garimpo that was the motive for entering th

in the first place. But some people who have succeeded once feel that they can succeed again on a bigger scale, now that they have acquired some experience and have a detailed knowledge of local conditions and personalities. They plough their winnings back into the garimpo, buying more machinery and barrancos. They conclude agreements with other donos looking for a sócio, the owner of a barranco who does not have the machinery to exploit it fully, for example. In this way they create for themselves a portfolio of holdings and investments in an analogous way to the expansion and diversification of a successful company in the business world. This is not easy to do; it demands experience, a detailed knowledge of local conditions, and, most importantly, a mastery of the way that economic transactions are conducted in the garimpo. An internal entrepreneur cannot simultaneously supervise all his investments, and it becomes imperative that he finds people he can trust to whom he can delegate responsibility, preferably close relatives. At the same time, he has to be aware of the often cutthroat nature of economic life in the garimpo, and have the experience and judgement to know when he is being swindled and what he can do about it.

The internal entrepreneur, then, needs not only an abundance of all the entrepreneurial virtues that an entrepreneur outside the garimpo might have, but also a deep knowledge of garimpagem and garimpeiros. The garimpo is, in many important respects, very different from the business world which other entrepreneurs inhabit. Outside the limited areas of federal intervention, it is not regulated by the state and its judicial apparatus. There are no such things as written contracts, only verbal agreements that may be twisted or ignored according to circumstances. Agreements will almost as a matter of course not be honoured if one of the parties sees advantage in cheating the other. But for the person who can operate successfully in this highly charged environment, the rewards can be enormous.

If investments are shrewdly chosen and successfully carried through, an internal entrepreneur can increase holdings and revenue almost exponentially. This is partly because of the high price of gold and partly because the levels of capital investment needed to set up operations in a garimpo are not, in absolute terms, very high. In the Amazon gold rush, in certain circumstances, it is possible to find the ideal combination of low capital costs and a highly valuable product. Internal entrepreneurs are therefore very important to garimpagem, at both the local and regional levels. They represent one of the very few examples in Amazonia of an authentically indigenous commercial

elite. They may not originally be from Amazonia, but they are umbilically connected to it, having risen through a social and economic structure that is unique to the region and which is in no danger of being bought or otherwise dominated by interests from the south of Brazil. And for a very few there is still one further rung to which they can aspire; the regional entrepreneur, a person who can be thought of, for want of a better term, as a macro-garimpeiro.

8   The Regional Entrepreneur

With the regional entrepreneur garimpagem literally enters the world of big business. In every goldfield there is a small number of people who have great importance in the economic structure of garimpagem in their area. Their interests go beyond any single garimpo or complex of garimpos, and their operations are of a regional or even a national ambit, rather than merely local. Although they will still be in the business of extracting gold in most cases, mining itself is often over-shadowed by interests in what can be called the ancillary sector of garimpagem, most importantly in air transportation and gold buying, but also including franchises for the hire and sale of machinery, gold refining, jewellery manufacture, retailing, hotels, prostitution and politics. Besides activities directly and indirectly related to garimpagem, regional entrepreneurs also move into other fields where venture capital in Amazonia is traditionally applied; land grabbing and land speculation in the countryside, dealing in real estate in urban areas, and involvement in political campaigns, usually as backers but occasionally (as in the case of José Altino Machado in Roraima and Marlon in Marabá) with political ambitions themselves.

The select band of regional entrepreners that the garimpo has generated are well known figures throughout Amazonia; Marlon, who began with a fabulous bamburro in Serra Pelada and went on to become a notoriously brutal landgrabber and estate owner near Marabá; Geraldo Rosaldo from the Gurupí, who probably buys more gold in the region than the local Caixa Econômica Federal; Machado in Roraima, one of the driving forces behind the infiltration of the reserve of the Yanomami, hoping to make another fortune with land expropriated from the Indians. The best known, and the most success-ful, is the legendary Zé Arara, whose real name is José Araújo. Today he divides his time between Itaituba in the Tapajós, Santarém and São Paulo, and he is unquestionably the richest entrepreneur that

Brazilian garimpagem has yet produced. He began as a garimpeiro in the Tapajós in the late 1950s, and since then has built up an empire that includes interests in garimpos throughout the Tapajós, fleets of private planes, and a chain of hundreds of gold-buying and retailing shops throughout Amazonia, covering every area of garimpagem, advertisements for which are amongst the first things that a newcomer to Amazonia sees in the entry hall of Belém airport. It is difficult to know the exact value of his interests, but they run into millions of dollars.

9 The Minor Sócio

One possible response for a dono who wishes to operate a barranco and not over-burden himself with debts in the process is to attempt to share the costs. This is done through a relationship called *sociedade*; somebody with whom this relationship is formed is called a sócio. In keeping with the small scale of most operations, the majority of sócios are minor investors, whose contribution, although possibly crucial to the running of an operation, is not in absolute terms very high. In return for their help, sócios have the right to a proportion of the gold produced. It is quite common for a dono to have more than one sócio, but this is avoided if at all possible, simply because the more people gold production has to be divided between, the less remains for the dono. Exactly what percentage of production the sócio will receive depends on the importance of the contribution, and has to be thrashed out between the dono and the sócio beforehand. A sócio may or may not be a garimpeiro, and may or may not be resident in the garimpo, although in most cases a non-resident sócio will visit at least occasionally to make sure that there is no cheating going on. Sometimes a sócio will be another dono, one common example being a dono who has a barranco and some machinery but not all the machinery needed to work the deposit effectively. Where possible, it is preferable that some previous connection should exist between a dono and sócios, ideally a kinship tie, or, failing that, a *compadresco* link (when Ego stands as godfather to a child, the child's father and Ego become *compadres*). This makes it less likely that one party will cheat the other, although disputes between kin and compadres do occur as well.

10 The Syndicate Member

For more capital-intensive forms of garimpagem, such as equipping a raft and keeping it supplied by air, or an exceptionally mechanised barranco, the costs may be shared between a small syndicate. When each member makes a considerable contribution, extraction can be much more sophisticated and profitable. Syndicates commonly move into an area of mature garimpagem some time after the initial fofocas have died down, buy a rich barranco with a proven track record, and mechanise production to a new level of sophistication.[3] Some syndicates may even be formally registered as small mining companies, although this is rare. External entrepreneurs may think it advisable to spread risks and costs by inviting one or two people to become partners. Syndicates are most common, as might be expected, in areas where both gold production and overheads are high, especially where garimpos have to be supplied by air.

One exception is Serra Pelada, where syndicates are a feature of the garimpo. This might seem surprising, as Serra Pelada is one of the more accessible garimpos and the level of mechanisation of gold production is not especially high. This is largely due to the historical accident of the growth of a large market in Imperatriz and Marabá in the buying and selling of barrancos in the mine. When gold production in Serra Pelada was at its peak, in 1980 and 1981, the demand for barrancos was so great that prices were driven up to a level where many donos had to form syndicates in order to acquire one.

Apart from the categories of garimpeiro described here, there are many other figures who can be found in garimpos; merchants of all kinds, gold buyers, prostitutes, police troopers, travelling photographers, cooks, pilots and doctors – to name but a few. These bit players will be considered in more detail in Chapter 9, when the effect of garimpagem on local and regional economies will be examined. They are mentioned here as an indication of the limitations of the model of the social structure of the gold rush that is being proposed. It is no more than a skeleton, which in any given case will be fleshed out by other figures arising out of specific local and regional contexts. But the model does include all the most basic types of garimpeiro, those involved directly in the social organisation of gold production. No model of this kind can fully reflect the richness and diversity of garimpagem, but it is proposed as a kind of core element, a basic social structure to which all the regional variations of garimpagem, save to some extent raft garimpos, can be reduced. While this process of reduction is in a sense impoverishing, it does provide an analytical framework for the local and regional ethnographies that can supply the gaps and omissions inherent in a model as general as this one.

As a postscript, it may be of interest to return to the survey data from the Gurupí and get an idea, in one specific case, of the relative numbers of each social category. As an arbitrary decision was made to restrict the sample size to fifty donos and fifty workers, the survey does not reflect the numerical superiority of workers over donos. Sócios were not included in the study, as the majority were non-resident. The survey also seriously underestimates the number of manual donos relative to mechanised donos. Manual donos are difficult to administer questionnaires to as they move around more and tend to work scattered along stream beds and banks some distance away from the centres of garimpos: since visits to them were more difficult and time-consuming they were somewhat neglected. Finally, as it was a sample carried out in a limited number of garimpos, all of which are within walking distance of one another, there is no regional entrepreneur; in the Gurupí as a whole there is only one garimpeiro who falls into this category.

When classification along the lines of the model of social structure presented here was carried out, the patterns were as shown in Table 4.7. Thirty of the fifty donos had at least one sócio involved in their operations, twenty-three of whom were either relatives or compadres. Points worth stressing include the small but strategic group of exclusively porcentista workers, most of whom will be the donos of tomorrow, and the small numbers of people who make it to the top. It illustrates the fact that, despite the glamour and potential rewards of gold extraction, the lot of most workers is unremitting hard manual labour and most donos have to struggle to stay solvent. The majority of them will eventually leave *blefado*, or, as garimpeiros say, *magro, liso, e doente* – thin, broke and sick.

Table 4.7   Distribution of Gurupí garimpeiros in occupational hierarchy

Internal entrepreneur	– 4
External entrepreneur	– 2
Gerente	– 2
Mechanised dono	– 31
Manual dono	– 11
Cantineiro	– 2
Porcentista	– 12
Diarista	– 36

SOCIAL MOBILITY IN THE GOLD RUSH

To complete this description of the social organisation of garimpagem it is necessary to include the types of mobility and patterns of exit that have been mentioned in passing above. This is done in Figure 4.5. It shows the paths that upwardly and downwardly mobile garimpeiros usually follow. It can be seen at a glance that there are more paths of upward mobility than there are of downward movement. Downward social mobility is rare in garimpagem. This is because those who fail tend to leave the garimpo altogether rather than descend to the lower reaches of the hierarchy. An external entrepreneur who fails will return to the other commercial interests he has outside the garimpo. A manual dono is usually not a full time garimpeiro in any case, and will return to smallholding for much of the year. A mechanised dono will usually choose to leave *blefado* rather than have the perseverance to continue as a manual dono or a worker, although some do choose to remain. Of the fifty Gurupí workers sampled, four had been donos at some stage, one manual and three mechanised. All the same, it is difficult for someone who once owned a barranco and machinery to come to terms with the fall in status that downward mobility entails. For somebody who was once an independent dono to have to hawk his labour around and accept orders in an area where it is very possible that people who once worked for him are now donos in their own right is a deep humiliation.

There are three characteristics of garimpagem as a social system which can be deduced from Figure 4.5 and which need to be stressed. The first is that it does offer real opportunities for upward mobility to the mass of people who do not enter the system at its upper levels, and this is a consequence of a second feature of garimpagem; it has an extremely versatile and flexible structure that can accommodate, at different levels, a wide variety of people who come to it with differing objectives and levels of resources. A poor man can be a garimpeiro as well as a rich man (the belief that 'the garimpo is open to all, to whoever wishes to enter' will be remembered), although initially at least he will not be the same type of garimpeiro.

To the potential dono, garimpagem can offer a choice of levels of investment, and, critically, the lower end of this range is accessible to the small investor. This is especially so because of the abundance of cheap second-hand machinery in garimpos that is bought and sold at prices below its true market value. This is because of the constant flow of bankrupted donos out of the garimpo, desperate to recover at least

Figure 4.5   Social mobility in garimpagem

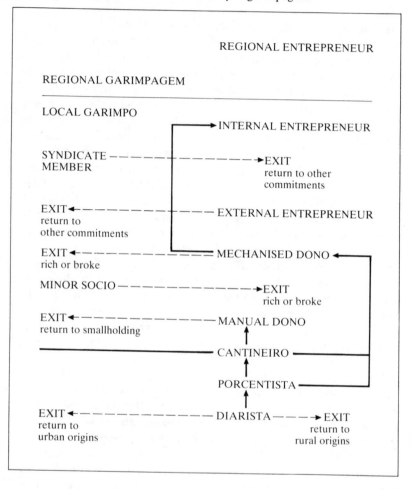

some of their losses through the sale of their machinery. It means that aspiring donos can strike hard bargains, as they know that the dono who is leaving is being hounded by creditors and will have to take whatever he can get. It is common for machinery to be acquired in return for assumption of a debt rather than for cash. Thus, paradoxically, the high rate of bankruptcy amongst donos is a mechanism which helps to replace those who leave with people coming up through the system, as it releases machinery to garimpeiros who might not have been able to afford to buy it new.

In Figure 4.5, upward mobility begins with the diaristas who decide to move towards working for a percentage share. A porcentista who earns enough to move higher up the scale has a choice of routes. Some decide to become cantineiros, initially on a small scale but hoping that their knowledge of an area and the personalities within it will allow them to expand later. Others may decide at an early stage to work independently as a manual dono, buying or constructing a cobra fumando. But the goal for most porcentistas is to get hold of the kind of machinery that can increase capacity and potential gold production many times over, and this means moínhos, chupadeiras, and, in an ideal world, a raft. This path from porcentista to mechanised dono is the most important channel of upward mobility in garimpagem. Once machinery has been acquired, ex-porcentistas are often in a better position to move up still further, compared to middle or upper class garimpeiros who enter the system at this level using machinery purchased with family backing. Although some of these arrivistes are classic urban hustlers, streetwise and hardheaded in a way that equips them to go far in garimpagem, many are naive and inexperienced, and the attrition rate amongst them is high. They are a tempting target for other garimpeiros and cantineiros who will encourage them to overcommit themselves. Somebody who has come up 'through the ranks' will not be deceived by their blandishments. If they decide not to take their winnings and leave garimpagem, they can aim for the routes from mechanised dono to internal entrepreneur, and from internal entrepreneur to regional entrepreneur, that have already been described.

Finally, it is important to grasp that the social structure of most garimpos is in a state of continuous ferment. A stream of workers constantly arriving is matched by the outflow of diaristas returning to their principal occupations and porcentistas moving on to other areas of garimpagem. The flow of bankrupted donos out of the system is balanced by new donos coming up 'through the ranks' as well as others coming in with machinery for the first time. External entrepreneurs shuttle back and forth between the garimpo and wherever their other interests are located, while internal entrepreneurs move about from garimpo to garimpo checking operations in barrancos where they have an investment. Manual donos constantly enter and leave the system according to their other commitments. In most cases a survey of a garimpo would be difficult or impossible, simply because the population is rarely the same from one day to the next. At certain times, during fofocas for example, this movement of garimpeiros is intense, so intense that it becomes hard to see any structural features beneath the turmoil. Nevertheless, the occupational hierarchy described here will always develop over time. It is the framework within which the social and economic relationships between different categories of garimpeiros that will be examined in the next two chapters takes place.

Before doing so, several points raised in this chapter bear directly on the wider political debate about mineral policy in Brazil. There are two issues in particular to which this discussion of the social structure of garimpagem is relevant. It has been contended for some time that garimpagem is a socially inequitable form of mineral extraction that concentrates wealth in the hands of an elite and offers little or no opportunity of advancement to the mass of people who enter it. Parallels are drawn with the rubber boom in Amazonia, and the best known regional entrepreneurs are compared with the rubber barons of the nineteenth century, figures whose personal fortunes were built on the direct exploitation of large numbers of small producers.[4] From this a related conclusion is drawn; it is asserted that garimpagem, as it becomes increasingly capitalised, is evolving into a capitalist or pseudo-capitalist social and economic system, with donos as employers of a mass of people who are effectively wage-earners. These theses have gained almost complete acceptance on the left and centre of the political spectrum in Brazil, and been the basis for fierce criticism of federal intervention in Serra Pelada, which, it is said, has resulted in the enrichment of the few at the expense of the vast majority.[5] The best known evidence that is quoted to support this view is a study of receipts issued to sellers of gold to the Caixa Econômica Federal in Serra Pelada in 1982 that was carried out by DOCEGEO technicians in 1983.[6] It found that 104 garimpeiros sold 27.3 per cent of all the gold sold to the CEF in Serra Pelada in 1982, while another 886 sold 45 per cent. As the average population in Serra Pelada in 1982 was 48 000, it was concluded that 990 garimpeiros concentrated something over 70 per cent of gold production in Serra Pelada in their hands, a result that was described as 'giving us some idea of the income distribution that garimpagem gives rise to, as unjust, probably, as income distribution in the most oppressive countries of the world'.[7]

It should be clear from the information in this chapter that both these ideas are misplaced. Garimpagem does have very important channels of upward mobility which even the poorest diarista may, if he chooses, enter. It has been shown that the transition from porcentista to dono, while it depends on skill, experience, and, to a certain extent but less than is generally believed, on luck, is one which many garimpeiros make (fully twenty-five out of the fifty donos sampled in the Gurupí did so, it will be remembered), and which can be realistically aspired to by porcentistas. Capital costs and overheads are not necessarily crushing, given the availability of credit and cheap second-hand machinery. It is also worth noting that the level of upward mobility in any one area of garimpagem which can be observed by researchers is below the real level. It is common for porcentistas to work in areas like the Tapajós and the river Madeira, but then to choose another goldfield nearer home, like the Gurupí or southern Pará, in which to set themselves up as donos. When upward mobility involves two or more goldfields, as is often the case, it will not show up in studies confined to a single region of garimpagem.

Furthermore, it is clearly wrong to think of garimpagem as in any way a capitalist enterprise; at best, such an interpretation confuses capitalisation with capitalism. Entrepreneurs and entrepreneurial activities are not specific to capitalism, and work regimes in garimpos are clearly neither capitalist nor becoming so. Most importantly, they are not conceived of as being so by garimpeiros, who make a radical distinction between themselves and the formal mining sector. Indeed, as Chapter 8 explains, garimpagem and the formal mining sector have to a great extent defined themselves in opposition to each other since at least the nineteenth century.

The DOCEGEO study of 'income distribution in Serra Pelada' is in any case deeply flawed, both methodologically and theoretically, and betrays a lack of knowledge of even the most basic features of the social organisation of garimpagem. In the first place, as an analysis of receipts issued by the Caixa Econômica Federal it refers only to official gold production. Theoretically, all garimpeiros in Serra Pelada are obliged to sell gold to the CEF, and are searched when they leave in order to make sure they are not taking any gold out. But there are many ways of smuggling gold out despite these measures, and all geologists and other technicians who have worked at Serra Pelada estimate that somewhere between a fifth and a third of all gold mined there is smuggled out. This 'unofficial' production is not included in the study. Even as it stands, saying that a certain number of people out of 48 000 appropriated 70 per cent of Serra Pelada's gold production does not take into account that the vast majority of those 48 000 would have been diaristas, whom one would not expect to sell gold in most cases, as they would be paid in cash. Those who did receive payment in gold equivalent would only have received a small amount. The real universe that it would have been interesting to examine should have been gold sales by porcentistas and donos, which would have drastically reduced the base numbers of the study.

But the fundamental flaw is that studies of this type, examining the commercialisation of gold, do not allow any conclusions to be drawn about the production of that gold nor about the distribution of the proceeds of its sale. The commercialisation of gold has to be distinguished from both production and distribution; it is a separate process. It does not follow that because 990 garimpeiros sold 70 per cent of the gold bought by the CEF that they either produced that 70 per cent or that they kept 70 per cent of the proceeds of all gold sales in Serra Pelada in 1982. In fact, almost all of those selling large amounts of gold to the CEF would have immediately returned with the money to their dwelling, where the diaristas, porcentistas, sócios and creditors of the dono in question would have been waiting. They would be paid off or receive their share, and the dono keep what remained. The person who sells a large amount of gold in Serra Pelada will never keep all the proceeds, and it therefore becomes nonsensical to use the receipts of gold sales to say anything about income distribution in the garimpo.

In this respect garimpagem is very different from the rubber boom. Although debt/credit relationships are important, even essential, in the functioning of a garimpo, taken together they do not constitute anything comparable to the *aviamento*, the system of debt/credit relationships in the rubber trade, which in its most extreme form ensured rubber workers could never pay the debt they contracted.[8] Workers, unlike seringueiros during the rubber boom, do not contract debts; their donos do. Furthermore, the fact that gold is so valuable means that even modest production is enough to stay solvent. Even regional entrepreneurs cannot seal off and dominate large tracts of land as the rubber barons did; the sheer scale of the post-1979 rush makes that impossible. In any case, the structure of activities that an entrepreneur in garimpagem builds up is governed by the existence of a broadly based system that includes both major entrepreneurs and large numbers of small and medium scale operators. It is much easier, for example, to get hold of large amounts of gold by setting up a cantina in a garimpo than by sealing off an area and physically and economically dominating gold production within it.

Entrepreneurs in garimpagem are not a select group of expropriators controlling production and dictating the terms of labour to those lower down in the hierarchy. The contemporary gold rush in Amazonia simply does not work like that. In garimpagem, a dono is by definition an independent producer. He is free to make his own production decisions inside the barranco, no matter how much he owes outside it and to whom he owes it. The diarista and porcentista are free to come and go as they please,[9] and never incur debts to donos if no gold is extracted. Unless it is specifically understood beforehand, they are not engaged for a definite period and may leave at any time, collecting what is due to them. This independence of the dono and freedom of action of the worker are core features of the social organisation of the garimpo.

The importance of this point cannot be over-stressed. Once it is taken on board, the true complexity of the social and economic structure of the gold rush can be perceived. Obviously the social organisation of gold production proceeds along a hierarchical axis in one sense; there is a definite occupational hierarchy which can be represented as a pyramid. But it would be a fundamental mistake to see those at the apex and upper reaches of the pyramid as controlling the base. They will have mined a certain proportion of the gold; in partnership with others they will have an interest in the production of an additional proportion; they will certainly buy a great deal of the gold that others produce. Nevertheless, their relationship to those lower down the hierarchy cannot be understood in terms of dominance, control or coercion,[10] and in this respect garimpagem is very different from the many other hierarchically structured extractive and agricultural activities in Amazonia, where those at the top really do (or did) dictate terms to those at the bottom; Brazil nut gathering, *latifundista* agriculture, and so forth. There may be an occupational hierarchy, but there is also a fair amount of upward mobility in the system, and, most importantly, people can move on or opt out at any time. From the point of view of workers, garimpagem has much to offer. Despite the backbreaking nature of the work, and the lack of work safety, working in the gold rush offers autonomy and even opportunity. This autonomy is central to economic life and social relationships in the gold rush.

5 Economic Life in the Garimpo

WORK REGIMES, PERCENTAGE DEALS, AND THE *REQUE*

Although social life in the garimpo is more than simply the aggregate of a series of economic transactions and relationships, it is impossible to understand it without considering the garimpo as an economic system. People work under several distinct labour regimes, deals are struck, operations are financed, agreements are honoured and broken, proceeds spent and invested in different ways, credit extended and refused, and in the process people get rich, get by, or go bankrupt.

The basic forms of economic organisation in garimpos – work regimes, patterns of investment and consumption, credit, liquidity and bankruptcy – are the backdrop against which social relations in the gold rush are played out. The purpose of this chapter is to explain how the garimpo, as an economic entity, works. Given the different forms of technology and the wide spectrum of types of people to be found in garimpos, it is a complex topic – but also a rich one. Success in garimpagem is not just a question of owning the appropriate machinery or having specialised knowledge. It also has much to do with how well garimpeiros can move in this economic universe, and manipulate the many different strategies and options that it presents them with. Garimpagem is nothing if not transactional, and skill in handling transactions can do much to compensate for lack of resources. It goes without saying that operating in this economic universe also entails entering into distinct social relationships, but that aspect will be treated separately in the following chapter.

In the last chapter the two basic forms of work regimes, the daily wage and percentage stakes, were introduced. There are variations on these two themes, but all workers in garimpos can be classed as diaristas or porcentistas of one kind or another. Which regime workers will choose, it was also explained, depends essentially on what they want from garimpagem. For the dono, however, deciding which work regime or regimes should be used is more complicated. There are advantages and disadvantages associated with each, and several factors have to be taken into account.

The first variable to be considered is how many workers will be required to carry through an operation. This depends on the nature of the barranco to be worked. The larger and deeper it is, the more workers it will need. It may be that the operation will require one or more *rebaixamentos*, deepenings of barrancos that are extremely labour intensive, except in the relatively few operations where excavators or bulldozers are deployed. It is common for rebaixamentos to last weeks; for example, one type of operation is the 'cleaning' of an old barranco, where an abandoned digging, filled with water, mud, and the remains of land slippings, is brought back into production. One operation of this type that was closely followed during fieldwork involved almost four months of successive rebaixamentos before gold-bearing material was reached, and only ten days of gold production was possible before a rain-provoked landslide made further work impossible. Obviously, operations of this type need more workers than usual. The types of machinery that a dono might deploy each require a certain number of workers to be effective: two or three for a cobra fumando, at least six for a lontona or dalla, three for a raft, six if it is to be operated twenty four hours a day, as is usually the case, at least four for a chupadeira, and at least three for a moínho. These are minimum figures; in an ideal world donos would like three or four men over and above the number required just to operate the machinery to help in rebaixamentos and bring out as much gold-bearing material as possible.

Then there is the nature of the deposit to be thought of. Alluvium requires fewer workers, as a rule, than a primary deposit. Rock often has to be chipped out with pickaxes and carried to the moínho in sacks, where it has to be reduced to a size that can be passed through the moínho. At least three workers, and often more, are needed to keep one moínho supplied with material. Generally speaking, mechanised garimpagem requires a work crew of at least five people, plus the dono, who in addition to supervising and directing operations will often work as well. Double or triple that number is not unusual. All workers have to be fed, accommodated, and supplied with tools, and donos are acutely aware that direct and indirect labour costs are usually the largest component of total costs (see Appendix). Exactly how high they are depends on what work regime is used.

With a rough idea of how many workers are needed and how long an operation is likely to take – estimations that often prove to be wrong even when made by experienced donos, slaves as they are to weather conditions and variations in deposits – a dono then has to consider actual or anticipated gold production. The objective of donos is to ensure that as much as possible of total gold production remains in their hands at the end of the day, so the decision between a percentage or a wage system depends to a large extent on what production is, or is likely to be. If production is low, a daily wage will tend to be uneconomic; on the other hand, a daily wage is fixed, and therefore if production is high it makes more sense for a dono to use diaristas. Too many porcentistas and a large bite would be taken out of the dono's share of the gold produced.

Nevertheless, it is not unusual to see a barranco with a good level of gold production being worked by porcentistas. This apparent contradiction is explained by the constraints that lack of resources can impose on a dono. Diaristas are normally short stay garimpeiros. They are entitled to leave in the middle of an operation, when gold production has not yet begun, and this poses a dual problem for the dono; they have to be replaced, and they have to be paid, at a time when it might be difficult to find the money – most donos have little cash or gold on hand. A porcentista, on the other hand, is not paid unless gold is produced, and so can usually be relied upon to stay with an operation until the end. The many donos who have liquidity problems may well opt for a percentage system even if anticipated production is high, because it means they postpone paying workers until gold is actually extracted, and this enables operations to be got off the ground more easily.

In choosing a work regime a dono is also to a certain extent choosing a type of worker. Even donos who have the resources to employ diaristas may decide that it would be better to work with experienced porcentistas than with rawer diaristas, especially if an operation is complicated. On the other hand, from the point of view of the dono, experience is a double-edged quality for workers to have. Experienced porcentistas will demand a higher standard of food and working conditions than is usually the case with diaristas. Furthermore, one aspect of experience is learning how to go slow on the job, or even pilfer gold that is being produced without the dono noticing; donos often say that it is better to work with an inexperienced crew because they are more honest, expect less, and work harder.

Theoretically, then, choosing a work regime is a complicated decision. In practice it is often less so, because lack of resources or difficulty in getting credit forces many donos to use porcentistas even if they would prefer to have diaristas. What often happens is that donos try to strike a balance between the two, using porcentistas for the more skilled jobs and diaristas for the rest; two or more distinct work regimes can thus be in use in a barranco at any one time. The more skilled a job, the more likely it is that it will be done by a porcentista. Workers who specialise in operating machinery are often porcentistas, and the most skilled and dangerous work, such as raft garimpagem, is exclusively porcentista. Equally, garimpeiros who are essentially manual labourers by another name tend to be diaristas.

Decisions for donos do not end with choosing between diaristas or porcentistas; they then have to decide between a number of different daily wage and percentage systems. The daily wage is the more uniform. Apart from a straight daily salary, the only variant is piece-rate working. There are some operations which involve carrying sacks of material out of barrancos, either taking gold-bearing material to where the machinery is set up, or, where overburden cannot simply be shovelled out of one barranco without interfering with operations in others, shifting it well away from the barranco grid. Piece-rate working applies to a work crew as a whole, and it gives an opportunity for every member to earn multiples of a daily wage. One *diária* is fixed as being the carrying of a certain number of sacks which contain a set number of spadefuls of material. In the Gurupí, a *diária* was equivalent to forty sacks of fifteen spadefuls or sixty of ten. A strong worker could achieve this mark in three to five hours. Once one *diária* had been earned, workers had the option of either knocking off for the rest of the day, or going on to earn multiples of a *diária*. Piece-rate working requires, besides those carrying the sacks, an *apontador*, who stands with a notebook wherever the material is to be deposited and records how many sacks each worker shifts, and at least two people filling the sacks in the barranco to be taken away. A fit and well-drilled work crew could achieve up to three *diárias* in a day. Piece-rate systems are thus popular with diaristas, who receive more than they otherwise would, and with donos who need a job doing quickly and are prepared to pay for it. It is most common towards the end of the dry season, when donos are anxious to get as much as possible done before the arrival of the rains makes working conditions more difficult.

The most common form of percentage system is simply to agree a stake in advance, five per cent being standard. Certain types of garimpagem, like rafts, are only worked on a percentage basis, because the skills needed and the dangers involved mean that no dono would find garimpeiros prepared to work merely for a daily wage. Rafts are worked in two twelve-hour shifts of three workers each, who take turns to dive and usually receive five per cent apiece.[1] Where gold production is high and the demand for skilled workers particularly intense – such as Serra Pelada in 1980 and 1981, parts of the Tapajós, and some garimpos in Cumarú, Mato Grosso and Rondónia – another system more advantageous to the worker called the *meia-praça* is used. Under this system, gold produced is split evenly between the dono and the work crew. This means, in effect, that the work unit receives more gold than the dono, as there are no claims upon the gold received by a *meieiro*, as a worker in the meia-praça system is called, while from the other half the dono has to pay for food for the workers and the other running costs of the operation. The meia-praça is especially common during fofocas or when gold production from an area is rising, a time when donos are desperate to attract labour and tend to be over-optimistic about the potential of their barrancos. The meia-praça thus tends to enjoy a brief flowering in the earlier stages of a garimpo, and is then replaced by other work regimes more advantageous to donos as gold production dips and the demand for labour lessens. This process occurs through natural attrition rather than being imposed: donos use the meia-praça when they have high expectations, and during a fofoca a form of collective hysteria can grip even experienced donos, who convince themselves and each other that they have found another deposit on the scale of Serra Pelada. When gold production does not live up to these high hopes, more donos using the meia-praça will go bust than those using any other work regime, because they get to keep a relatively smaller proportion of the gold extracted.

The best example of this was Serra Pelada. In the period when gold production and demand for labour was at its peak, from the second half of 1979 until early 1982, the meia-praça was the most common work regime there. However, as barrancos deepened costs rose, and the emphasis shifted more to the enormous number of manual labourers who were needed to move the overburden out of barrancos and away from the barranco grid, who were either diaristas or piece-rate workers. By 1986 there were few meieiros left; most of them had moved south to newer garimpos in Cumarú and Mato Grosso.

Under both daily wage and percentage regimes, workers receive food, accommodation, are provided with all tools, and are free to come and go as they please. They must work every day except Sunday, from about an hour after dawn to an hour before sunset, with an hour's break for lunch at noon. Outside these hours and on a Sunday, diaristas are paid *hora extra*, overtime, at a rate agreed with the dono. They cannot be compelled to work overtime, although generally diaristas will jump at the chance to earn more money. Politeness dictates that a worker should say roughly how long he will be available, and donos can try to come to agreements in advance about the length of time to be worked, although such agreements are invariably informal and non-binding: should workers wish to leave at any time they are free to do so without notice and do not forfeit their accumulated wages. However, a worker will generally give at least a few days notice of intention to quit, because it is in his interest to do so; it gives the dono a chance to make arrangements for paying him. Donos have similar privileges: they may dismiss a diarista at any time, although again convention dictates that a few days notice should be given.

Diaristas are generally paid in a lump sum in cash or the gold equivalent at the end of the period they work. Refusal to pay wages, even in situations where no notice is given, is only justifiable when a worker has been caught stealing or sabotaging an operation; refusal in any other context can quickly lead to violence. Donos can dismiss diaristas at any time, provided that they are paid for the work they have done. This is sometimes done without notice, but again, as it is not in a dono's interests to acquire a reputation as bad employer, at least a few days notice will generally be given.

One of the advantages of porcentistas, from the point of view of the dono, is that because their earnings depend on gold actually being produced they can usually be relied upon to see an operation through until the end. If a porcentista does leave temporarily, he has to pay for a diarista to take his place until his return if he wishes to retain his percentage stake. If a porcentista leaves before any gold is produced the dono has no obligation to pay him anything, although in special cases, such as a porcentista who has to leave because of sickness, injury, or family crisis, most donos will pay him at diarista rates for time worked. Some may even pay the costs of medical evacuation and treatment.

To a certain extent, this altruism is self-serving. It gives a good impression of the dono to the other workers in the crew, making disputes with them less likely. At the same time, actions like this quickly become known. Workers entering a region of garimpagem will know about garimpos and the donos within them long before they arrive. On jungle paths, in bars and brothels, on buses, planes and boats, workers on their way out are constantly in contact with workers on their way in, bringing them up to date on the latest situation in the garimpos they have left. Even amongst garimpeiros these informal information networks are proverbial for the speed with which they transmit news and events, and are known by the sardonic nickname of *rádio peão*. It is very much in a dono's interests to acquire a reputation as a dono who takes care of workers; it means that they will be sought out by incoming workers, especially by experienced porcentistas, and have the option of picking and choosing from amongst those who present themselves. Conspicuously generous gestures are in any case, as will be seen, a way of signifying success at gold extraction; they confer prestige and command respect.

Once a dono and a worker come to an agreement on the work regime to be used, it cannot be changed except by mutual consent, although if a dono wants to shift from a diarista system to a percentage one he has the option of paying off the diaristas and engaging porcentistas in their place. A porcentista cannot be dismissed before production begins unless he is caught in a gross breach of norms, like stealing. Once production does begin, at least one porcentista will be present during despescagem at the end of the day, and the gold will usually be weighed in their presence by the dono in the evening; disputes over the actual amounts of gold being produced are thus very rare.

Once gold production begins, porcentistas will leave after a certain time. In the case of a poor dono with low production levels, a percentage system will only be used because of lack of resources to pay diaristas, and so porcentistas are often disguised diaristas, short-stay garimpeiros who would return to other rural and urban occupations after a few weeks or months in any case. In the contrasting example of a rich dono with high production levels, porcentistas will invariably be professional garimpeiros whose objective is to set up as an independent dono: once they have made enough gold to make this possible, they will leave. But even the richest donos will rarely go over completely to diarista or piece-rate labour, partly because the more complex jobs are best done by professionals, who will not work for a daily wage, and partly because, as will be seen, there are certain strategic advantages for donos if they can divide their workforce into two or more groups which do not have identical interests.

There is also a way that manual donos can get the use of machinery to work the material they excavate, in the process allowing owners of machinery to make a good living in a garimpo without ever owning a barranco or financing an operation proper. Sandoval, an ex-taxi driver from Belém, explains how it works:

Waldomar was one of the first people to arrive here in Sedral and he has several barrancos, but I don't have anything against that because all the barrancos that he has, he works. He arrived early on, marked out several barrancos, and put three men in one, four in another, five in another, working meia-praça with cobra fumandos. In my barranco today we were doing a rebaixamento, and so my moínho was idle. He came to me this morning and suggested that I put his material through my moínho, and that's what I was doing today. Half the gold went to his meieiros, and Waldomar and I divided the other half. I had to pay fuel costs, but that wasn't anything just for one day, and I didn't pay labour because I did it myself. Everyone wins; Waldomar gets his material processed faster and more efficiently, I get more than enough gold to cover my costs on a day when I wasn't using the machinery anyway, and Waldomar's meieiros get their half of the gold. Perfect.

A fair number of mechanised donos will not be using their machinery at any one time because they are doing rebaixamentos. On top of that, there are some owners of machinery who specialise in processing other people's material, because it allows them to dispense with labour costs altogether. In return for taking on the running costs of machinery – fuel and spare parts – they will usually receive 25 per cent of the gold extracted. On the debit side, only large garimpos would generate enough work to keep this type of operator constantly occupied, and most of them have to laboriously dismantle and transport their machinery to fofocas, where the demands for the service they provide are greatest.

Apart from their wages or percentage stakes, workers can supplement their income through an institution known as the *reque*, Reque means, essentially, incidental gold extraction. It can be thought of as a kind of bonus, or fringe benefit. When a moínho is in operation, the joints where the lid fits over the mounting are lined with strips of sacking so that nothing can escape through the narrow gap. Over the days and weeks that a moínho is in use, small pieces of gold lodge in the sacking. Exactly how much depends on the material being processed, but it can be as much as ten grams. Flecks of gold also lodge in the *peneira*, the metal filter at the bottom of a moínho. Then there is the sacking used to line a caixa. Although it is beaten with a stick during despescagem to remove the gold that is lodged in it, a little always remains. It can be extracted if the sacking is vigorously scrubbed in a bucket filled with soapy water, and the solution is then panned in a bateia. The small amounts of gold that can be obtained in this way are in the gift of the dono. They have the right to keep it for themselves if they wish, or they can *liberar* – allow individual workers or the work crew as a whole to extract and keep it. In addition, the dono may give permission for individual workers or the crew as a whole to work in the barranco on Sunday, provided they use only manual technology. If a dono is especially pleased with the performance of workers, he may even allow them a few hours on the moínho or the chupadeira on Sunday, letting them keep what they produce. Reque is a generic term for all these bonuses on top of the wage or percentage stake.

The reque is an important element in the relationship between donos and workers. It is simultaneously carrot and stick. For diarista workers especially, it can be a significant addition to their wages. But being allowed to 'work the reque' is a favour, not a right. Withholding it causes grumbling and resentment, but no complaints that the dono has no right to do so. It is thus a sanction at the same time as an incentive. Workers know that if they work well they can count on a reque, and if they work badly the dono can punish them by refusing it. Furthermore, the fact that the reque can be granted to some workers and withheld from others means that it can be used very subtly; an astute dono can divide a work crew, creating tensions and jealousies within it, more effectively by shrewdly granting and refusing the reque than by any other means. But it is a sanction that ought to be used with restraint. Donos who are sparing with the reque will not only alienate a work crew to the point where they will work as slowly as they can get away with. They will also get a bad reputation on rádio peão. One of the first pieces of information that incoming workers will try to get hold of about donos is whether or not they are reasonably generous with the reque. A dono known to be miserly will have more difficulty finding workers than one who is not, and will find it especially hard to get hold of skilled porcentistas, for whom denial of the reque is tantamount to an accusation of professional incompetence.

Work regimes in garimpagem, then, are complex and variegated. That variety is especially striking when it is contrasted with the relative uniformity of labour regimes in other traditionally important extractive activities in Amazonia, such as rubber, timber, and Brazil nuts, or within the increasingly important ranching industry. They are certainly remarkable for the freedom of action they allow to workers, and, to a lesser extent, donos. When compared to *latifundista* agriculture, timbering, forest clearing, cattle ranching, the rubber industry, or the Brazil nut estates – in other words, the principal non-urban sources of employment before 1979 in Amazonia – the work regimes and conditions of employment in garimpagem appear positively benevolent. Workers never get into debt with their employers, except for when a dono pays a fare for a worker to go to an air-supplied garimpo. They are not usually engaged for a fixed period, and, although there are some conventional politenesses that should be observed, they can come and go more or less as they please. In the reque, they even have a type of bonus incentive. The income of porcentistas rises in accordance with any increases in production. In certain systems, such as the meia-praça, a work crew can even end up with a significantly higher proportion of gold production than the dono.

The implications of all this are important. Firstly, the variety of work regimes is both in keeping with and a reflection of the variety of types of garimpeiro and the different levels of technology and investment that one finds in garimpos. Secondly, that very diversity is important in the functioning of garimpos; variety and diversity in economic structure in themselves open up opportunities for transaction and manipulation, whether it be in garimpos or Wall Street. Finally, and most importantly, although the work is often backbreaking and dangerous, it is carried out under work regimes that afford more advantage to the workforce than any other they could enter, with the exception of smallholder agriculture. This in itself is part of the explanation for the sheer scale of the post-1979 rush.

LIQUIDITY, CREDIT AND BANKRUPTCY

Running a gold operation is not just a question of having machinery and workers. Workers have to be fed, which means that during an operation donos have to lay in supplies of staples like rice, beans and farinha, and also coffee, sugar, cooking oil, meat, salt, okra, onions, and peppers. Donos who can afford it hire a cook; those who cannot have to prepare food for the workers themselves. They must also provide whatever tools might be needed – spades, pickaxes, crowbars, large chisels, mallets, sledgehammers and sacks – as well as fuel and spare parts for the machinery. Moínhos are especially demanding, as a ready supply of replacement steel flails is essential. On top of this donos need large amounts of plastic hose and pipes, and plastic sheeting for the lining of water tanks. If these supplies are bought in bulk outside the garimpo, donos have to pay lorry drivers, pilots or mule drivers to bring them in. They buy large amounts of mercury, and occasionally acid to scrub gold clean of impurities. And all this takes no account of the initial capital investment necessary to buy machinery.

In the Appendix, basic budgets from three operations are reproduced.

All were mounted by experienced mechanised donos, and were judged typical of operations at the lower end of the mechanised scale. The results of two of these operations were also entirely typical; a small profit which could equally well have been a small loss. In Barranco 2, gold was found at an early stage and steady production maintained, but in the others corners were cut and donos had to improvise solutions to problems as they arose. In spite of this, considerable sums were spent over the course of these operations. Even though the sums are not in absolute terms very high, especially when compared to the formal mining sector, they are still large amounts of cash and credit for small and medium scale donos to have to find.

It is often striking how threadbare an existence many donos lead. For months on end they eat nothing but rice, beans, and farinha, with the occasional bird or small animal they manage to shoot. To say that they have liquidity problems is in many cases putting it very mildly; many donos live in a state of acute economic crisis, with a fair proportion apparently teetering on the edge of bankruptcy. Nevertheless, not as many actually do go bankrupt as an initial analysis of costs and resources might suggest. This is partly because of the availability of credit, but in many cases what makes the difference between success and failure is a quick mind and a glib tongue. A surprising number of donos have the knack of conjuring up the resources needed to start operations and keep them going from a seemingly hopeless economic position.

The story of how Santos Neto managed to finance and run the operation that appears as Barranco 3 in the Appendix is a case in point. This was an operation of the type garimpeiros call *limpeza*, the 'cleaning' of an old barranco that at one time had produced a lot of gold, but which in August 1985 was filled with water and the remains of old land slippings to a depth of about twenty meters. Santos Neto estimated that it was going to take at least two months to bring into production again – it would take almost double that as it turned out – and it would be a labour-intensive job to boot. He did not have to think a great deal about the work regime he was going to use, as he knew he could not hope to pay diaristas for so long. When I left the garimpo of Cerqueiro at the end of June, Santos Neto was drawing towards the end of an operation in another barranco which had made a slight loss. Although he was talking of moving into the other barranco, I very much doubted that he would be able to do so. I was surprised and delighted when I returned in September to find him in mid-rebaixamento, getting on with 'cleaning' the barranco. When I asked him how he had managed to set up the operation, this was the reply:

I began with the other barranco when you were here the last time. I worked there for two weeks after you left with the moínho, only making small amounts daily, three grams, four grams, not more.

How much did that leave in your hands after paying costs?

I couldn't tell you, because what I was doing was this; I'd produce a little gold and immediately leave to buy supplies outside [the garimpo], diesel oil, food, and then come back in. Then when I'd made another few grams I'd do the same, buy supplies and keep them for the time that I'd start in the other barranco. I wanted to have at least the food and fuel bought before I started, so that I wouldn't have to worry about it. It was like a cantina in here. That little room was full of sacks of rice and drums of fuel. Then I spent two weeks with the moínho in another abandoned barranco, where there was some really low grade rock that nobody else wanted to work.

Did you make anything?

A little, one *puxada* [daily production] of six grams, another of five. It was more of a reque than working a barranco proper, just working rocks that had been thrown away there. With the money I bought food and fuel again, food and fuel, food and fuel. It was when there was no rock left that I was really stuck; I still needed to lay out money but I'd already spent all my gold production and there was nowhere else I could put my moínho to work. I had a small house in Geraldo [a smallholder village eighteen kilometres from Cerqueiro] that I got in exchange for a boat and outboard motor that I bought when I first arrived here in 1982 to make the journey downriver to Maracassumé. I exchanged the house for a cow with a woman in Geraldo, with a cash sum on top as well. I sank the cash in this operation straight away, and then put the cow together with an old chainsaw I had, and exchanged them with a smallholder for a field of planted rice. He was going to pay me in rice that I was going to sell in Maracassumé, but as the price went up then[2] he wanted to pay me money instead, so as I didn't really have the time to go to Maracassumé we agreed 3.5 million cruzeiros [about $400]. I gave

2.5 million as down payment to Chico [another dono] on a more powerful motor, because cleaning this barranco is a heavy job. The million that was left went on the final supplies that I needed to start.

How are you going to pay the other instalments for the motor?

I probably won't. I only need it for this job; my other motor is fine for most things. I'll just use it here to get a reasonable production, and then, when the next payment is due, I'll give it back. He won't complain, as I'll agree to him keeping the down payment as hiring fees. And if gold production is better than I expect, well, I'll have the money to pay, won't I?

This is an experienced dono talking, highly skilled at overcoming apparently insurmountable obstacles. His achievement was impressive; by wheeling and dealing both inside and outside the garimpo he managed not only to lay in enough food and fuel to support a lengthy operation, but also to get hold of a more powerful motor, without which the barranco could not have been worked. His entrepreneurial abilities were obvious in his management of the complicated series of exchanges he performed, and in his shrewd decision to make a local smallholder the final link in the chain of transactions. He knew that with rice he could not go wrong: he could either have used it directly to feed his workers, or marketed it himself, selling it either to the COLONE colonisation project or on the free market in Maracassumé. As it turned out he did even better than he thought because of the rise in rice prices, and was able to conclude a very advantageous cash settlement. At the same time, he knew that local smallholders would not be interested in a house in Geraldo, as they live in their forest plots, but also that they would find it hard to resist a deal involving both a cow and a chainsaw. It is also worth noting that by handling all the necessary transactions himself, accumulating supplies gradually and paying cash directly to outside suppliers, he avoided the local cantineiros and thus cut down his costs considerably by not using credit. A more inexperienced dono would as a matter of course have laid in supplies on credit from a cantineiro and accepted the interest on debts contracted as part of total costs. He kept labour costs to a minimum by contracting five porcentistas at five per cent each, only hiring two diaristas for five days when extra help in a rebaixamento was vital. The result was a tribute to his skill; total costs of under $700 for an operation that lasted four months, when a comparable operation like Barranco 1 in the Appendix cost $3,008.

Despite this, the operation was only a limited success. Santos Neto could not fully overcome the disadvantages of lack of resources and liquidity. Throughout the four months he was hamstrung by not having enough workers; with no money for diaristas, and reluctant to take on more porcentistas because it would eat into his share of gold production, he tried to make do with five workers in an operation that really required ten. This meant that certain jobs – such as removing overburden away from the barranco so that it would not be washed into it again by the rains, and shoring up the sides of the barranco with logs – could not be done effectively. In the long term this led to the premature closing of the operation. It also meant that part of each day had to be spent clearing out material that had slipped into the barranco overnight, and this slowed the descent towards paydirt. Once gold-bearing material had been reached, it was only possible to remove enough to keep the moínho going for ten days before the rains caused the collapse of one side of the barranco and put an end to the operation for the year. A small profit was achieved all the same, but for Santos Neto, who had stripped himself of some assets to finance the operation, it was a disappointment.

This operation was a textbook case of reasonable success gained by the skilful deployment of limited resources, backed by entrepreneurial inventiveness. Even so, Santos Neto could not fully overcome the constraints which his straitened circumstances imposed. If even Santos Neto's virtuosity led to only limited gains, the difficulties faced by less experienced and resourceful donos can readily be imagined. Their costs are generally higher, partly because they tend to use the credit facilities extended by local cantineiros, and partly because one consequence of inexperience is getting the type of deposit and estimations of time and numbers of workers needed wildly wrong, and thus using diaristas when porcentistas would have been better, or vice-versa.

At the same time, the inexperienced are targetted both by cantineiros and other garimpeiros, workers and donos, as likely people to conclude unduly advantageous deals with. Even experienced donos use local cantineiros to some extent, when they do not have the time or money to lay in supplies themselves; inexperienced donos are often completely reliant on the supplies they can get on credit at a local cantina to keep going. In many cases donos try to reduce their dependence on credit by involving sócios in their operations, but the dono who can operate purely on the strength of sócios is rare. Getting something on credit is called *comprar fiado*, and it is one of the most common phrases one hears in garimpos. Credit is the lubricant of the economic system in all garimpos; without it, most operations would never get off the ground.

But the fact that credit is easily available in garimpos does not mean that it is indiscriminately given. It would not be in a cantineiro's interests to supply an operation that was being so incompetently run that it would collapse before the dono could pay off the debt. Cantineiros need donos to succeed for another reason; an important part of their business is supplying goods, especially alcohol, to workers. If a dono goes bankrupt, not only does the cantineiro have to write off the large debt the dono has run up, but also the several smaller debts the workers have run up. Supplying goods on credit in a garimpo is thus a subtle business that demands fine judgement on the part of a cantineiro. They have to strike a balance between avarice and prudence; interest on loans is an important part of their income, but if they allow donos to go so far into debt that they decide to flee, the cantineiro will usually have to write off most of the original loan and all of the interest. In addition, cantineiros do not finance operations from scratch. They do not, as a rule, extend credit for the purchase of machinery. Donos must already have made this initial capital investment before cantineiros will consider supplying an operation. Machinery can be obtained on credit, with instalments to be paid *da produção*, from gold as it is extracted, but from other donos or outside suppliers, not from local cantineiros.

Cantineiros, then, are important figures in the garimpo. One of the consequences of the strategic position that the cantina occupies in both social and economic life is that cantineiros are just as important to visiting anthropologists as they are to garimpeiros. If anybody knows who is producing gold and who not, who is a skilful garimpeiro and who not, who is having trouble with workers and whose workers are contented, which barrancos might be worth 'cleaning' and which should be left alone, it will be a cantineiro. It is literally their business to know. A cantineiro will cast around for information on a new client, as they might be opening an account because they have been refused elsewhere, and it is in every cantineiro's interest to respond to requests for information from other cantineiros: they may compete with each other on one level, but this does not preclude them from acting as an informal cartel to preserve their common interests. This quiet vetting continues once the account has been opened. Thus the giving of credit

1. Basic instruments: 'cuia' (l) and 'bateia' (r)

2. The bateia in use: panning

.3. Cobra fumando: note bateia being used to catch overspill

4. Supplying water to a cobra fumando

5. The moinho, a portable mechanical crusher, with motor and pile of alluvium in background. The caixa in the foreground is being cleaned for gold, with riffles laid out on the right

6. Caixao, as used in chupadeira and raft garimpagem

7. A chupadeira (foreground) with pipes going up to caixao and down to barranco

8. High pressure hoses in use during a chupadeira operation. The two men sitting in the water are ensuring that no stones are sucked up into the chupadeira

9. Manual 'rebaixamento', showing terraced shape it typically assumes

10. A good haul: mercury saturated with gold resists water flow at bottom of caixa

11. The final stages: excess mercury being drained off in a bateia, with 'pancake' of gold and mercury lodged in centre

12. Mercury being burnt off with butane torch. Note it is being done in area of food preparation: gas cooking rings top left

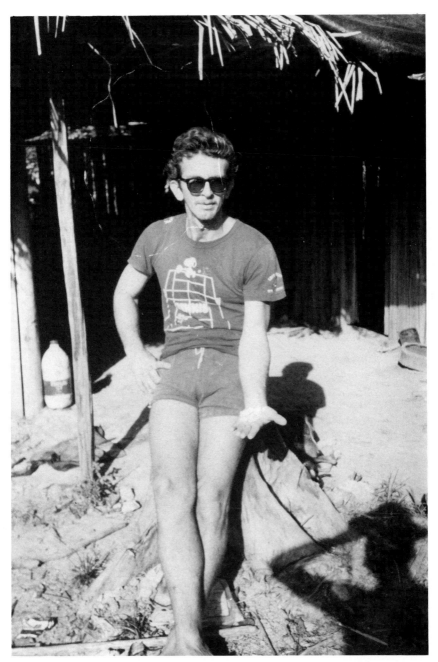

13. Gold. Santos Neto is holding about 100 grams, worth around $1,000 in 1985

14. Montes Aureos. Earth dam constructed by British in 1859 now planted with banana trees in foreground, modern barrancos cut into hillside behind

15. Detritus from earlier rushes: in Montes Aureos a steam boiler and cogwheel abandoned by the British in the 1860s rusts in the middle of a modern garimpo

16. Serra Pelada

17. The 'fofoca' of Trinta Cinco in its early days: moinhos amid forest only partially cleared in rush to get into production

18. Cigarette break

in garimpos is as tightly structured and controlled as its strategic importance in the running of operations implies, although the mechanisms are informal and unobtrusive.

All the same, people do go bust, and often. To a certain extent the post-1979 rush would not be on such a grand scale if this were not so, as the cheap machinery bankrupt donos release into the system is one factor that ensures a steady stream of replacements for them. Bankruptcies are potentially explosive events; the conflicting claims of creditors from outside the barranco and workers within it have to be resolved at a time when all parties are feeling tense and mutual recriminations are flying around.

What happens depends on the way the bankrupt dono pulls out. There are three alternatives. The first is to flee, secretly by night, or openly by day, saying it will only be a brief trip outside to get more supplies or a spare part and never returning. In this case there will be a free-for-all involving creditors and workers, which can easily spiral out of control. Secondly, a dono might persuade another dono or a cantineiro to take over the barranco and machinery and assume all debts, in which case the dono will change but otherwise the transition is a seamless one and the workers remain happy, provided that the new dono gives them no cause for concern. Thirdly, a dono might redeem at least some debts and pay off workers by selling machinery and any other assets; the only possible problem here is if the sale does not cover the debts. During the course of fieldwork several bankruptcies were witnessed; the most convoluted, and in some ways the most interesting, was one which involved Chichico, a cantineiro in Cerqueiro.

What happened was this. Bernardo, a mechanised dono, ran up an account with Chichico for $500 in an operation that involved three porcentistas and seven diaristas. After three months no gold had been produced, some of the workers were clamouring to be paid off so they could leave, Bernardo's sócios were refusing to have anything further to do with the operation, no other cantineiro was prepared to advance Bernardo any credit – in other words, things were on the point of collapse. Bernardo still believed that the barranco had potential, but knew that he did not have the resources to continue. He went to see Chichico and said that the only thing he could do was to try and find another sócio outside the garimpo. In the meantime, he proposed, Chichico should temporarily take over his barranco, machinery, and workers, and try to recover the debt himself. In return for Chichico assuming his debt to his workers, Bernardo shrewdly suggested, any gold produced on top of the $500 would go to Chichico as well. It was a deal Chichico, despite some misgivings, could not resist. He suspected that Bernardo might simply not return, and thought of selling his machinery once he had gone to recover the debt and pay off the workers, but as the machinery was worth more than $500, even when sold at a reduced price, he decided to give Bernardo the benefit of the doubt. Most importantly, Chichico knew the history of the barranco and believed that Bernardo had been working it in the wrong way; he thought he might make a killing.

Two months later, Chichico himself was in serious trouble with the operation. On top of the $500 he was owed, he had invested a further $1600, paying off the diaristas who wanted to leave, engaging replacements, and putting his ideas about how the barranco should be worked into effect. He was funnelling supplies from the cantina into the operation, thus doubly damaging himself because they would normally have been given out on credit to other donos, and he was himself running up ominously high bills with outside suppliers.

In the end, despite a few close calls, he managed to pull through. He produced enough gold to pay off the workers and cover most of his costs, although if the original debt of $500 was included he made an overall loss of around $200. He had saved himself because, as a cantineiro, he could use income from other sources to underpin his own operations. What he essentially did was to transfer debts from the work crew to his outside suppliers, an option not open to donos who are not entrepreneurs. There was a postscript to the story. Bernardo, it turned out, having failed to arrange another sócio, was keeping in close touch with developments from a nearby town. When he found out that Chichico had managed to pay the workers and reduce the original debt, he waited until Chichico was away, came in with a mule driver, dismantled the machinery, and hurriedly took it away. As they had already been paid and the operation was about to be closed down anyway, the workers did not stop him. When he returned, Chichico was furious; he was especially angry when he heard that Bernardo had said he had repossessed the machinery because Chichico was about to sell it to recover a debt that was less than the price he would get for the machinery. This was a lie, Chichico said, as a cantineiro who did that – in effect, stealing from a dono in trouble – would immediately lose the custom of many donos. Chichico said he had merely wished to keep the machinery as a surety, thinking that as long as he had it Bernardo would pay the $200 he still owed.

This illustrates several points about bankruptcies. Firstly, cantineiros are almost always involved, as the most important local creditor will usually be a cantineiro. Secondly, the workers did get the money they were owed in the end, and there was enough gold produced to keep the porcentistas happy, although many had to stay with the operation for considerably longer than they had originally intended. Both Bernardo and Chichico were aware that in the final resort the machinery could be sold, but since the original debt was less than the likely sale price of the machinery, there were strong constraints on Chichico not to take such a drastic step. Bernardo took action before the debt had risen to the point where he might have had to flee and lose his machinery, although he was not above subterfuge to get it back. The episode was certainly a problematic one, but all parties ended up in a better postion than had at one time seemed likely; the workers were paid, Bernardo managed to keep his machinery and Chichico reduced his loss to $200.

Some bankruptcies do result in workers never recovering what they are owed, but this is not as common as might be expected. In two of the possible outcomes, where the original dono sells up and closes down, or where another dono takes over, they can expect to receive at least some of what they are owed. In the worst case, when a dono flees, they will still enjoy the advantages of physical possession of the barranco and machinery, and what happens afterwards depends on how well they can fend off the demands of other creditors. The two cases of a dono fleeing that were witnessed during fieldwork had opposite outcomes. One involved only five workers, who were owed a great deal less than was due to each of three creditors, who also happened to be prominent figures in the garimpo. They simply arrived in the barranco the next day with their own workers, and took away everything they could find that had belonged to the dono, ignoring the protests of the workers. The next day the creditors offered to pay for the workers to return home and, disgruntled and out of pocket, they had to accept.

The other case involved a larger work crew, eleven diaristas, who were owed for three months. They mounted guard on the machinery, but at the same time went to see the main creditor, a cantineiro, and asked to be left to try and extract enough gold to pay their wages without interference, pointing out that if they succeeded they would also be able to pay off the debts they had individually run up at the cantina. Provided that they did not expect any more credit, the cantineiro replied, he was agreeable. For two weeks they used what supplies the dono had left, and managed to pay themselves. Then they left, and the cantineiro and other creditors took the machinery.

The general point here is that whether or not workers recover what is due to them in bankruptcies depends on how many of them there are, whether they can act in a united and co-ordinated way, and how powerful the creditors from outside the barranco are. When a large work unit stays together and announces it will try to pay itself, other creditors will usually accept the fact, because the only way of enforcing their claim would be violence, which would be foolish when the workers are not asserting any permanent claim on the machinery or barranco and can be expected to leave as soon as they extract enough gold to pay themselves. If the workers attempted to sell the machinery rather than use it, however, the situation would be altogether more serious. No such case was seen during fieldwork, nor could any garimpeiros quote me an example from their own experience, which suggests that this theoretically most problematic type of bankruptcy is fairly rare.

SELLING GOLD: PATTERNS OF INVESTMENT AND CONSUMPTION

Garimpeiros have a number of choices when it comes to selling the gold they earn or produce. As a general rule, the further away from the garimpo gold is sold, the better the price will be. Occasionally, as in a closed fofoca or garimpo, garimpeiros are forced to sell at an artificially low price to a single dominant local figure. All cantineiros buy gold for cash, or accept it in payment for goods, and travelling gold buyers constantly circulate through areas of garimpagem. Both they and cantineiros pay prices slightly below the market level, which garimpeiros accept for the convenience of receiving cash on the nail. In all villages, towns and cities near garimpos, gold buyers are thick on the ground. Many of the smaller gold buyers pass on the gold they buy at a slightly higher price to the gold buying networks set up by regional entrepreneurs like Zé Arara. These bulk buying operations turn a profit by refining the gold, which involves a loss in volume but an increase in value, and then selling it clandestinely overseas or to jewellery manufacturers elsewhere in Brazil.

The biggest gold buying network of all is the official state gold buying programme run by the Caixa Econômica Federal. The Caixa, almost uniquely for a state institution, is trusted by garimpeiros. They know that the price the Caixa quotes is the latest world market price, daily converted into Brazilian currency at the current exchange rate. The only slight disadvantage is that one per cent of the value of the sale goes to the state in the form of the IUM, the *Imposto Único de Mineração*, a tax on all mineral sales. Nevertheless, the Caixa's price is still highly competitive, and where possible garimpeiros will sell to the CEF, if only because they know that there the scales have not been doctored with. Selling to the Caixa is, unusually for Brazil, a simple and non-bureaucratic process, since in its anxiety to buy as much gold as possible, and thereby increase tax revenues, the CEF routinely waives the strict legal requirements on mineral sales by garimpeiros, such as the production of a membership card of a garimpeiro union.

Once a dono has the proceeds of a gold sale in hand, what remains after workers, cantineiros and sócios are paid off can be employed in a number of different ways. It can be ploughed back into the garimpo; Santos Neto was seen in action doing just that, and it is the constant reinvestment of proceeds in other operations that characterises entrepreneurs and most mechanised donos in garimpagem. However, not all garimpeiros choose to follow this route.

In villages, towns and cities in or near areas of garimpagem, like Imperatriz in southern Maranhão or Marabá in southern Pará, there are many recently built luxury homes, with large cars parked in the drive. Many belong to *bamburrados*, those who have struck it rich in garimpos, and to garimpeiros about to leave for the goldfields this ostentatiously displayed affluence is a concrete reminder of the wealth that garimpagem can bring to a select few. Stories of bamburros and bamburrados are recounted time and again in garimpos, with their themes of perseverance rewarded and overnight changes of fortune serving to bolster morale when operations hit low points. They are all very similar; a rich strike and tumultuous celebrations, followed by the purchase of an array of consumer durables, land, houses, cars, cattle, and so forth. The level of detail that is common knowledge is often surprising. In Marabá it is easy to walk down one of the streets that contains the houses of bamburrados with somebody who can, like a tour guide, name the owner of each house, say where the bamburro occurred, and how many kilos of gold it involved, no doubt somewhat exaggerated. These houses (and the cattle ranches, private planes and plots of land that could be found with a little more time) are not necessarily purely for show. In an economy plagued by hyperinflation, transforming large amounts of money into property as quickly as possible makes a good deal of economic sense, and many bamburrados buy property to speculate with rather than display. Nevertheless, in many cases this affluence does embody an alternative economic ethos to that held by hardheaded reinvestors like Santos Neto. In certain circumstances nobody consumes quite so conspicuously as a successful garimpeiro, and even unsuccessful garimpeiros often consume as conspicuously as they can.

The case of Maria is typical of this kind of behaviour. Maria is a widow, and was one of the spontaneous smallholder migrants who moved into the Gurupí in the late 1970s and was absorbed into the COLONE colonisation project. In 1982 she found gold in a stream that she had used to irrigate her rice fields. She began to work it with an experienced garimpeiro she made her sócio, and it turned out to be one of the richest strikes in the area, provoking a large fofoca and leading to the establishment of a garimpo which still bears her name. Over the next three years Maria and her partner extracted eleven kilos of gold from her barranco, worth about $110 000 at 1985 prices. The effect this sudden wealth had on Maria was poignant. She showered money, goods and cattle on her extended family. For herself, she bought some cattle and roofed her wattle and daub house in Geraldo with aluminium sheeting. She drank and gambled. A succession of hangers-on and lovers took what they could worm out of her. At a time when the 'road' between the settlement of Geraldo and the town of Santa Teresa on the BR-316 highway could only be travelled by mule or on foot for most of the year, she bought two Chevrolet pick-up trucks and a car for herself, with the idea of running a service for passengers and goods between the two settlements. Inevitably, as soon as the rains arrived the Chevrolets were stranded, like beached whales, in Geraldo, and Maria sold them the next year for a fraction of the price she had paid for them. She became more and more disillusioned with requests for help from all and sundry and took refuge in rum drinking, neglecting her barranco. In 1985 a syndicate from Serra Pelada offered to take over her barranco for two years, giving her ten per cent of production; this guaranteed her a high income and freed her of the worries of running a barranco. She went away to live in Nova Olinda, a settlement about thirty kilometres away, where she would go on drunken sprees during which she smashed up bars. Despite this she was a very popular figure amongst local bar owners, who would vie amongst themselves for the privilege of having their bars wrecked. They knew she had more than enough money to pay for any damage caused, and they could make a killing by presenting her with inflated repair bills, which she would pay as she could usually not remember what she had done.

I thought what had happened to Maria tragic, a view that was shared by all entrepreneurs and most mechanised donos, who regretted seeing all that money go to waste, as they saw it, and would explain in detail exactly how it should have been reinvested. However, not everybody shared that view. Most workers, and many donos, felt that Maria had acted as a garimpeiro should, and said that she was much better off and happier than would have been the case if she had remained an ordinary smallholder. Those who felt this way repeatedly quoted a proverb, *dinheiro do primeiro bamburro tem que ser gasto em puta e cachaça*, literally, 'the money from the first bamburro has to be spent on whores and rum.' If the money from the first bamburro was not dissipated in this way, they said, you would never have another. Garimpeiros with money in their pockets often take this dictum to heart.

There are many examples of this. The discovery of a nugget or rich material is often announced by jubilant pistol shots and followed by everybody repairing to the cantina, where the proud dono stands drinks for all comers. Ghettoblasters and expensive radios obviously unsuited to life in the forest are common in all garimpos. Many garimpeiros wear enormous gold watches, in a place where knowing the exact time is never important. It is a point of pride to wear gold bracelets and chains, the chunkier the better, made up from gold garimpeiros have extracted themselves. Gold teeth are ubiquitous: in one case witnessed during fieldwork, the wife of a garimpeiro went so far as to have perfectly good teeth extracted and replaced by gold ones. Some garimpeiros will pay hand over fist for airfares to garimpos that could easily be reached by river or road. In my particular case, donos would take pleasure in giving me *pedras cravadas*, gold-veined stones, from their barrancos, and many times I had to decline offers of small amounts of gold by explaining that I could not take them out of the country. This type of behaviour has a long history; von Eschwege describes the practice of the 'honorary bateiada' in eighteenth-century Minas Gerais, where visitors to a barranco were invited to observe a bateia full of material being panned, and offered the proceeds; the larger the amount of gold that was given away, the more prestige accrued to the dono.[3]

The stories which garimpeiros most like to tell and hear are not detailed histories of how famous bamburros were discovered, or heroic tales of endeavour in the jungle, although these types of story do exist. The most popular are accounts of how the proceeds of a bamburro were spent. The more spectacular the extravagance, the greater the appreciation with which the story is greeted. One tells of a bamburrado who hired two taxis for the day, one for himself and the other to carry his hat. There is another about a bamburrado who smeared honey on a dog and then covered it with banknotes. When he took it for a walk and was asked what he was doing, he replied, 'All my life I have run after money, and now money can run after me'. Spectacular generosity is often the keynote to this kind of story. One of the most typical is of a bamburrado who walks into a hotel or bar, closes the doors, and orders everybody to continue drinking until the stock is exhausted, at his expense.

Stories like this, the belief that money from the first bamburro has to be spent on 'whores and rum', the conspicuous consumption that is represented by the gold watches, chains and imported ghetto-blasters in jungle clearings, are all evidence of a rather different approach to the economics of garimpagem than the ones considered in this chapter so far. They demonstrate that for many garimpeiros gold extraction is not just a matter of profit and loss; it is tied into notions of prestige and codes of appropriate behaviour. The vision of the ideal garimpeiro to which many aspire is not just of a person skilled in finding and extracting gold. It also includes being somebody who can afford to be mythically generous, in a way that ensures they will become celebrated figures in garimpagem's oral pantheon. If they have the wit to combine the extravagant gesture with telling comment, as in the story of the garimpeiro who dramatised his liberation from worries about money by covering a dog with banknotes, so much the better.

A value system which goes so far as to say that the money from the first bamburro ought not to be reinvested in the garimpo, and that spectacular generosity is an appropriate way to denote success at garimpagem, clearly has little to do with the mercantile outlook of many garimpeiros. But it does constitute an alternative model of appropriate consumption for the many who choose not to see garimpagem only in terms of maximising profit. Of course, for entrepreneurs, both actual and aspiring, this perspective seems naive and regrettable, the sort of thing that gives garimpagem a bad name outside garimpos. But it is entirely in keeping with the diversity of backgrounds from which garimpeiros come that there should be different cultural beliefs and practices concerning investment and consumption, and the division between reinvestment and conspicuous consumption reflects this.

SERIOUS BUSINESS: ECONOMIC TRANSACTIONS IN THE GARIMPO

It has already been mentioned that there are no written contracts in garimpos, only verbal agreements, and that there is no external regulation by the state and its judicial apparatus outside the limited areas of federal intervention. Some idea of the wide variety of transactions that take place in garimpos should have been conveyed by the previous sections of this chapter, but the picture would be incomplete without devoting some attention to the way transactions are conducted and how they are structured. The aim of this section is to do this while attempting to convey something of the intense, cut-and-thrust atmosphere which surrounds them. Garimpagem is extremely transactional, and skill both in making deals and knowing when and how to break them is one of the prerequisites to success in the garimpo.

In some ways garimpos are ideal environments for the hustler, but it should also be clear by now that they are not anarchic and loosely organised communities where anything goes. Norms, constraints and sanctions do exist, and one consequence of the frequent lack of external regulation is that aggrieved parties can resort to open violence more easily: this in itself is a powerful restraining factor. Economic transactions, like other areas of social life in garimpos, are shaped by the tensions that result from the desire to make a killing on the one hand, and fear of the consequences of going too far on the other.

When garimpeiros themselves talk about the way they conduct transactions, a word that recurs a good deal is *esperteza*; it is a quality that garimpeiros value highly, and everyone would like to be considered *esperto*. Although the usual translation of *esperteza* is cleverness, in this context it is better rendered as cunning. As one garimpeiro pointed out in an interview

> Here in the garimpo, being good in a fight isn't the most important thing. You can lose a fight but still come out on top in the end if you're *esperto*. And if you're really *esperto*, you'd never get into a fight in the first place.

Esperteza is essentially the art of bending norms without breaking them.

The following transaction, or, more accurately, series of transactions, is a good instance of *esperteza* in action. It is a commonplace example, of a kind that occurs daily in garimpos of any size. It begins with Duarte, a mechanised dono. Duarte was an experienced garimpeiro and was relatively successful in the garimpo, but he was a family man and hated the enforced separations from his wife and children. In the end he decided he would prefer to go back to his previous occupation, which did not involve such long periods away from home. He owned a lorry and used to buy loads of fish in São Luís, pack them in ice, drive them to Teresina in the neighbouring state of Piauí, and sell them. So he agreed to sell his machinery, a moínho and two motors, to a buyer from the town of Santa Teresa, about thirty kilometers from Duarte's garimpo. He locked the machinery in his storeroom, gave the keys to Marcos, a trusted worker, and left instructions to hand the machinery over when the buyer arrived. He said it would be within a couple of days, made his farewells, stood his friends a final drink at the cantina, and left.

Another dono, Sousa, knew that besides the machinery Duarte had also left 300 grams of mercury, a few kilos of rice, a fanbelt and various other spare parts locked up in the storeroom, worth about $70 in all. He also knew that Duarte had only mentioned the machinery to the buyer. He went to see Marcos and offered to buy the mercury, rice and spare parts for one gram of gold, about $10. He would have paid more, but guessed that Marcos, for whom the gram would be an unexpected windfall, would not hold out for more, and in fact that was exactly what happened. Sousa kept the mercury for his own operations, sold the rice to a cantineiro, used the fanbelt to replace one he had borrowed from another dono and broken, and sold the remaining spare parts to other donos whom he knew needed them. There was no way Duarte or the buyer could know what had happened. When Sousa told me the story he was contemptuous of Marcos for not thinking it up for himself; anyone with a little *esperteza*, Sousa said, would immediately have tried to sell the goods, or at the very least should have seen that they were worth a lot more than one gram of gold and held out for more.

This incident reveals a lot about transactions in the garimpo. Firstly, it characteristically turns one apparently simple transaction – Duarte's sale of machinery to an outside buyer – into the starting point for a series of secondary transactions – between Sousa and Marcos, between Sousa and a cantineiro, between Sousa and a number of donos – which were accomplished so rapidly that they almost became a blur. Garimpagem has a remarkable capacity for generating transactions, with goods being resold almost as soon as they are acquired, changing hands many times before arriving at a final destination. Each stage in this chain of transactions involves profit for somebody.

Secondly, it shows the importance of detailed local knowledge and information networks. Without the knowledge that the mercury, rice and spare parts were there, and that Duarte had not mentioned them to the buyer, Sousa could not have begun to operate. Nor would he have been able to dispose of the spare parts so quickly if he had not known who would snap them up. The fact that Duarte was leaving the garimpo was common knowledge, as was the identity of the buyer. Sousa, who knew Duarte quite well, knew that there were other things besides machinery in his storehouse. From that it was only a short step to go down to the local cantina and ask the cantineiro (another friend of Sousa) whether the buyer knew about them. Once Sousa knew that he did not, he could begin to move in.

Finally, although certainly devious, the whole series of transactions did not actually break any norms of conduct, although it was skating close to the edge at times. The crucial question here was whether or not Duarte had sold the rice, mercury and spare parts together with the machinery. Strictly speaking, most garimpeiros would agree, the fact that he had not mentioned them to the buyer meant that he had not, although Duarte clearly expected that the buyer would collect them as well, or he would have left specific instructions for their disposal when he left, or have sold them separately to someone else. When Sousa went down to the cantina to check whether the buyer knew about the spare parts, what he was essentially doing was seeing if the transaction he had in mind with Marcos would be 'illegal' or not. If Duarte and the buyer had come to an agreement that included the spare parts, rice, and mercury, what Sousa did would have been theft, a clear transgression of garimpo norms. It would have entitled the buyer to set the police on Sousa when he was next in Santa Teresa, or exact retribution more directly. It would also have marked out Sousa as a bad lot, and he would have been watched carefully by everyone, especially cantineiros, from that time on. Rádio peão would in addition have ensured that Sousa was branded as a thief throughout the region.

If the story of Duarte's exit from the garimpo and what it led to has a moral, it is the importance of being on the spot if you enter into a transaction. This in itself tells us something about the attitudes and assumptions garimpeiros bring to economic transactions. They know very well that the usual condition of most donos is acute financial crisis, and that workers are in garimpos with the object of making as much money as they can in the shortest possible time. Combine this with the very high stakes that are often involved, and one has a recipe for mutual distrust and suspicion. Unless dealing with somebody they are prepared to trust – kin, compadres, or close friends, for example – the prudent garimpeiro will work on the assumption that the other party, if not actually cheating at present, is looking for an opportunity to do so in the future. If somebody is not actually on the spot to monitor progress, the chances that they will be cheated are quite high, although of course the cheater will do everything possible to ensure the absentee victim knows nothing about it.

One reason why the attrition rate amongst inexperienced donos is so high is that it takes time to learn how to conduct transactions properly. Although some people come to the garimpo with more than their fair share of *esperteza* and feel at home more or less immediately, the majority have to learn how to operate in a garimpo, and while they are doing so they are highly vulnerable. They might buy a barranco on the basis of gold showing up in the bottom of a bateia filled with material from it, which later turns out to have been the pulverised remains of empty brass cartridge cases fed through a moínho. They might buy mercury that has been diluted with silver paint, or a piece of machinery that breaks down on the first day of operations. They might accept that an obviously bankrupted dono is leaving to get supplies rather than fleeing. In short, they might trust somebody when it would be wiser to suspect them until they prove their honesty over time. It is often difficult to draw the line between *esperteza* and deception, but when one of the parties to a transaction is either inexperienced or periodically absent, it is much more likely that cunning will slip into deceit.

It might seem from all this that transactions in garimpos are rather cynical affairs, with all parties manoeuvering ruthlessly to ensure that their interests prevail, each making the worst possible assumptions about the intentions of the other, and everybody being prepared to break norms as well as bend them if they think they can get away with it. To a certain extent this Machiavellian picture holds good; transactions are, literally, a serious business, conducted by hardheaded people who are often struggling to stay afloat. It is therefore only to be expected that many transactions take place in a charged atmosphere where slight disagreements can ignite into full-blown conflicts. Nevertheless, it is important not to go too far and think of the garimpo, and economic transactions within it, as a Darwinian universe where only the ruthless survive and prosper. There are two important qualifications to be made here; the first concerns norms and constraints in general, the second has to do with the core transaction in the social organisation of gold extraction, the contracting of labour.

The whole question of norms and constraints will be dealt with more fully in the next chapter, but it should be pointed out here that although in many cases norms in garimpagem are somewhat vague and general, outright theft and deception is strongly and universally condemned, on the ideological plane at least. It is not just a question of moral disapproval, as the sanctions and constraints that operate in cases of this kind are concrete, immediate, and powerful. As has already been mentioned, there is the possibility that such conduct will provoke a direct and violent response. Even should the attempt succeed, there are costs. A reputation for dishonesty is a serious handicap. It makes getting credit much more difficult. A dishonest dono will have problems getting workers; dishonest workers do not find donos willing to employ them; dishonest cantineiros find their customers deserting them. Just as rádio peão magnifies an honest or generous action, so it enlarges trivial transgressions into major sins and passes them on at almost unbelievable speed; awareness of this is a strong incentive to tread carefully. Obviously, as the case of Duarte's exit from the garimpo shows, the line between *esperteza* and illegality is a difficult one to draw at times, and there can be differing interpretations of transactions; it was seen how it was possible to have a quasi-juridical argument over the finer points of whether the spare parts had really been sold or not. Nevertheless, certain lines cannot be crossed without immediate negative consequences, and the wise garimpeiro remembers that even the appearance of wrongdoing can be as damaging as wrongdoing itself, once facts become exaggerated and distorted on rádio peão. The pure Machiavellian would not, paradoxically, last for long in a garimpo, although every garimpeiro needs a little of the Machiavellian to survive.

Finally, there is the basic point that some transactions are very different from others. A full analysis of the types of transactions that are to be found in garimpos would be a book in itself, but it is enough to note here that in the garimpo there is a great difference between transactions that are essentially about the acquisition and reselling of goods, machinery, and gold, and a transaction that centres on the sale or contracting of labour.

The agreements struck between donos and workers are easily the single most important type of transaction in garimpos. It is on them that the extraction of gold depends, and they are central elements in the social and economic structure of garimpagem. In the first part of this chapter a great deal of material about work regimes was presented. From that information, it is clear that, in contrast to the rather freewheeling nature of other types of transaction, the norms and

constraints surrounding the contracting of labour are extremely detailed
and specific, covering not just payment but also features like the
reque, accommodation and even diet:

> At that time we were really in a bad way. Getting hold of meat was a
> real problem. Somebody would slaughter a cow or a pig, and we
> didn't have the money to buy the meat. So what we used to do was go
> there and get hold of the hide once they'd thrown it away. We'd
> bring it back here where nobody could see us, and scrape it with
> knives to get those little bits of meat that were still on it, maybe half a
> kilo if we were lucky. Then we'd serve it up to the workers. They
> never knew where it came from.

> *Why go to so much trouble? Why not just eat rice, beans, and farinha?*

> It would have been better, but you have to give workers meat every
> now and then. If they don't get it, they grumble, and don't work so
> well. It's expected. It's a type of obligation that donos have.

Thus transactions between workers and donos are more closely
hedged about with norms and constraints than any other type of
transaction in the garimpo. They do not take place in a grey area where
the enterprising can try to turn an advantage by exploiting the vague
and elastic generalities that pass for norms in other types of transaction, and they afford little or no room for disagreement over what
does or does not constitute acceptable behaviour. Disputes between
workers and donos occur regularly, but they are about matters like
thefts, pay arrears, the quality of the food, and so forth, not about the
terms of a work regime, which are accepted as given by both sides.
Workers may occasionally not receive what is due to them, but only
because of bankruptcy, not because a manipulative dono alters the
terms of a work regime. When workers contract themselves to a dono
they enter the most highly structured transaction in garimpagem, in
which the potentially destabilising urge to make a killing is severely
restricted. *Esperteza*, for a change, is not a factor. As a result, the
central transaction in the social organisation of gold production tends
not to be problematic, even though it sometimes appears as an island
of stability in the midst of a mass of more peripheral transactions that
often seem on the point of exploding, and occasionally do. What
happens when tension finally boils over into open conflict is one of the
themes of the following chapter.

6 Social Relations in the Garimpo

One of the most confusing things about garimpeiros for the visiting anthropologist is that they seem highly individualistic at one moment and yet insist at another that garimpagem is a collective, cooperative enterprise. As we have seen, the notion of individual freedom of action is central to the social organisation of garimpagem. When constraints on that freedom come from another garimpeiro, such as a dono da fofoca, the position is at best ambiguous: in some situations, like the early stages of a fofoca, donos will consent to one of their number holding authority over them; in others, such as production decisions within the barranco or the later stages of a fofoca, they will not. State intervention provokes a similarly dualistic response. It was resisted by garimpeiros in Rondônia in 1970 and Roraima in the mid 1970s and 1985, but welcomed by them in Serra Pelada in 1980 and Cumarú in 1981. This dualism surfaces again in the conceptions garimpeiros have about the type of life they lead and about the nature of garimpagem itself.

Sometimes garimpeiros represent themselves as free men working in autonomous and self-regulating communities which are 'open to all, to whoever wishes to enter', a brotherhood braving the difficulties and dangers of a pioneer life far from the comforts of civilisation. But equally often garimpeiros complain about the harshness of life in garimpos, painting it as a dog-eat-dog struggle for survival, where men who were once honourable are corrupted by greed and the rule of law gives way to anarchy. Even in relatively peaceful and accessible garimpos like those of the Gurupí one often hears comments like 'in the garimpo, the strongest are always in the right',[1] or 'here we live at the edge of the world, a garimpo is the end of the world'.[2] The way that garimpeiros represent social relations and social life in the garimpo to themselves and to outsiders is through two opposed and mutually exclusive philosophies, one individualistic and the other collective.

The collectivist view of garimpagem emphasises that no man is an island. Both the technology and the social and economic structure of garimpagem, it asserts, force interdependence on garimpeiros, and it is only through cooperation and mutual support that life in garimpos can be made tolerable. Only those who recognise this truth can be

133

successful in the garimpo, because when they are in trouble or need advice they can turn for help to those they have helped in the past. Equally, a true garimpeiro will respect the norms of the garimpo, keep his word and be honest in his dealings with other garimpeiros, and stand shoulder to shoulder with his fellows in the defence of the garimpo against outside interests if need be. Food must be shared, even when it is in short supply. Those in trouble should be helped. A true garimpeiro, for example, will make it a point of honour to see to it that an ill or injured colleague gets the medical care he needs, even if it means having a whip-round to pay for evacuation to a clinic, since the next time it might be him who catches malaria or is injured in an accident. In garimpagem an experienced garimpeiro is called *manso*, literally 'tame', which reveals a conception of the garimpo as a place that socialises those who work within it for any length of time. People enter as raw individualists, are transformed by the collective nature of garimpagem, and come to realise that in such a difficult and hostile environment cooperation and unity are absolutely essential for survival.

Another perspective, in direct contrast, argues that life in garimpos is *brabo*, wild and anarchic. It sees other garimpeiros as competitors rather than comrades, with each pitted against the other in a Darwinian struggle for survival. Gold is seen as fundamentally corrupting. It ignites greed and amorality in people who seem, and may even once have been, honest and likeable. Perhaps the best-known example of this process to a Western audience is Humphrey Bogart's memorable performance as the American garimpeiro Dobbs, in John Huston's superb film *The Treasure of the Sierra Madre*, which represents just such a moral decline. Thus in dealing with other garimpeiros one should assume that they will break agreements if they feel they can get away with it, and breaking norms is justified on the grounds that everybody else does so as a matter of course. This does not necessarily mean that a garimpeiro will never act altruistically, but he will do so out of self-interest, evacuating a casualty in order to acquire a reputation as a good employer, or lending a spare part to somebody in order to be free to borrow from them in the future. Relationships with other garimpeiros are seen as similar to the nitroglycerine many donos keep in their storerooms; inherently unstable and liable to explode if handled wrongly. Confrontation and conflict are seen as inevitable, as a natural state of affairs.

It should be evident from the three chapters before this one that there are elements of truth in both of these perspectives. This only makes things more confusing for the anthropologist, as it means that all garimpeiros are able to draw on convincing examples from their own experience of garimpagem which are wheeled out to support whatever point of view they feel like expressing. Garimpeiros are full of tales about how they or others were taken for a ride or managed to put something over on somebody else, but also come up with many examples of generosity, collective action, and mutual help. And despite all the bloodcurdling stories, anybody who spends time in a garimpo will sooner or later witness genuinely altruistic acts, like a group of friends carrying out an injured colleague in a hammock strung from a stout pole. The fact that there are such widely differing representations of the nature of social life in the garimpo points to the difficulties and ambiguities that attend any analysis of social relations within it.

As good a place as any to begin is to consider the relationship between the individual and the group in the garimpo. It is extremely complex, with some factors stressing individual over group identity and action, and others doing the reverse. Although individual autonomy and freedom of action are highly prized, very few garimpeiros work individually. The only garimpeiros who truly work on their own are occasional lone prospectors, but even an accomplished desbravador will usually operate with at least one companion. All other garimpeiros work as one of a unit of several people. Equally, the garimpo is hierarchical, even though there is more social mobility than is often the case in wider Brazilian society. This might lead one to expect some form of collective identity and action within the garimpo, as donos and workers line up against each other along 'class' lines.

Thus several questions emerge. To what extent can social life and social relationships in the garimpo be viewed in terms of 'class politics', of rival social categories negotiating and mobilising? Do workers act collectively in relation to donos, and vice versa? In what circumstances does collective action take place? What happens in conflicts between donos and workers? Who, if anybody, exerts authority in the garimpo? In what contexts are the two views which garimpeiros themselves cite, the garimpo as state within a state, a self-regulating community of free men, or the garimpo as a violent free-for-all, expressed and acted upon?

SOLIDARITIES AND DIVISIONS

Although there is a basic division between donos and workers in every garimpo, any analysis of social relations in garimpos has to begin by stressing the heterogeneity of both groups. There are different types of donos and workers, working a range of machinery under different work regimes. They come from disparate backgrounds and have varying levels of commitment to garimpagem. Within a single barranco the position can be complicated enough; extend the analysis to the garimpo as a whole and things can become very complicated indeed.

To get an idea of the kinds of problem that can arise, take the hypothetical but entirely typical example of a mechanised dono with six workers. Imagine that to work the barranco the dono has had to get backing from a sócio outside the garimpo, and has also needed to get a heavy-duty pump from a dono inside the garimpo, who had to be made a sócio with a right to ten per cent of the gold extracted. Two of the workers are used to operating machinery and are porcentistas, while the other four are diaristas, although every now and then all six work on a piece-rate basis for a couple of days. All the workers expect decent food and accommodation and are disgruntled because they think that what they are getting is substandard. All the workers resent it when the dono loses his temper and complains that 'peões' know nothing about garimpagem. On the other hand, the four diaristas are short-stay garimpeiros and try to get away with as little work as they can manage, which conflicts with the commitment of the porcentistas to the operation, who tend to back up the dono in his efforts to get the diaristas to work harder. One of the porcentistas in particular is anxious to stay on good terms with the dono, because he has ambitions of setting up on his own and needs to widen his knowledge of barranco operations.

For the dono's part, although he knows that he could not continue without the supplies the sócio pays for and the motor pump on loan from the other dono-sócio, he resents them making any comments or suggestions about the operation, and when they do he complains that they are interfering in production decisions which are his alone. He suspects that one motive for the other dono lending his motor pump was to get acquainted with the deposit in the area around his barranco with a view to moving into the general area at some future date, and he feels uneasy about having him as a neighbour.

On top of the tensions arising directly from work, there are always others lurking in the background. Imagine, for example, that the dono comes from a middle-class family and together with one of the porcentistas hails from a big city, while the others are from rural districts in the interior. To make matters worse, two of the diaristas are

Pentecostalists who disapprove of the dono's foul language (which gets more blasphemous when they complain about it) and his liking for marijuana. Evidently, in this barranco tensions and solidarities exist in several different dimensions at the same time. While identifying with his fellow workers when they complain about the food and the dono's short temper, the urban porcentista might sympathise with the dono when he mutters darkly about having to work with country bumpkins and swear at his evangelist comrade when he disapproves of him bringing a bottle of rum back from the cantina on Saturday night, especially if the dono is acute enough to imply that he and the porcentistas share a common identity as 'real garimpeiros', as opposed to short-stay labourers. Imaginary though this example is, it is representative of the kinds of cross-cutting tensions and bonds that arise within barrancos, and in no way exaggerates the complexity of social relations within them.

At this point it would be useful to look in general terms at the three relationships that are most important to the social organisation of the garimpo; relations between donos, relations between workers and relations between donos on the one hand and workers on the other.

1   Dono-Dono

All donos are forced into relationships with other donos whether they like it or not. Sometimes, as in the example quoted above, this relationship is a formal sociedade, with more than one dono having a stake in an operation. When barrancos are being worked in close proximity to each other, as is very often the case, donos have to deal with each other to make sure that boundary lines between barrancos are not crossed, that pipes and hoses do not obstruct operations, and that overburden is disposed of somewhere where it does not interfere with work in neighbouring barrancos. But underlying these everyday concerns are deeper imperatives that force donos into contact with each other. Most donos operate in straitened circumstances and need to construct relationships which allow them to turn to other donos when in need. And all donos, rich and poor, depend on information. They have to be able to tap into a communal pool of knowledge about local personalities (which cantineiros give the best terms, etc.), the history of barrancos (so-and-so spent X months using a chupadeira in barranco Y and extracted Z amount of gold, etc.), and the types of deposit in a given area and their quirks (the alluvium shifts direction in

João's barranco, so it might be worth opening up a barranco on the hillside over in that direction, etc.). Without information like this garimpagem in a micro-area would be almost impossible, and so the more experienced and knowledgeable donos are constantly being approached for advice and information by their less experienced peers. This tends to restrain the more individualistic donos, as if they alienate their colleagues they will not be able to profit from the shared experience of others.

The most concrete example of the way that donos do form co-operative relationships amongst themselves is reciprocal lending networks. If a dono runs out of fuel, or if a part on a machine breaks and he has no spare on hand, he can approach a colleague for what he needs. Most donos will comply with these requests if they can, as any material handed over is given on the explicit understanding that the next time the dono in need leaves the garimpo to get hold of supplies he will replace what he takes. It is a convenient arrangement for both parties. It means that one can keep working until it is more convenient to get more supplies, while the dono who gives knows that he will be repaid in goods that have not been marked up by a cantineiro. Most importantly, he knows that if at some future date he needs something he can approach the other dono for it.

There are certain limitations on this form of mutual assistance. Reciprocal lending networks involve only relatively minor items – small amounts of food or fuel, fanbelts for a motor, steel flails for a moínho, and so on – because it is universally recognised that donos cannot be expected to prejudice their own operations for the sake of other donos. It is perfectly legitimate for a dono to apologise and say that although he would like to help he needs what was requested for his own operations. Although requests for spare parts are acceptable, requests for entire items of machinery are not; a dono contributing an item of machinery would be making a significant material contribution to an operation and would therefore be entitled to demand to be made a sócio. A dono might lend an item of machinery not in use, but only for a couple of days and only to a close and trusted friend. Even close friends would have to pay to use it for more than a day or two.

When something is lent in this way, it is a signal that the donos involved are on good terms. Requests are not made between donos in conflict. Consequently, a dono perpetually on bad terms with a number of colleagues is significantly limiting the extent to which he can turn to reciprocal lending networks, and his operation will suffer as a result. Equally, it is counter-productive to try to renege on replacing what was taken. Any dono who tries to wriggle out of this sort of commitment rapidly gets a reputation as somebody to whom it is not worth lending items, and donos will go to considerable lengths to avoid this image. Several times during fieldwork donos were seen receiving requests for items which they had borrowed in the past at times when they had none on hand to give. They would only admit they could not reciprocate for the time being if the request came from somebody they knew very well. In the majority of cases, they actually borrowed items from a third dono in order to pay back the original loan.

Reciprocal lending networks also provide a field of collective action by donos against one of their number. If a dono consistently behaves in a way that makes other donos feel that they want nothing to do with him, he will be frozen out of both lending and information networks. Requests from him will not be refused directly, as this would provoke a potentially dangerous confrontation, but he will find that his requests come at times when all machinery is in use, everybody's fuel stocks are running low, and that particular spare part has already been lent out to somebody else. It is violent behaviour which more than anything else produces this kind of communal sanction. While other donos will not usually interfere in a violent dispute between other donos, they will have opinions about who is in the right. If a dono uses violence which other donos think unjustifiable, especially if it is done to move in on another dono's barranco, he is marked as a danger to everybody. Donos will stop sharing material and information with him, and will try to turn workers and cantineiros against him by fueling rádio peão with details of his transgressions. A dono targetted in this way could only remain in a garimpo if he was sufficiently well off to be economically autonomous, and even the richest donos still depend on access to the pool of knowledge and experience of garimpagem in the area around their barrancos.

There are certain other contexts in which donos will act collectively. If a number of donos wish to enter an area that is sealed off for one reason or another, they may co-ordinate a mass invasion; an example of this was seen in the fofoca of Trinta Cinco described in Chapter 3. If the existence of the garimpo is threatened, as it was in Serra Pelada, donos may unite to fight the external threat; it will be seen in the next chapter just how important the contribution of donos was in the campaign to keep Serra Pelada open. It also often happens that all donos agree that their garimpo needs a certain facility, such as an airstrip or a trail to a neighbouring garimpo, in order to become viable. Such needs are met by *mutirão*.[3] In a mutirão, donos agree to suspend their own operation for a few days and bring their workers to help on the project. However, a mutirão in a garimpo is a fragile institution. Most donos cannot afford to be working outside their barrancos for more than a couple of days and drift back there within a short time, leaving the richer donos to complete the job. This leads to ill-feelings and tension, with the best off feeling they were taken advantage of, and the ordinary donos reasoning that as the richest stand to gain most from communal facilities it is only right that they should make the greater contribution.

However, against all these examples of collective action and reciprocal help one has to set the fact that disputes between donos are frequent and remember that a dono can view another as a competitor as well as, or rather than, a colleague. Relations between donos whose barrancos border on each other are especially problematic. They are not necessarily tense; neighbours often become friends, cooperating closely, sharing information and experience, lending reciprocally, and dropping in on each other in the evening to chat, play draughts, or listen to the radio. Equally, things can go wrong. Neighbours are more likely to clash over barranco boundaries, especially if one is producing gold and the other not, and donos can, often unintentionally, prejudice operations in neighbouring barrancos. The collapse of a barranco wall disrupts operations in barrancos that border on it, and is invariably followed by recriminations and accusations of carelessness and irresponsibility. Donos get irritated when too many hoses and pipes carrying other people's water supplies festoon their barrancos, or when workers from another barranco have to pass through his to dump overburden. Many of the economic relationships that donos enter into with other donos turn sour. One party may feel that the other could have done more, that the machinery should have been deployed in a different way; in short, there are dozens of ways in which the failure of an operation that brought two or more donos together can poison relationships between them temporarily or permanently. Once relationships go sour, what was once perfectly normal becomes sinister. What were once friendly enquiries from a neighbouring dono about the behaviour of the gold deposit in a barranco are construed as evidence that he is deciding whether it would be worth encroaching. Donos who were once proud to demonstrate their prowess by showing off the gold they produced during good times may think other donos who ask how things are going during a lean streak are gloating at their ill fortune.

Jealousy, for example, can be a potent source of bad feeling between donos. There are a number of beliefs in garimpos that reflect this. Many garimpeiros divide donos into two categories, those who are *feio para ouro* and those who are *bonito para ouro*, literally 'ugly for gold' and 'pretty for gold'. Briefly, ugly for gold means someone who can never find or produce gold, and pretty for gold means the opposite. Donos are thought to be pretty or ugly for gold irrespective of their skills; they are qualities which derive from personal beliefs and certain kinds of behaviour. Unsurprisingly, when garimpeiros who have come into contact with these ideas are asked how it is possible to tell a dono who is pretty for gold, the answer is a dono who acts in the collective and cooperativist manner described above. The surest signs of a dono who is ugly for gold are greed and jealousy, and those who conspicuously hunger for gold and are envious of other donos' success are called *ambicioso*. They are thought to have *olho grande*, a phrase that outside the garimpo means both the evil eye and covetousness. They bring bad luck and in extreme cases can bewitch both people and barrancos.

Most donos do not take beliefs about olho grande or people being pretty or ugly for gold very seriously; more often than not they serve as raw material for jokes and banter between donos. They talk about them as ideas held by 'ignorant peões' and usually dismiss them as superstitious nonsense. They do agree that a dono who is greedy, or jealous of others, is less likely to succeed than one who is not, but they back up this assertion with material rather than supernatural explanations. Donos who are ambicioso, they say, tend also to be aggressive, short-tempered, and to think only of the short term. Not only do they prejudice their own operations by alienating other donos, but their method of working a barranco will be shortsighted. They will desert a barranco if a fofoca occurs nearby when it might be better to persevere. If they find gold, they will lower the barranco faster than advisable in their eagerness to extract as much as possible, without reinforcing the barranco walls in a way that would allow gold extraction to proceed safely at greater depths as well.

Thus although donos can and do act collectively, relationships between individual donos may well be tense, especially if they are working in neighbouring barrancos. Further fragmentation occurs as a result of the heterogeneity of donos as a group. Manual and mechanised donos may well have little in common, and entrepreneurs will not necessarily feel much kinship with a run of the mill mechanised dono. Conflicts between donos are common, and may even lead to violent confrontations, but that does not mean dono-dono relations are necessarily confrontational. There are powerful constraints on donos, and individual disputes have to be placed in the context of a social environment that recognises the inevitability of conflict but which also throws donos together, making the sharing of information and material a powerful imperative if success in the garimpo is to be achieved.

2 Worker-Worker

While there are certain circumstances which will unite all workers in a barranco against the dono irrespective of labour regime, the importance of the division between porcentista and diarista cannot be overstressed. Nowhere was the difference between the two clearer than in Serra Pelada. A DNPM geologist who worked there from 1980 to 1983, for example, was struck by the way meieiros formed an interest bloc within the garimpo separate from both donos and diaristas:

> In 1981 I already thought that the meia-praça was in decline in Serra Pelada. This was for several reasons, but I think the most important was that the meieiros were far more trouble to the donos than the diaristas. Usually with diaristas there are few problems. Provided they get a bare minimum of food and are paid at the end of the time they spend, they leave happily enough. Not the meieiro. In Serra Pelada, as elsewhere, the meieiro is a semi-dono. He wants to eat meat every day, has to have a good breakfast, a lunch with meat, if you serve up fish they won't accept it. They lost my respect because of this. I lived there for some time and I felt that the meieiro was really a problem, the donos would complain about them all the time, and of course it meant that their overheads were much higher. So I wasn't surprised when the diária became the main work regime there.'

It was explained in the previous chapter that in many ways diaristas and porcentistas have conflicting interests and represent opposing types of worker; diaristas tend to be short-stay garimpeiros for whom garimpagem is a complement to other occupations, whereas porcentistas tend to stay longer and have garimpagem as their principal or only occupation. Porcentistas tend to do more skilled work inside barrancos and they typically stay with an operation from beginning to end, often working with several different sets of diaristas in the process. Thus their relationship with diaristas can be more than a little ambiguous.

Porcentistas do make common cause with diaristas on issues that affect the barranco as a whole, such as the standard of food and accommodation and the way the dono treats workers. On the other hand, they will tend to have a strong sense of identity as garimpeiros, which they will invariably share with the dono but only rarely with diaristas. On top of this, their own economic self-interest will inevitably induce them to link their fate with that of the operation, and by extension with the dono. This does not apply to diaristas. They are basically interested in working for a certain period and being paid at the end of it. Usually they know little about the finer points of garimpagem, such as, for example, how to lower a barranco in such a way that excavation will be possible at greater depths. From the point of view of a diarista it is immaterial exactly how much gold an operation produces, or indeed whether it produces any at all, provided that the dono can pay them. But for both the dono and the porcentista it is a question of vital importance. As a result, porcentistas often get angry with diaristas if they think they are slacking, and will criticise their work without any prompting from donos in a way that forcefully reminds anybody watching that many porcentistas are donos in the making. This can lead to little love being lost between diaristas and porcentistas in a barranco.

The fact that so many porcentistas have ambitions of becoming donos themselves has another important consequence. As a rule, there is not much contact between diaristas from different barrancos. The working day is more or less from sunrise to sunset, six days a week. Diaristas may meet socially in cantinas during evenings or on a Sunday, and often travel to and from garimpos in large groups, but for the most part they are atomised into barranco work crews, living as a unit in accommodation provided by the dono, who more often than not lives there as well. Many diaristas do not even make much of an effort to get to know people outside their barranco, reasoning that there is no point forming relationships when they will be moving on soon in any case. Porcentistas, on the other hand, make a point of getting to know porcentistas in other barrancos and often form close friendships with them.

It is not difficult to see why porcentistas gravitate towards one another. For obvious reasons, many of them have a deep interest in the practicalities of garimpagem and are eager to learn more by sharing notes with others. Some of the knowledge and experience they hunger to absorb comes from sympathetic donos, but most of it comes from conversations with fellow porcentistas. It is no exaggeration to say that informal chatting is one of the most important social processes in garimpagem. It largely explains, for example, how garimpeiros move from region to region with such ease, travelling distances which seem immense to a European but which a porcentista will regard as phlegmatically as a Scot might contemplate a journey between Edinburgh and Glasgow. Very often a porcentista with no experience of an area will travel there with another porcentista met in a garimpo who knows the area well. Even when travelling alone, a porcentista will invariably, through previous contact with a porcentista who has worked in the region, have some idea of the best route to travel, the best garimpos to head for, and the sorts of problems that he is likely to encounter. This information is often very specific, extending down to the names of hotels and donos with a good reputation. It makes moving between regions of garimpagem very much less problematic.

Porcentistas, then, have a strong sense of group identity. Diaristas, while they may act collectively against a specific dono in specific circumstances, are fragmented into work units that do not have very much contact with each other. They will not make common cause with diaristas in another barranco who are in conflict with their dono; they may have opinions about who is in the right, but ultimately it is seen as something which has to be settled by the parties concerned. Thus while collective action by workers within a barranco is common, collective action across barrancos is not. The fragmentation of workers into barranco units is overlaid by the differing economic interests that diaristas and porcentistas have within the barranco. Donos are not slow to recognise this fact and exploit it.[4]

3   Dono-Worker

Although conflicts between workers and donos do take place regularly in garimpos, it has to be remembered that no economic relationship in garimpagem is as highly structured as that between donos and workers. This means, paradoxically, that the conflicts which do not take place are in some ways more important than those which do. Donos and workers do not have disputes about the choice of work regime, the terms of a work regime once chosen, the length of time that workers are engaged for, their right to move on when they feel like it, or the amount of gold which is being produced. Both donos and workers take the economic parameters of their relationship as given, and generally speaking conflicts between them occur when one or both parties believe that the other is not living up to binding commitments. There is no question of each side having a radically different conception of social relations within the barranco and attempting to impose it on the other. While disputes between donos and workers can reach a frighteningly intense level all the same, this means that they are usually resolvable. When conflicts happen, both sides know what corrective action should be taken to return matters to normal because they share a vision of what a 'normal' relationship between donos and workers is. Metaphorically, dono-worker relationships are like a football match. The two teams play against one another, the play often gets heated, even occasionally violent, but both teams play to the same set of rules and nobody thinks of moving the goalposts.

In some ways the relationship between donos and workers seems more egalitarian than it actually is. Usually, the lifestyle of a dono does not differ very much from that of his workers. They live in the same hut, eat the same food, sleep in neighbouring hammocks and much of the time even do the same work; many donos do not shrink from doing manual labour when it is necessary, and one regularly sees donos covered in mud wielding a spade or a pickaxe shoulder to shoulder with workers. Indeed, many donos are vehement in their belief that it is impossible to work a barranco in any other way; they say that operations have to be directed from the inside and by example, in order to gain the respect of the workers by demonstrating that you yourself are not too proud to do the dirty manual work, as well as the planning and the administrative chores that running a barranco entails. The more fastidious external entrepreneurs, most of whom regard manual labour as demeaning and literally direct operations from above, standing on the rim of the barranco issuing orders to those toiling below, are regarded by both workers and donos as the worst kind of dono.

Nevertheless, the fact that they have similar lifestyles and often do similar work does not mean that donos are not scrupulous in maintaining a social distance between themselves and their workers:

The problem with peões is that if you get too friendly with them they start taking liberties. They become very demanding, and start complaining about the food, or saying the work is too hard, and this makes things very difficult. If you keep showing your teeth [smiling] and chatting to them, they take liberties. The way to treat them is to be serious, correct but serious. . .Right when they arrive a dono should make clear the way he runs his barranco. You should be honest with them, firm but fair. That way the peão will respect you. He will see that you're honest, that you won't mistreat him but at the same time that you won't stand for any nonsense.

The other problem about getting friendly with a peão is that it creates tensions with the others. For example, I once had an excellent peão, Bernardo. He was an extremely hard worker but at the same time never took any liberties. I liked him, we became friends, and I used to let him have reques. But this caused great problems with the other workers, who wanted the same privileges that Bernardo was given. I used to say, look, if you work as well as Bernardo does, then you'll get reques as well. They never did, of course. Bernardo was a porcentista who took care of the moínho. The dono isn't necessarily around when something goes wrong with the moínho, so Bernardo had to know what to do. Obviously, a skilled peão like this has to be treated with a little more care and consideration than you would a diarista. Diaristas don't understand anything about machinery. And they rob you if you don't keep an eye on them. To be honest, I don't have much time for diaristas.

This quote is a good example of the way that donos tend to look down upon workers. Like virtually all donos he uses the word peão throughout to refer to both porcentistas and diaristas (although he might not have done had there been a porcentista present while he was talking), but at the same time he makes very clear the practical differences from the point of view of a dono in dealing with porcentistas and dealing with diaristas. The line that one has to be 'firm but fair' is one that donos constantly repeat when talking about how workers should be treated, but as this dono kept talking the contempt he felt for diaristas became increasingly obvious – and in fact this particular dono was notorious for being high handed in his treatment of workers. Several conflicts with his workers occurred precisely because his over-bearing attitude irritated the 'peões', and what with most people would have been minor quibbles tended in his barranco to blow up into major confrontations that united both porcentistas and diaristas against him.

When there is dissatisfaction within a barranco porcentistas tend to be the ones who articulate grievances and press demands. This is only partly because they are more demanding when it comes to food and conditions. The typical diarista is young, has little experience of garimpagem and would usually not have the confidence to complain directly to a dono, although he might express his discontent in other ways, like going slow on the job. But although porcentistas often find themselves talking to a dono on behalf of diaristas, the reverse is also true. Partly this is because their economic interests coincide with those of the dono, but it also has much to do with a shared social identity. Donos may exploit the fact that both they and porcentistas see themselves as 'real' garimpeiros, skilled craftsmen as opposed to diggers of dirt. This is reinforced in many cases by the tendency of porcentistas to stand in relation to the dono more or less as an apprentice stands in relation to an artisan. In a way porcentistas have a foot in both camps, and this means they are well placed to mediate between the dono and diaristas. A particularly blatant breach of the universally understood commitments that bind both sides together will drive the porcentistas into one camp or the other, but blatant violations of the social contract are rare. Most of the time conflict between donos and workers is low level, expressed as grumbling and footdragging rather than outright argument. In this situation porcentistas are a stabilising influence, as they can identify with both donos and diaristas and thus constitute a channel of communication between the two.

Of course, things do not always work out so neatly. Some donos are too quick tempered, or too insensitive, to make any concessions to porcentista sensibilities and alienate all their workers as a result. In many cases discussions between donos and workers are complicated by the fact that the workers can see that no gold is being produced or is likely to be produced in the near future. They know that there is little the dono can do to improve food, work conditions, and accommodation. Worst of all, the diaristas may decide to desert what is clearly a sinking ship and demand their money, which is likely to reduce an already hard-pressed dono to desperation. With hardship shortening tempers on both sides, the tension can swiftly escalate to dangerous levels, especially if there happen to be no porcentistas in the barranco to mediate.

This was exactly what happened in a barranco in the garimpo of Cedral in 1983. This conflict is interesting for several reasons. Although it reached an extremely dangerous pitch of tension, it began as most conflicts within a barranco begin, with one party, in this case workers, feeling that the other was not fulfilling its commitments. That the commitment – payment for work rendered – had to be fulfilled was not at issue. While it is a vivid demonstration of just how confrontational relations between donos and workers can become, in the manner of its resolution it also demonstrated how conflicts that do not directly involve people outside the barranco but which threaten to have ramifications for them will provoke outside intervention.

Once I was working with nineteen diaristas. For some time before it happened I'd been having problems. That's just like a peão; when they see that you're in trouble they start not wanting to do any work, complaining about the food, and then from one hour to the next they decide they want to leave and ask for their money. 'I'm leaving today and I want what you owe me now!' and not bothering about whether you can actually pay them. That's what happened in this case. There was a group of eight peões, who all came from some damn place in the interior, Vargem Grande I think. One morning when I woke up all of them came in and there I was, as if I wasn't in enough trouble already, with eight peões all wanting to go home and demanding their money. I mean, hell, paying all eight at the same time for a month of work, that's a fair amount of money. I didn't have it, they could see I didn't have it, and they knew that damn well when they asked for it, they did it just to bugger up my operation. They were even wanting to attack us. There was me, my brother, and Benedito [a friend who was a sócio in the operation in question].

Were they armed?

Of course. You know what people from the interior are like, they all had a *facão* [a long knife used for cutting wood and undergrowth]. They said they'd beat us up if we didn't pay. So we had to be macho as well. I said that if they tried I'd shoot them. My brother had a stave in one hand and a knife in the other, I had a rifle, and Benedito unsheathed his facão. I said I'd shoot the first man who came against us, that if they were the men they said they were then they should come against us, and that if I missed they'd get theirs with the knife, staves, or even fists if they wanted. I was talking like that, but I was frightened all the same. I mean, shit, eight against three, and I couldn't see a way out of it. If I could have paid them I would have, but I simply didn't have the money.

So what happened next?

Well, there was another dono, Ivan, who had a hut nearby and he must have seen what was happening because he called me over to his place and gave me a lump of gold to pay them with. So I paid them and they left that same day. What could I have done if he hadn't lent me that gold? It's not as if he had any obligation to help me, he just saw what was going on and called me over. And although he gave me the gold early in the morning, I didn't pay them until the afternoon because I was so angry with them I wanted to make sure they had to spend a few hours walking in the forest at night if they were going to get out that day. When I had the gold in my hand, when I knew that I'd be able to pay them, I thought, right, you bastards, you fucked me over, and now it's me that's going to fuck you over.

This confrontation is a typical example of a dispute that threatens to have ramifications beyond the barranco where it takes place. Barrancos and huts are grouped together, and what goes on in one happens under the eyes of other donos and workers living and working in the vicinity. It is not difficult to see why Ivan acted as he did. Partly it was the understandable desire not to have stray bullets flying around him, but equally important would have been his recognition that he was faced with a situation which could have gone horribly wrong. With two armed groups facing up to each other in the way that they were, it would not have taken much to touch off a pitched battle which might well have resulted in deaths. Murders complicate things for every-body. Relatives of the dead seek vengeance on the killers, and the police would become involved. Within a few days Cedral would have been full of heavily armed military policemen confiscating arms, beating up anybody thought to be connected with the incident and probably a few who were not for good measure. Equally disastrously, the garimpo would have acquired a reputation for violence, the flow of workers would slacken and everybody's interests would be damaged. Lending a lump of gold to the dono in trouble would to Ivan have been a small price to pay to ensure that none of this came to happen.

This chapter began by noting the contrast between the two opposing ways that garimpeiros represent social relations in the garimpo to themselves and to outsiders. It should by now be clear that both these perspectives can be supported by a selective reading of social life in garimpos. Somebody wishing to stress the collectivist, socialising nature of garimpagem could point to the mutirão, to the sharing of information, to the similar lifestyle of donos and workers, to reciprocal lending networks, to the way garimpeiros always share food and evacuate casualties, to communal sanctions against wrongdoers, to a social identity that unites donos and porcentistas, and to many other equally convincing factors. Somebody wanting to argue the opposite line could cite the frequency of conflicts between donos and other donos, between porcentistas and diaristas, and between donos and workers, the equally frequent bending and breaking of norms, the construction of a social identity by donos and porcentistas that excludes diaristas, the self-interest underlying the apparent altruism of lending networks and medical evacuation, the naked greed of some donos, and so forth. We have seen how social life and social relationships in the garimpo are, predictably, neither one nor the other. The point is rather to understand why garimpeiro representations of social relations in the gold rush should be so strikingly dualistic. It seems to reflect a series of existential contradictions that are part and parcel of being a garimpeiro.

On the one hand garimpeiros have a highly developed ethos of individual autonomy and freedom; on the other they live in communities and must form relationships with others because they cannot work individually. These relationships can be neither wholly individualistic nor wholly collaborative. Individualists find out the hard way that no man is an island and that they cannot afford to alienate too many of their colleagues, while collectivists find out the hard way that there are social divisions and clashes of interest within the garimpo which make it a nonsense to think of it as a community of free and equal men. No single ideological representation could possibly reconcile or sublimate such glaring contradictions. Normative dualism is the only way around this dilemma, each element of which can be solidly rooted in life in garimpos as it is experienced by garimpeiros.

Another point that emerges from this examination of social relations in the garimpo, and garimpeiro representations of them, is the impossibility of 'class war', collective action by one social category in a garimpo against another, say between donos and workers. The preconditions for class politics do not exist in garimpagem. The heterogeneity of both donos and workers is one reason for this, together with the high rate of attrition amongst donos and the rapid turnover of workers. In a situation where both workers and donos move around or out of the system with such facility, stable and coordinated collective action over any period of time is clearly very difficult. Then there is the fact that the interests and objectives of any one type of dono or worker are not necessarily the same as any other, a point best exemplified by the relationship between porcentistas and diaristas. Finally, and perhaps most importantly, both donos and workers are atomised into barrancos, and this fragments both social categories still further. There is only one situation that can generate a sense of shared identity which embraces everybody in the garimpo and lead to the simultaneous mobilisation of all social categories within it: an external threat to the existence of the garimpo, either from a mineral company or from the state.

CONFLICTS: MEDIATION AND A SMALL WAR

Garimpeiros may not engage in class politics as such, but all garimpos are political arenas of a kind. Some garimpeiros are more powerful than others, and powerful garimpeiros have dealings and rivalries with each other that are essentially political in nature. Thus no analysis of social relations in garimpos would be complete without looking at garimpos as political arenas where some garimpeiros have political prestige and influence. The relevant question here is whether, apart from the relationships of dominance and subordination that arise directly from the workplace, some garimpeiros have authority over others with whom they do not necessarily have a direct economic relationship.

One way of approaching the question of power and authority within the garimpo is to look at conflicts. If somebody not directly involved in a conflict is called in by both parties to mediate, those called in are obviously playing a directly political role. The issue of mediation in conflicts is also interesting, because it has fascinated many observers of the gold rush, social scientists as well as journalists and administrators. Many sources, together with all the geologists, politicians, lobbyists and administrators interviewed, talk about what they call '*a lei do garimpo*', the law of the garimpo.[5] This is said to be an informal but binding legal system which operates within garimpos, which states, for example, that food should always be shared, that barranco boundaries once demarcated are inviolate, and that theft is punishable by death – which prompted one DNPM geologist to remark in an interview that 'there are no thieves in garimpos, only murderers'. Yet at the same time, many of the same journalists and politicians were painting an image of the gold rush as proverbially lawless and anarchic, an image it still bears today, and which is a constantly recurring theme in virtually all coverage of the gold rush by the Brazilian and international media. The question of what happens in conflicts in the garimpo is thus more important than might appear at first. In what circumstances does this alleged 'law of the garimpo' come into play? Or is it the case, in the words of the garimpeiro quoted above, that 'in the garimpo, the strongest are always in the right'? Who has power in the garimpo, and when do they exercise it?

Rich donos are automatically influential figures within the garimpo purely on the strength of the greater economic resources which they possess. As they have more on hand to lend, they are central figures in reciprocal lending networks, if they choose to participate in them. A mutirão is usually organised by a rich dono, as it is not as problematic for them as it is for poorer donos to deploy their workers outside their barrancos for a while. If they also acquire a reputation for fairness and generosity in their dealings with other garimpeiros, then their opinions about the rights and wrongs of individual conflicts will do much to shape the climate of public opinion in a garimpo. If, for example, a rich and respected dono imposes sanctions against another dono, others will tend to follow his lead in order not to prejudice their relationship with him. At the same time, even the most economically powerful dono has to be careful about doing anything that could be construed as unsolicited interference in a dispute where his own interests are not directly involved. This would contravene the deeply held principle of the autonomy of the dono within his own barranco. Because of this, many donos whose economic position would qualify them for a political role within the garimpo refuse to take it on, regarding it as a thankless distraction from the more important task of extracting gold. Interventions made to defuse a potentially explosive situation before it gets out of hand, as Ivan did in the previous section, are the only exceptions to this. Long experience of garimpagem also confers prestige, whether or not it is accompanied by economic success, and the opinions of such *garimpeiros mansos* are presumed by others to be more authoritative.

In the particular case of the dono da fofoca, one finds the most highly structured form of mediation in garimpagem. Before a dono da fofoca loses authority, any disputes that occur in his area of jurisdiction are referred to him to be settled – often with a heavy heart, since donos da fofoca know that one of the classic ways of precipitating the final dissolution of their authority is to have their verdict rejected by one of the plaintiffs in a dispute. Mediation is highly structured in certain other contexts as well. There are the special cases of closed garimpos, where a dominant figure continues to mediate in disputes long past the fofoca stage, and garimpos under federal intervention, where mediation is taken over by the state.

But in the majority of garimpos that are neither fofocas nor under federal control, mediation is far less structured. To begin with, important types of dispute never go to mediation. Conflicts between workers and conflicts between workers and donos have to be settled by the parties concerned. Somebody else may intervene to resolve the dispute by lending money or gold, but they are not really mediating in any real sense. Conflicts which are internal to the barranco have to be settled within it. The only disputes which might go to mediation are those between donos, and even here most of the disputes where mediation takes place are minor. A major breach of norms would not go to a third party to be resolved; the wronged dono would view the process as legitimation of an illegitimate act.

Mediation in garimpos is never automatic and even when it takes place it has to operate under strict limitations. Nevertheless, when garimpeiros are asked if conflicts are often mediated by a third party, most say that they are. They say that the opinions of the most experienced and the most prominent donos are sought by the parties in dispute and their decision respected, making the process sound rather like adjudication by tribal elders. Not only was no mediation of this type observed during fieldwork, but garimpeiros who described this system were unable to come up with a single example from their own experience that stood up to close questioning. What mediation there is on the part of prominent donos is much more informal and much less structured than garimpeiro accounts suggest. Firstly, any initiative must come from the donos concerned; mediators have to be called in and do not offer their services. Secondly, there is never more than one mediator; mediation does not take place by panel. Thirdly, the verdict is not automatically respected, and mediators have no means of enforcing their decision.

What happens when a dispute goes to mediation is that the two donos involved recognise that they are not going to agree, and decide to take the argument to a third figure, with whom they already have some connection. The last point is important, because it would be unthinkable for a dono to involve somebody with whom he had no previously existing social relationship in a question that directly affected his barranco. As rich donos have dealings with more garimpeiros than poorer ones, partly because of their prominence in lending networks and partly because they will have interests in more than one barranco in the garimpo, it is to donos who combine social prestige with economic importance that parties in conflict will usually turn. But mediation can be a difficult business for even the most prominent dono. On the one hand he will be flattered at being asked to adjudicate, as it is concrete evidence of his elevated standing within the garimpo, but on the other he has no means of enforcing his decision and will lose face if one of the donos involved refuses to accept it. He will therefore try to conciliate rather than hand down a decision from on high, looking to find a compromise that will be acceptable to both sides rather than seen in terms of victory or defeat by one or the other.

Mediation, then, is in practice much less important in the settling of conflict in garimpos than might be thought from the comments of observers about the 'law of the garimpo', or even from what garimpeiros themselves say about how conflicts are settled. It is not common, and only a relatively narrow range of disputes are subject to it. Even when it does take place, the verdict is not necessarily accepted by both sides and the mediator has no means of enforcing it.

The reason that decisions have a merely moral force behind them is that even the most prominent dono cannot physically mobilise garimpeiros in his support if he relies exclusively on relationships forged within the garimpo. This is initially surprising; patron-client relationships are very common in Brazil and one might have expected to see an economically powerful dono evolving into a *patrão*. *Clientelismo* is in fact of very little importance in garimpos, and on reflection it is not difficult to see why. Firstly, the idea that workers could be in any sense retainers is anathema to a garimpeiro. It would contradict the central tenets of individual autonomy and freedom of action. The social relationship that a worker enters into when he is contracted by a dono revolves exclusively around the workplace, and does not imply any form of allegiance beyond the barranco. On top of this, relationships in garimpos are extremely transient; workers come and go, donos move around and many of them end up leaving garimpagem altogether. In these conditions, the formation of anything resembling a patron-client relationship is extremely difficult, because dono-worker and dono-dono relationships are usually not permanent enough to allow them to develop. It has been shown how confrontational relations between a dono and his workers can become, with workers frequently making life difficult for the dono because they believe that the terms of their work contract are not being honoured. If donos often have problems in maintaining their authority even in the barranco, it follows that getting workers to put themselves at risk in conflicts which they would regard as having nothing to do with them is well nigh impossible.

This was dramatically illustrated by an incident that took place towards the end of 1985 in the area around the village of Geraldo in the Gurupí. It was instantly christened the *guerrinha*, the little war, by the people of the region, and it was the only time during fieldwork that large scale mobilisation took place during a conflict. Significantly, it was not garimpeiros who were doing the mobilising, although it directly affected several garimpos and one of the prime movers in the conflict was a garimpeiro. We have already met the two main protagonists once before; Zé and Luisão. Luisão was the dono who organised and led the invasion of the fofoca of Trinta Cinco, where he publicly humiliated Zé, an incident described in Chapter 3. Zé had been waiting for a chance to take his revenge ever since, and nearly three months later it came. At one level the guerrinha was a settling of old scores, but it was much more complicated than simply a feud between two powerful donos. Both Luisão and Zé were much more than garimpeiros, and the story of how their animosity played itself out cannot be understood without seeing their rivalry within garimpagem in the context of political conflict between them and the social forces they represented in several other arenas besides the garimpo.

The invasion of Trinta Cinco was merely the catalyst in a long-running power struggle between Zé and Luisão which had begun almost as soon as Luisão arrived in the garimpo of Nadí in early 1984. But the roots of the conflict go back much further. The dispute had three important strands. One of them was the enmity between Zé and Luisão as a result of clashes within garimpagem, of which the invasion of Trinta Cinco was merely the most serious example. The other two themes in the story predate Luisão's arrival in the area by more than a decade. One of them had to do with the political consequences of the settlement of the area during the 1970s; the other involved Geraldo, the founder of the village that bears his name, and a stand of timber.

Zé was not only a dono in garimpagem; he was also the leader of the local rural trade union, the sindicato, and the representative in Geraldo of COLONE, the Companhia da Colonização do Nordeste, a state land agency that had regulated the process of land occupation in the west of Maranhão since the 1970s. COLONE was a product of the accelerating movement of smallholder migrants to western Maranhão during the 1950s and 1960s. This was a movement which, as in other parts of Amazonia, was accompanied by a great deal of violence. The construction of the Belém–São Luís highway through the region in the 1960s attracted landgrabbers as well as smallholders to the Gurupí. The large landowners of the rural oligarchy already present there made common cause with the landgrabbers in attempts to appropriate land for speculation and ranching, which involved denying migrants access to land and expelling those who were already there. The smallholders met violence with violence, and by the 1970s a situation had been created that was seen by the federal authorities as a threat to public order; their response was to set up COLONE with funds from the state of Maranhão, the federal POLONORDESTE programme, and the World Bank, and give it responsibility for regularising the process of land occupation in the area. By the mid 1980s it had largely succeeded in creating one of the few areas in Amazonia where large numbers of smallholders were given official title to their lands and provided with basic health and agricultural extension facilities, but land speculators from outside the area and large landowners within it were still not prepared to admit defeat. Led by the *prefeito*[6] of the municipality of Godofredo Viana, who controlled the local police and could rely on backing from powerful figures in the state government in São Luís, they were still looking for opportunities to weaken COLONE's authority and encroach upon the lands it had titled to the smallholders.

Zé was one of the figures upon whom COLONE relied to maintain its position at the sharp end, in the smallholder communities which since 1982 had been deeply involved in garimpagem as well. He was the COLONE agent for the communities of Geraldo and Alto Alegre, responsible for coordinating malaria control and the voicing of small-holder complaints and suggestions to COLONE. He was also the first line of mediation in disputes between smallholders, as COLONE held to the philosophy that disputes were better settled internally, and would only intervene if the differences seemed irreconcilable. Zé was also the leader of the local *sindicato rural*, the rural trade union. Since the 1970s the Catholic church had worked together with the small-holders, painstakingly helping them to organise to resist landgrabbers, and later working together with COLONE to consolidate smallholder control of the land. This was a long process that lasted more than a decade, and was carried out with considerable courage in the face of often violent opposition from landowners and land speculators, who controlled the local police and used both them and hired guns to terrorise and occasionally kill. Zé was important to the church organisers. He had physical courage, a gift for organisation, and was a charismatic public speaker. In addition to this Zé had, like many other smallholders, adapted very well to the growth of garimpagem in the area. He had acquired machinery and effectively utilised the garimpo as a complement to his agricultural activities. He was thus an im-portant figure in regional politics. He was a prominent dono in the garimpo of Cedral, and was the person to whom smallholders who had any problem with garimpagem would turn. Outside the garimpo, he was an important actor on the political stage that pitted the small-holders, the church, the sindicato and COLONE against the prefeito, the landowners, the police, the landgrabbers, elements of the state government in São Luís, and Rosaldo, a powerful garimpeiro entrepreneur in the garimpo of Cachoeira, just over the Pará border, who was beginning to turn his eye to other areas of investment.

As soon as Luisão arrived in the area in 1984, Zé distrusted him. Rumour linked him to Rosaldo, and it was certainly true that Luisão immediately became a major gold buyer and regularly travelled to Cachoeira. Rosaldo in his turn was linked directly to a group of Paraense landgrabbers who in early 1984 after years of violence and political controversy had finally been expelled from the Gleba Cidapar, a large estate on the Pará bank of the Gurupí river. Zé suspected that Luisão was passing on information about the situation in COLONE territory, and feared that the Paraense landgrabbers might form an alliance with their Maranhense colleagues, heralding a new attempt to move in against the smallholders. This suspicion crystallised into certainty in November 1984, when the elections for officers of the sindicato took place.

On the day of the election, Luisão turned up in Geraldo together with the prefeito and a few military police. They said they were there to guarantee a free election, but in fact they ostentatiously positioned themselves outside the hut where balloting was taking place and buttonholed those coming in to vote, suggesting they might prefer not to vote for Zé if they knew what was good for them. Zé suspended the voting and went to the town of Santa Helena to fetch the local priest, who returned with him to Geraldo and had to threaten Luisão and the prefeito with legal action and denunciation in the São Luís papers before they agreed to leave. From then on Zé went around armed and never travelled alone.

At the same time, Luisão's behaviour in Nadí was unusual. Although he had machinery and a barranco, he spent more time and energy buying gold from others than on extracting it himself. He always had large amounts of cash on hand to do so, but the money did not come from the sale of gold from his barranco, where production was only modest. The profit margin on the resale of gold was also too small to account for all the money he seemed to have on tap, and it was generally assumed, although never proven, that it came from Rosaldo. He had a stock of spare parts which he lent out willingly without borrowing very often in return. He even lent money to other garimpeiros at uneconomic rates of interest, and seemed to be trying to put as many garimpeiros as possible under an obligation to him. He was always accompanied by Bernardo, a mysterious figure who was always armed and seemed to be his bodyguard, which made other garimpeiros a little suspicious of his motives. No other garimpeiro met in the Gurupí during fieldwork had a bodyguard.

All the same, the spark that ignited the guerrrinha had nothing to do with garimpagem; it resulted from a tactical move in Geraldo by Luisão in conjunction with the prefeito. They took advantage of a longstanding division in the community between COLONE and the founder of the village, Geraldo. Geraldo had once been a companion of Eduardo, the founder of the garimpo of Cerqueiro. Like Eduardo, he had been one of the first settlers to arrive in the area in the mid 1960s. He had cut trails, hunted jaguars and sold their pelts, panned for gold, and planted crops for some time before other settlers trickled in and a community began to form around him in the early 1970s. But all the time that Geraldo was 'taming' the area, as settlers say, he was unaware that COLONE to the east had already marked the area down for future land settlement and got the state government in São Luís to pass a decree giving it title to what Geraldo believed was common land. When COLONE surveyors appeared in 1974 and told him that they were about to take over land distribution in the village, Geraldo refused to accept it. He held to the view that the land had been unoccupied and therefore belonged to whoever worked it, and refused to allow COLONE to dictate where he could clear fields and plant crops. COLONE had an equally cogent reading of the situation; unoccupied land belonged, legally, to the state, and thus COLONE, as a state agency with the specific brief of regulating land occupation in western Maranhão, was perfectly entitled to move into the area over which it had legal title, which included the settlement of Geraldo. What made the situation especially poignant was that although Geraldo and COLONE had opposing philosophies of land occupation, COLONE was acutely aware of the debt it owed to him for doing so much to open up the area and help the first migrants who arrived there, and was not unsympathetic to his position. It made great efforts to win him over, promising him a titled plot of the regulation area (250 metres by 2500) wherever he wanted it, a feeder road from his plot to the highway, credit and technical help. But Geraldo was adamant; he had been the one who 'tamed' the area and therefore he had the right to plant wherever he pleased. Although several members of his family gave in and accepted plots, Geraldo did not. So, with regret, COLONE was forced to omit Geraldo from its plans.

The result was that the founder of the village became a marginalised figure within it, just as Eduardo became a marginalised figure within the garimpo that he founded. To a certain extent, the way that Geraldo was frozen out of the subsequent development of the community he had founded split the village. In Amazonia, the founder of a community enjoys considerable prestige and respect within it, and the fact that Geraldo was the only smallholder left without a titled plot of land after COLONE had taken over was generally perceived as unjust. Zé and others connected with COLONE felt extremely uncomfortable about it, and Geraldo's large extended family formed a bloc of smallholders who felt bitter towards COLONE and, by extension, towards Zé personally.

After 1982, when non-smallholders began to arrive in some numbers after the establishment of garimpos in the area, the unity of the community was fractured still further. In 1985 Geraldo consisted of about 500 households. Although the majority were still smallholders, a considerable minority were not connected to the land; they were hoteliers, gold buyers, retailers and merchants of various kinds, and mechanics. The days when the entire community united and fought the landgrabbers were succeeded by more complex dealings between a number of different social groupings within the village as its economic base and social composition diversified. A wave of conversions to evangelical Protestant sects broke the Catholic church's previous monopoly on the religious affiliations of the settlers, and the old enemies of the sindicato and COLONE began to use subtler means to divide the community. The prefeito donated money to build evangelical halls, and attempted to turn anti-Catholic feeling against the local padre, an Italian liberation theologist. In 1984 a good quality dirt road was built by the army linking Geraldo with the BR-316 highway, and the prefeito and the local landowners claimed credit for it. While the church, COLONE and the sindicato were still very active, they were no longer the only political force in the village.

It was an attempt by Luisão and the prefeito to exploit these divisions that led to the explosion. In October 1985 Luisão approached Geraldo with a tempting offer. He was interested in the large amounts of commercial timber that still existed in plots surrounding the village. If Geraldo could get the timber to the road, Luisão suggested, he would get a lorry to collect it and sell it in the nearby town of Maracassumé, and cut Geraldo in on the proceeds. Geraldo agreed, and together with two nephews began to cut a trail through various smallholder plots in order to get at the timber. The owners of the affected plots went straight to Zé and demanded that he put a stop to it.

Luisão's offer had been a shrewd one, well calculated to put the cat amongst the pigeons. In the first place, it would guarantee a furious row amongst the smallholders, which Zé would have to sort out. Secondly, it was an outright challenge to both Zé and COLONE. One of the conditions which smallholders had to accept to receive a plot was that they should leave forest enclaves within them, and one of Zé's jobs was to enforce this rule. The idea was that COLONE would market all timber, with the proceeds going towards the various agricultural extension schemes it ran for the benefit of the smallholders as a whole. Luisão was taking a calculated gamble. He knew that legally COLONE owned the timber, but also that this would if anything be an incentive for Geraldo to harvest it. He also calculated that the local police was in the hands of the prefeito, whereas COLONE would have to get the distant authorities in São Luís to act, and even if this could be done the timber would have long since been transported and sold by the time anybody from the capital arrived to see what was happening.

He did not, however, anticipate the furious reaction this would provoke amongst the smallholders and the sindicato, nor imagine that Zé would seize upon the issue to kill two birds with one stone; to reassert COLONE authority over the timber at one level but, more importantly, to expel Luisão from the region, thus gaining full revenge for his humiliation at Trinta Cinco and serving notice to landgrabbers and the prefeito that the sindicato was still capable of seeing them off by force.

Zé realised immediately that there was no point in taking the dispute to São Luís and decided to take direct action. He chose a day when Geraldo was staying with relatives in Santa Helena. On the morning of 28 November 1985 the village awoke to find that scores of smallholders from the nearby settler community of Alto Alegre had arrived to join their colleagues in Geraldo. They were all armed, and set up barriers on the trails leading to the garimpos. Although people were allowed to pass freely, mules carrying the supplies on which the garimpeiros depended were not. Zé sent a message to Nadí ordering Luisão, Bernardo and one dono who had been closely associated with Luisão to get out of the area within twenty-four hours. He sent another message to Geraldo saying that nobody would do him any harm as he had been an innocent pawn in a wider game and that he should not be afraid to come back to the village.

Later that day, a patrol of smallholders on the road between Geraldo and the highway spotted a lorry coming in to collect the first load of timber. Without any warning they fired on it, shattering the windscreen and disabling the engine. They were undoubtedly shooting to kill, although luckily the driver was only slightly injured by flying glass. Pulled from the cab paralysed by shock, he managed to convince his attackers that he was only an employee of the timber company who knew nothing of what was happening, whereupon the smallholders drove him to Santa Helena and left him at a clinic.

That evening, a colonel of the military police together with a dozen troopers arrived in Geraldo to find out what was happening. Zé told them that the community regarded them as hopelessly compromised by their association with the prefeito, that the attempt to shift the timber was clearly illegal, and that until the arrival of senior COLONE personnel the sindicato was going to ensure that no timber would be sold for private profit. The police, helpless in the face of so many armed and angry smallholders, prudently withdrew and took no further part in the conflict.

These developments had immediate repercussions in the garimpos near Geraldo, especially in Nadí. While garimpeiros were concerned that the blockade would wreck their operations if it continued for any length of time, there was a complete lack of sympathy for Luisão and his two associates who had been named by Zé. Still less did those whom Luisão had helped in the past feel any obligation to put themselves at risk on his behalf. Luisão and his two associates did not even attempt to rally support; they reasoned, correctly, that their lives were in immediate danger and fled by a circuitous route, avoiding the more frequented trails where vengeful smallholders might be lying in ambush.

In short, the mass of garimpeiros reacted by putting a curse on both houses. They believed Zé had used unnecessary force, unaware as most of them were of the larger interests at stake, and asserted they would remove the roadblocks by force if they remained in place. At the same time they had little sympathy with Luisão and the others; if they were foolish enough to get mixed up with politics and timbering when they should have been preoccupied with their barrancos, the consensus went, then they deserved what they got. The absence of any solidarity with Luisão, despite his diligent cultivation of his peers, was striking. The impression was of a man who had thought he could buy himself a clientele being rather cynically exploited as an economic resource by his fellow garimpeiros: a Machiavelli fallen amongst more seasoned Machiavellians.

The conflict blew over almost as soon as it had begun. On the second day, once news of the flight of Luisão and the others was confirmed, the blockade of the trails ended. COLONE officials and lawyers descended on Geraldo, and the prefeito, realising he had been decisively beaten, stayed away. The timber remained under COLONE control, writs were served on the timber company offices to prevent further attempts to ship out timber, and Geraldo returned to the village. The padre negotiated the return of one of the figures expelled by Zé and arranged for the machinery Luisão had left behind to be shipped back to him. The sindicato, through Zé, had demonstrated that it was still the dominant political force in the community, and had shown anybody with designs on COLONE land that they would be better advised to seek out other areas where smallholder organisations were less formidable.

Nevertheless, Ze's mobilisation of the smallholders was not without costs. Although he had shown that Luisão had been wrong in thinking his alliance with the prefeito, and by extension the local police, would be enough to assure victory, he had earned the enmity of the garimpeiros amongst whom he still had to work for the high-handed way in which he had imposed an indiscriminate blockade. This would make life in the garimpo more difficult for him in future. He had also alienated a section of the community in Geraldo. Those not directly linked to the sindicato, who relied to some extent upon the garimpo for their living, and who had arrived after the struggles with the land-owners, were deeply worried by what had happened. They thought they were living in an area of Maranhão that was unusually peaceful, and for them it was a shock to go to bed one night with little indication of trouble and then to wake up and find the village full of armed men setting up roadblocks along the trails upon which they relied for part or all of their livelihood. Zé would have to cope from that point on with the image of a belligerent man who was prepared to put smallholder interests above those of the community as a whole. His standing amongst the smallholders had never been higher, but he seemed not fully to have realised that the smallholders were no longer the only constituency with which he had to deal as a community leader.

The 'little war' demonstrated that conflicts within the garimpo can happen as a result of rivalries between garimpeiros who bring their differences in other arenas to the garimpo, which becomes one locus of a more generalised crisis. Just as no man can be an island in the garimpo, so the garimpo itself cannot be treated in isolation from the social and political context in which it is inserted. Wherever garimpos are established they become part of the fabric of local and regional political life. In the case of the most powerful garimpeiros, garimpos are often only one of a number of political arenas in which they move. In this respect, as in others, it would be a mistake to think of garimpos as self-contained universes. As the most powerful garimpeiros operate in other spheres besides the garimpo, rivalries that have their origin outside the garimpo can still precipitate conflict within it. They constitute one more political arena which influences and is influenced by the flux of political activity in other spheres.

The guerrinha was decided not by the relative strengths of Zé and Luisão within the garimpo but by their capacity to mobilise support outside it. It illustrated just how problematic mobilisation of garimpeiros is for even the most powerful dono. Luisão lost because when the decisive moment came he found he could not mobilise support in the garimpo. He completely misread the nature of the social relationships he believed he was constructing with his fellow garimpeiros: he thought he had become a *patrão*, and for that presumption he almost paid with his life.

7 Serra Pelada: The Gold Rush on the National Stage

With this chapter we leave the ethnography of garimpagem and begin to consider it in a wider economic and political context. The garimpo of Serra Pelada has already been mentioned in passing several times in this book and will now be dealt with at greater length. This is only partly because Serra Pelada is the most dramatic and the most visually startling example of the scale and the importance of the gold rush that has taken hold of large parts of Amazonia since 1979. It was also the first garimpo to be taken over by the state, and a knowledge of the history of state intervention in Serra Pelada and its consequences is fundamentally important to the analysis of the relationships between garimpeiros and the state, and between garimpagem and mineral companies in contemporary Amazonia. Serra Pelada redefined those relationships.

Serra Pelada is a garimpo about ninety kilometres as the crow flies from the city of Marabá, in the south of the state of Pará (see Map 3). Since 1979 it has been in turn an enormous fofoca, the first garimpo to be taken over by the state, an electoral battleground, a national political controversy and a kind of co-operative. At its peak, in 1983, it was producing more than a metric ton of gold a month and had a population of between 80 000 and 100 000 garimpeiros and traders. It has been variously portrayed as a place where people become fabulously rich overnight, or as a 'hellhole' where thousands work in semi-slavery for a pittance; as an escape valve for social tensions or as a powder keg of social tensions waiting to explode.

It was television programmes and newspaper features about Serra Pelada that first alerted most Brazilians to the fact that there was a large scale gold rush going on in Amazonia, and in journalistic terms it was an excellent story. Photographers and television reporters were able to show remarkable, Dantean images of tens of thousands of garimpeiros removing entire hills with pickaxes and shovels (see Plate 16), report the discovery of gold nuggets weighing up to forty kilograms, and document the further transformation of a part of Amazonia that was already in an advanced state of social ferment from the changes that the construction of the highway network had precipitated. It was not surprising that foreign journalists followed the lead of their Brazilian colleagues in beating a path there. Television documentaries have been made about Serra Pelada by Jacques Cousteau, the BBC, West German television and several US networks. Lavishly illustrated features on Serra Pelada have been run by *Time*, *Newsweek*, the *Sunday Times*, and *Die Zeit*. Both in Brazil and abroad Serra Pelada has come to symbolise the Amazon gold rush, despite being a uniquely atypical garimpo.

One might be excused from the coverage for thinking that Serra Pelada suddenly appeared from nowhere, mushrooming up overnight as camps of gold miners do. In fact Serra Pelada, like most places in Amazonia, does have a history. It is a history not only of the site of Serra Pelada itself, but also of garimpagem and other extractive activities in southern Pará as a whole.

Serra Pelada is located in what is usually called the Araguaia–Tocantins by geographers and administrators, the part of southern Pará which is dominated by the Araguaia and Tocantins rivers, tributaries of the Amazon but huge river systems in their own right (see Map 3). Much of it is still dense tropical rainforest, although its removal has been proceeding at an alarming rate since the 1960s. The river plains are broken in several places by ranges of hills, called serras (highlands) in Portuguese. It began to be settled by the Portuguese and Brazilians towards the end of the eighteenth century, although bandeirante expeditions had passed through the region since the early seventeenth century. Settlers arrived in greater numbers during the first half of the nineteenth century, and a pattern developed that was to last until the modern period of an economy based primarily on extraction rather than cultivation: the *drogas do sertão*, vanilla, sasparilla and vegetable dyes, palm nuts, timber, and above all *castanha*, Brazil nuts. The Araguaia–Tocantins is, literally, where the nuts come from: the region where many of the world's Brazil nuts are gathered and shipped. Until the 1970s Brazil nuts dominated the regional economy and are still an important element within it. As early as 1870 natural scientists like C.F. Hart were describing the Brazil nut trade in the Araguaia–Tocantins and lamenting the killing of castanha trees by felling them to get at the nuts.[1] By the end of the nineteenth century rubber was also being produced in the region, although the main centres of rubber production were to the west and north of the Araguaia.

As it turned out, the fact that its extractive economy was based

primarily on Brazil nuts rather than on rubber meant that the Araguaia–
Tocantins did not suffer as much dislocation as other areas of Amazonia
with the winding down of the rubber boom. Marabá, which had been
founded near the strategic junction of the Araguaia and the Tocantins
in 1895, became a regional centre of the Brazil nut trade and the seat of
a *município* in 1912. It was the point where Brazil nuts were stocked
and shipped north to Belém, and where the *donos dos castanhais*, the
owners of the Brazil nut estates, had their town houses and contracted
seasonal labourers. Over the decades the *donos dos castanhais* became
a landed oligarchy and a few powerful families, the Mutran clan
foremost among them, dominated regional politics. During the first
half of the twentieth century, at a time when most of the Amazonian
interior was economically stagnant or in decline, the economy of the
Araguaia–Tocantins was actually expanding and diversifying. Cattle
ranching began to establish itself; leather and hides were being exported to Belem from the 1930s and the expansion of ranching was
accompanied by an increase in timbering. The other feature of the
Araguaia–Tocantins, which would come to dominate the regional
economy by the 1980s, was mineral wealth.

The first specifically geological survey carried out in the interior of
Pará had been done further west, in the Tapajós, by Friedrich Katzer
in 1897. He refers to popular beliefs about the presence of gold in the
area which suggest that garimpagem was a feature of the local extractive armoury long before the discovery of gold there in 1956. He says
that 'the river Cupary, near to Aveiro, is, according to popular belief,
very rich in gold. But it seems to me on the basis of my examination of
the area that the legends can only be based on experiences of gold
extraction that took place long ago, and not on positive results
obtained recently'.[2] In this case, the legends were proved right: the
river Crepurí, in modern orthography, has been one of the richest
areas of raft garimpagem in the Tapajós since the 1970s. In the
Araguaia–Tocantins, the earliest detailed reports of garimpagem
document the presence of garimpos of diamonds and rock crystal on
the upper reaches of the Araguaia and near Marabá, which were
visited by DNPM geologists in the 1930s and 1940s but judged by them
to have been in existence since at least the 1920s.[3]

The DNPM, alerted by the presence of the garimpos and with the
reports of their field geologists in hand, began the first systematic
attempts to explore the mineral resources of the Araguaia–Tocantins
in the 1950s with a long term mapping programme called the Projeto
Araguaia. It began in 1954 and ran until 1962, and has some claim to

fame as a precursor of the far more sophisticated RADAM and Landsat surveys that would be used in Amazonia from the 1960s. As a result of findings from the Projeto Araguaia, the area around Marabá was selected for a more detailed follow-up survey, the Projeto Marabá. Its report, drawn up in 1971, mentions gold garimpos already present in the area and noted that, 'for a long time rudimentary working of gold has been a feature of the region. Garimpos of alluvial gold exist on the Praquequerinha creek off the Tocantins, and along the headwaters of the Itacaiúnas river.'[4] 'The headwaters of the Itacaiúnas river' means, as a cursory glance at Map 3 shows, the vicinity of Serra Pelada. Although gold would not be found at the site which became Serra Pelada until 1979, it is clear that garimpeiros of gold have been active near Serra Pelada since at least the late 1960s. Serra Pelada was thus the product of an established tradition of garimpagem in the Araguaia–Tocantins, more specifically of gold extraction up the Itacaiúnas, and so has to be seen as much as a culmination of an old order as the beginning of a new.

However, by 1971 the Projeto Marabá had long been overtaken by events. In the 1960s private mineral companies, both Brazilian and international, were turning their attentions to Amazonia. They could work untrammelled by the lack of resources that has always plagued the DNPM, and in 1967 something happened that was to transform the Araguaia–Tocantins. A helicopter containing a team of geologists from the Brazilian subsidiary of a US multinational put down with engine trouble in a range of hills south-west of Marabá called the Serra dos Carajás. One of the geologists noticed that there was little vegetation on the hill the helicopter had landed on, and this turned out to be because that hill and the ones around it consisted largely of billions of tons of high grade iron ore, bauxite, manganese, copper, nickel and cassiterite. The delighted military regime took over the area and set up the Projeto Carajás, a massive operation run by the state-owned mining company, the CVRD, the Companhia do Vale do Rio Doce. It involved the investment of billions of dollars in the construction of a chain of projects, dams, railways, roads, power lines, ports, and factories, in order to mine and export the Carajás deposits.

Carajás ensured that the Araguaia–Tocantins would from then on become a region of more than passing interest to Brasília, but although it was Carajás which sparked off that interest it was a small guerrilla uprising, the so-called *Guerrilha do Araguaia*, which began the pattern of direct military intervention in the affairs of the region which the federal takeover of Serra Pelada was to continue. The Guerrilha was a quixotic attempt by a Maoist offshoot of the Brazilian Communist Party to set up rural guerilla foci along Cuban lines. It began in 1969, a time when military repression after the 1964 coup was reaching its height, and was a very unequal contest. Between 1969 and 1972 Marabá and the area around it was flooded with troops, several thousand of whom confronted communist militants numbering no more than a few score. The guerrillas, most of whom were not from Amazonia, never managed to win over the local population and were never a serious military threat; most of them were killed. To the people of the region, the vast majority of whom never came into contact with the guerrillas, the operations of the army were bewildering and frightening, as one ex-Brazil nut gatherer working near Marabá in 1971 remembered:

> Well, round about then this business of the terrorists happened. I was working with some companions in a Brazil nut grove about fifty kilometers from Marabá. One day the army passed by our hut and took away all the arms we had, shotguns and even knives and machetes, which meant that we were left without the means of working, because we depended on the shotguns to kill game. So we had to leave and return to Marabá, but on the way we were stopped by army patrols four or five times. Every time they searched us, and they went through what we were carrying on our backs very thoroughly. Afterwards, things calmed down, I don't know how it all ended. But you couldn't really call it a war. The army was there, right enough, but we never had any contact with the terrorists. There were rumours of attacks, but it was more everybody being searched, roadblocks, police business, you know? Everybody who didn't have identity documents had to get them. A lot of us didn't even know what an identity document was in those days, you know.

It was the operations against the Guerrilha which first brought Major Sebastião Rodrigues de Moura, or Major Curió as he was nicknamed, to the Araguaia–Tocantins. He would later, in 1980, command the federal takeover of Serra Pelada and become for a while the dominant political figure in Marabá and southern Pará. He was a major in the Serviço Nacional de Informações, the SNI, the Brazilian security service, and from 1972, when the guerrillas were finally wiped out, he was part of a continuing SNI and military presence in the Araguaia–Tocantins. It was only partly because of Carajás and the wish to ensure that there was no recurrence of the Guerrilha that the military continued to keep an eye on the region. During the 1970s the level of rural violence in the region had risen sharply, and in Brasília this was seen as a potential threat to national security. In this sense too the intervention in Serra Pelada was the continuation of a long-running process of direct federal involvement in the affairs of the region, rather than something entirely new.

The 1970s were a time of extremely rapid change in the Araguaia–Tocantins, precipitated, as elsewhere in Amazonia, by the construction of the highway network. Smallholder migrants, ranchers, and land speculators moved into the region, large tracts of forest were turned into cattle pasture, intense land conflict resulted, and there was very rapid urbanisation in Marabá and elsewhere: Marabá's population mushroomed from roughly 10 000 in the 1950s to around 200 000 by the late 1980s. All the time that this was happening, mineral companies, alerted by Carajás, were intensively surveying the entire region. They, together with the DNPM, the CVRD and DOCEGEO registered hundreds of claims for mineral rights in the area. One of them, Decreto de Lavra 74.509, awarded to the CVRD in September 1974, would prove to be controversial: it gave the CVRD the right to prospect for and mine iron in the area which included Serra Pelada. Gold was first discovered by the DNPM in 1976 in the Serra das Andorinhas, within the Carajás project area, but because of worries that garimpeiros might be attracted to the strike news of it was kept secret until 1978, when garimpeiros discovered gold there independently. The DNPM reacted swiftly, calling in the federal police and expelling the garimpeiros from the Carajás project area. It was the first time that the federal police had been involved with garimpeiros in southern Pará.

Then, in November or December 1979, at a ranch called Tres Barras, owned by a not very rich cattleman called Genésio Ferreira da Silva, gold was discovered at the site which was to become Serra Pelada. The exact circumstances of the discovery are already encrusted by legend, and there are various versions. Some say a garimpeiro panning a stream on the ranch came to Genésio after discovering gold, others that Genésio contracted a geologist to examine his land after hearing of gold strikes in the area, and still others that a labourer called Aristeu went to Genésio with a strange stone he had found, which turned out to be a large gold nugget. Although Genésio tried to keep the news of the discovery secret, the fofoca, as always, was impossible to contain. Genésio became the dono da fofoca, and began to lay in supplies, build an airstrip, and assign barrancos to newcomers. It very soon became clear, as bamburro followed bamburro, that it was an exceptionally rich deposit. By March 1980 there were already about 5000 people working several hundred barrancos. DNPM and DOCEGEO personnel based in Carajás became aware of the garimpo, and DOCEGEO set up a gold-buying post there in March. The SNI also had their eyes on Serra Pelada from an early stage; in late March Curió flew in by helicopter and stayed for a few hours asking questions.

The period between the end of 1979 and the 1 May 1980, when federal intervention took place, was one of frantic activity in both Serra Pelada and Marabá. One person who was present in the region throughout this time was Luiz Bandeira, a sociologist working for DOCEGEO:

In October 1978 I was put in charge of an administrative unit in Serra Norte, part of the Carajás project, and from that date I frequently travelled to Marabá by car along the PA–150 road, which had been built by the CVRD to link Carajás and Marabá. In 1978 and most of 1979 this road was practically deserted, except for a few smallholders who cleared land and planted along either side of the road. But around the end of 1979 we began to notice a difference. Besides the smallholders, there were now numbers of garimpeiros going to and returning from Serra Pelada, as we later discovered the garimpo was called.

Do you think it was the presence of the CVRD and DOCEGEO in the area which had attracted the garimpeiros?

No, because the road had been open since 1977. Smallholders arrived soon afterwards, but not garimpeiros. It was only by the beginning of 1980 that we saw that the population movement on the road had changed in character, and it came to our attention that there was a group of garimpeiros in Serra Pelada. Our people, geologists and technicians, began to visit Serra Pelada in February to see for themselves what was happening, because the rumours were so contradictory. I remember that by March I had already written reports for DOCEGEO and the DNPM alerting them about the problems it was likely to cause, this sudden influx of people without even the beginnings of an infrastructure there to support them. In March I went to Marabá to contract people to work in Carajás, and spent two weeks there. It was from there that I first saw from close up the new reality which had come to exist in the region with the excellent gold production which was already coming out of Serra

Pelada. Two things especially struck me. The first was the large number of aeroplanes arriving at Marabá airport, taking off and landing incessantly, from light planes to executive jets. From them men got out with suitcases full of money to buy gold in the city. This really caught my attention.

Where were these planes coming from?

Mostly from São Paulo, with quite a few from the state of Goiás. The other thing which struck me was the complete freedom of trade in gold, buying and selling, the entire city seemed to be dedicated to gold commerce. The hotel where I was staying was completely full, every room taken, and in every room it seemed there was a gold buyer. Already by seven in the morning the coming and going was intense, with queues of people selling gold in front of every room. The doors were all open, and you could see the buyers there in the room weighing the gold and then paying out with bundles of notes, as if it were a bank counter. Just to give you an idea of what it was like, in the evening the kids who swept out the rooms showed me small glasses full of gold dust that they had swept up from the floor when they cleaned the room. It was what had fallen on the floor from all the weighing in the rooms where the gold buyers were. They had about ten grams each. I saw this personally. Another thing was that once I went to the chemist. A woman in front of me bought something and paid in gold. The chemist weighed it on precision scales and then gave her change in cash. I had never seen this in Marabá before. And then I saw that wherever you went all the shops had precision scales.

The people flooding into Serra Pelada, 30 000 of them by May 1980, were not for the most part seasoned garimpeiros. The Pará newspapers were already by April carrying stories about the 'economic dislocation' the rush to Serra Pelada was causing. *Castanheiros*, Brazil nut harvesters, were abandoning the Brazil nut estates for the garimpo, shops had to close down because the shop assistants had left en masse and could not be replaced, and the local chamber of commerce tried to get the mayor to shut the garimpo down. Banks found themselves short of tellers, and the most spectacular example of the sudden labour shortage was the temporary closure of the main post and telecommunications office in Marabá in April, because many of the staff had left for Serra Pelada. The lower rungs of the occupational hierarchy in Marabá were swiftly denuded.

More seasoned garimpeiros arriving in Serra Pelada from Maranhão were struck by the size of the garimpo, but taken aback by the lack of experience of most of the people there:

I was at home. Somebody came by and told me they had found a new garimpo, a good one, called Serra Pelada. So I got my things together and went there with him. We arrived in January 1980. I didn't think the garimpo was any good. You know why? It was full of people and we couldn't get a barranco. The only work there was carrying sacks of dirt out of barrancos. Shit, me do that? A garimpeiro who's worked in the Tapajós, Amazonas, and Mato Grosso, and produced more than a kilo of gold? So I left. Everybody there was *brabo* [inexperienced]. Most of them from Marabá. They didn't know anything, and went around with two .38 revolvers on their hips (laughs). They were violent, they didn't want people passing through their barrancos, none of that. There were some experienced garimpeiros there. We prospected a lot in the area but didn't find much. We were used to the Tapajós, Mato Grosso and Amazonas, and the people from Marabá were useless, so we went back.

Seen from Brasília, Serra Pelada was a very worrying development. It was convulsing an area which had a history of causing problems to the federal authorities since the time of the Guerrilha. Worse still, it had attracted thousands of garimpeiros to an area bordering on Carajás, the most expensive and the most important federal development project in Amazonia, which by 1984 was on the point of coming on stream and earning the government large sums of desperately needed foreign exchange. In addition, it was plain that the state was losing tax revenues from the unregulated selling of gold. Nobody knew how much gold Serra Pelada was producing, but it was clearly a considerable amount. The DOCEGEO post had by the end of April bought 208 kilos of gold, and this was only a fraction of total production.[5] The DNPM and DOCEGEO, realising that in Serra Pelada they were faced with the richest gold discovery in Amazonia in living memory, were already thinking that the gold could be mined more efficiently by the state mineral agencies. This was an especially enticing prospect for the CVRD, which had invested a great deal of money in Carajás and in 1984 was looking for extra sources of revenue to tide it over until Carajás came on stream.

Faced with all this, the Conselho de Segurança Nacional, the inner sanctum of the military regime, recommended federal intervention to President João Figueiredo. It would prove to be a momentous decision, not only for the Araguaia–Tocantins but for garimpagem throughout Amazonia, and much would later be written about the motives that lay behind it. No doubt pressure from the DNPM, DOCEGEO and the CVRD did play a part as did a desire to tax the gold trade. But the essential fact about state intervention in Serra Pelada was that it was conceived and executed by the military. To them, Serra Pelada was a concentration of tens of thousands of people in an area of rural conflict dangerously close to Carajás which had already seen one guerilla uprising. It constituted a spontaneous social movement unregulated by state bodies, and given its location this was in itself sufficient reason for military intervention. Serra Pelada was seen by the military as first and foremost a potential threat to national security, and this would be a theme in the subsequent history of the garimpo.

'THE GUN THAT SHOOTS THE LOUDEST IS MINE': FEDERAL INTERVENTION AND ITS CONSEQUENCES

On the 1 May 1980 the federal authorities took over Serra Pelada in an operation co-ordinated by the SNI and commanded by the SNI's Major Curió. Legend has it that the takeover began when a helicopter touched down at Serra Pelada and disgorged a group of armed federal police and Curió. Curió assembled the garimpeiros, and then fired his Magnum pistol into the air with the words, 'Here, the gun that shoots the loudest is mine'. Whether this ever happened or not, the phrase aptly encapsulates the intimidating directness which marked the take-over. A military cordon was thrown around Serra Pelada, entry and exit was temporarily forbidden, all women were expelled, all arms confiscated, and the sale and consumption of alcohol forbidden. A body called the Coordenação, the Co-ordination, was set up to administer the garimpo, headed by Curió and staffed by the DNPM, the federal police, and SNI agents. All garimpeiros had to register with the Coordenação, and possession of a work card became a condition of residence in Serra Pelada. The takeover was equally uncompromising in Marabá. The airport was closed down for a few days, all gold buyers were arrested, and those not from Marabá were expelled; even Zé Arara's wealth and importance did not save him from a couple of hours behind bars and expulsion to Itaituba. The haemorrhage of people from Marabá to Serra Pelada was stopped overnight.

Curió and a staff of around 150 police, geologists and administrators then set about turning Serra Pelada into a new kind of garimpo.

Facilities undreamt of in other garimpos were installed: a free clinic and malaria control post, a branch of the Caixa Econômica Federal, where all gold had to be sold, a post office, telephone lines and a government store where basic foodstuffs were sold at cost price. Thanks to these improvements, the garimpeiros had few qualms about the new daily regime the Coordenação imposed upon them. Each day began with a mass meeting in front of the office of the Coordenação, the singing of the national anthem, regimented callisthenics, and a pep talk from Curió before the crowd dispersed to start work. However, much more important than this were the changes the DNPM introduced in established work practices in garimpos, taking many aspects of the social organisation of garimpagem out of the control of garimpeiros and putting them in the hands of the Coordenação in general and the DNPM in particular. It was the first time any state body had been able to intervene in garimpagem in such detail and on such a scale.[6]

The DNPM geologists and mining engineers in Serra Pelada were mostly young and politically liberal. They had been dealing with garimpeiros increasingly since the 1970s, and for the most part believed garimpagem to be inegalitarian and exploitative. This was a point of view which came over strongly in all the interviews carried out during fieldwork with DNPM, CVRD and DOCEGEO personnel. With the federal police to back them up, and armed with the power of expulsion from the garimpo, they were given their first chance to put their reformist ideas into effect. The most important changes were the appropriation by the DNPM of the process of barranco demarcation and allocation, and the enforced arbitration of disputes by the Coordenação. In addition, no garimpeiro was permitted to own or have interests in more than one barranco. Those who did were forced to select one and hand the others over to the Coordenação, without compensation. These were then distributed by lot, with only those who did not own barrancos eligible to take part. The same was done with new barrancos. When the Coordenação decided to allow garimpeiros to move into an untouched area, the DNPM first surveyed it, divided it up into demarcated barrancos, and held a lottery for non-donos only. The evident fairness of this system made it very popular amongst the garimpeiros, but its explicitly egalitarian objectives proved impossible to maintain. Nothing could prevent the growth of a market, in Serra Pelada, Marabá, and Imperatriz, in the buying and selling of barrancos. Multiple ownership again became common through the simple expedient of selling all but a one per cent stake, which ensured that the barranco would continue to be registered with the Coordenação in the name of the original owner, despite his effective withdrawal from the operation.

Nevertheless, the reforms that the DNPM introduced did have some success: conflicts over barranco boundaries were rare, despite the enormous size of the garimpo, because a central register of the location and dimension of all barrancos could always be referred to. The DNPM also had the power to forbid garimpagem altogether in areas which it considered unsafe, and its prestige was considerably enhanced by incidents where the DNPM enforced the evacuation of an area literally minutes before the collapse of a barranco wall that would certainly have proved fatal.[7] It was also able to enforce a ban on the use of mercury and educate garimpeiros in gold extraction without it. Finally, it compelled garimpeiros to use only manual technology, because of the difficulties of water supply and the dangers created when water was allowed to run off near barrancos, threatening to provoke landslides. Despite these measures, over 100 garimpeiros had been killed in Serra Pelada by the end of 1989, almost all of them buried alive in land slippages. High though this toll was, without the DNPM presence in the garimpo it would have been much worse.[8]

The majority of the garimpeiros in Serra Pelada, impressed by the range of facilities and services installed for their benefit, were quite prepared to allow the Coordenação and the DNPM to run the garimpo at first. Curió, a man of great natural charisma, had the power to speak to the garimpeiros in terms they understood and very soon became extremely popular: '*Deus no céu e Curió aqui na terra*', God in heaven and Curió here on earth, was a common garimpeiro saying at the time. Thus the federal authorities found themselves in the rare position of having launched a large scale military operation in Amazonia which was generally welcomed by the mass of people in the region affected by it. The garimpeiros in Serra Pelada were relieved to find they were not going to be expelled, the tens of thousands of people in Marabá and elsewhere who became wholly or in part economically dependent on the garimpo were equally relieved, and the hundreds of thousands of people in Amazonia and beyond who were involved, directly or indirectly, with the Amazon gold rush, were delighted by the promise of state support for garimpagem which the takeover of Serra Pelada seemed to imply. In November 1980 President Figueiredo visited Serra Pelada and was carried on the shoulders of the appreciative garimpeiros, who cheered his speech to the echo. Figueiredo, naturally lachrymose and unaccustomed to warm demonstrations of popular affection, was moved to tears and declared that he would keep Serra Pelada open for the garimpeiros indefinitely. It was a promise that would come back to haunt him.

For the time being, however, the takeover was yielding unexpected dividends. Not only were considerable amounts of gold being produced by garimpeiros and bought by the state, but it also became clear that the garimpo was functioning as a kind of escape valve for some of the social tension in the region. A left-wing state deputy explained the situation succinctly:

> The idea was to put all the tension in the south of Pará into an area of a few thousand square meters. Southern Pará is a region of great social tension, there are conflicts between ranchers, smallholders and landgrabbers, all that sort of thing. Serra Pelada became an escape valve: they put everyone together in the same place, there was work for all. It was a way to relieve the social tensions in the area.

Serra Pelada was also, as the federal authorities began to realise, a large concentration of potential votes. As the important elections scheduled for November 1982 approached, Serra Pelada was increasingly drawn into state and federal politics. But to understand why Serra Pelada became politically important to Brasília, and thus how it came to precipitate a political upheaval in the Araguaia–Tocantins, a little background is necessary.

In 1979 the military regime began a process of gradual political liberalisation, with the aim of eventually transferring power to a civilian president, but in such a way that the military could continue to dominate from behind the scenes. One of the ways in which the military hoped to control the transition was through the election of a President from amongst the ranks of the parliamentary arm of the military regime, the PDS, the Partido Democrático Social. Since the PDS was tainted by association with the military in the eyes of the electorate no PDS candidate could be elected by direct popular vote, so the military decreed that the election for the next President would be indirect. It was set for 1985, but in order to ensure a PDS victory then the PDS had to win the congressional and state elections in 1982, as the electoral college would be composed of all federal senators and deputies together with state delegations.

In Pará, the struggle between the PDS and the opposition PMDB, the Partido do Movimento Democrático Brasileiro, was very close. The PMDB was strong in the state capital of Belém, the PDS in the interior. The picture was made still more complicated by splits within the PDS. Around Marabá the PDS had been the vehicle of the *donos dos castanhais*, especially the Mutran family, who controlled the city council. They represented the conservative, clientelistic politics of a landowning oligarchy. However, this oligarchy was under pressure from two fronts. One was the PMDB, which had been organising itself in the interior through the church, rural trade unions, and community associations. The other was from interests within the PDS which were antagonistic towards the landed oligarchy.

The development policies that the military regimes had followed in Amazonia were extremely technocratic, aiming to modernise through the implantation of large scale capitalism in both urban and rural areas: Carajás was one expression of this philosophy. But despite the visceral anti-liberalism which the technocrats and the rural oligarchs shared, the modes of production represented by people like the Mutran family and the *donos dos castanhais* were believed by the technocrats to be feudalistic remnants which would have to be swept away if Amazonia was to be modernised. On top of this, the federal authorities were by the 1980s beginning to feel that the domination of the PDS by the Brazil nut oligarchy in southern Pará was becoming an electoral liability. Thus, faced with a PMDB in the ascendant in Pará, the federal authorities came up with an astute new electoral strategy. Rather than allow the PDS's electoral chances in southern Pará to rest with an unpopular rural oligarchy, why not base their campaign on the newer, thrusting, entrepreneurial elite which had established itself in the region since the construction of the Belém–Brasília highway, and which was now investing heavily in Serra Pelada? And who better to head the PDS campaign in the Araguaia–Tocantins than Curió, whose charisma and speaking abilities fitted him for the task and whose popularity amongst the garimpeiros was great?

Thus, at the personal suggestion of President Figueiredo, Curió became a candidate for Congress and organiser of the PDS campaign in southern Pará, leaving the Coordenação in July 1982 to devote himself to the elections. From mid-1982 onwards, the strict entry controls which had kept the population of Serra Pelada down to around 40 000 were lifted. It was suddenly very easy to get a work card, provided entrants registered to vote at the same time. In October Figueiredo made a second visit to Serra Pelada and again promised to keep it open indefinitely.

In November, the strategy was vindicated. Curió was elected to Congress with a huge vote, and at the same time the domination of regional politics by the *donos dos castanhais* was definitively broken, by the man who had fought on behalf of that same landed oligarchy in the region only a few years before. '*A bancada do Curió*', Curió's slate, as it was known locally, took eight out of nine seats on the Marabá council and elected two state deputies. Allies of Curió took control of the council in Imperatriz, and for the Mutran family and the *donos dos castanhais* the November 1982 elections were more than just a reverse; their political domination of the region, which had still seemed secure at the beginning of 1980, was broken. Garimpeiro votes had achieved what over a decade of rural unionisation, church activity and PMDB organisation had thus far been unable to manage.

Initially it seems strange that the collapse was so sudden. In fact, given the way in which Serra Pelada had transformed the local economy, it could have been foreseen, as a PMDB congressman elected from the Araguaia–Tocantins at the same time as Curió explains:

> *In the late 1970s the castanha oligarchy still dominated the political structure of the Araguaia–Tocantins. Then, suddenly in 1980, there is military intervention in Serra Pelada and Curió springs up as the embodiment of a new political order. In the 1982 elections the power of the Mutran family is practically annihilated on the municipal level, let alone the state and federal levels. How do you explain such rapid decomposition?*

Easy. Traditional politics really did exert a great deal of influence in the interior of Pará, but with Serra Pelada there was an important modification in the political structure of the region. It came to happen that the interests of thousands, tens of thousands of people, became bound up with the continuation of garimpagem at Serra Pelada. I'm not talking just of the mass of people who depended upon it as a place where they could sell their labour, although that was obviously important. Serra Pelada became so famous, generated such a powerful myth, that thousands of medium and small scale entrepreneurs bought into operations there without knowing anything about the investment they were making. In Marabá, if you appeared with the document showing that you were the owner of Barranco Number such and such, registered with the Coordenação, you could go to a chemist, a trader, a doctor, a car dealer, or anybody with a little capital to spare, and sell a five or a ten per cent stake in the operation. In 1982 there was a clear threat, obvious to everybody, that if Curió were not elected the garimpo would close.

Everybody knew that this was the case. This was what led to the fall of the Mutran family.

Thus, by the end of 1982, Curió had become the dominant figure in regional politics. He had a large base of support in Serra Pelada, he controlled the council in Marabá, he could play an influential role in the state assembly in Belém and he was on excellent terms with Figueiredo and the military regime in Brasília. Nevertheless, there was a sense in which his election had been paradoxical. The problem was that for short term electoral reasons the government had made Serra Pelada into the cornerstone of its political strategy in southern Pará. In so doing, it was supporting a form of mineral production which ran directly counter to its technocratic, capital-intensive ethos of economic development, represented by Carajás, and articulated very forcefully by agencies within the Ministry of Mines and Energy, not to mention mineral companies accustomed to a sympathetic hearing from the state. Serra Pelada was thus a very disturbing development for the formal mining sector, highly conscious of its proximity to Carajás and deeply suspicious of any state action that appeared to institutionalise garimpagem. Counter measures had in fact been taken as early as late 1980, when the CVRD began to put pressure on the Ministry of Mines and Energy to declare that the takeover had been only a temporary measure, and that the area would be handed over to it in due course. This was certainly the assumption of all DNPM and DOCEGEO personnel involved with Serra Pelada before the electoral imperative became clear in 1982.

The CVRD, as we have seen, did in fact have some legal claim to the site of Serra Pelada from a claim registered in 1974. Other state mineral agencies, such as the CPRM and DOCEGEO, had in any case viewed garimpagem in Serra Pelada with some antipathy from the start. They argued that garimpeiros were technically incapable of extracting gold efficiently at the depths which the main pit in Serra Pelada had reached. In their support they could cite the patent lack of work safety, despite the best efforts of the DNPM, and the frequency with which work had to be stopped altogether to allow expensive contouring of the pits with bulldozers, without which garimpagem would have been impossible. In 1981, for example, Serra Pelada had to be closed in October until April 1982, and official gold production in the garimpo fell from 6.836 tons in 1980 to 2.591 tons in 1981 for precisely this reason.[9]

The pressure to expel the garimpeiros and begin mechanised mining was increased by the lobbying of IBRAM, the Instituto Brasileiro da Mineração, an association representing both public and private sector mineral companies in Brazil. To IBRAM, accustomed to having the state expel garimpeiros from areas wanted by the formal sector, as had happened in Rondônia in 1970, Serra Pelada was a dangerous precedent. Clashes between mineral companies and garimpeiros had become increasingly frequent since the 1970s, and now it seemed that the state was institutionalising garimpagem in the very region which both IBRAM and the CVRD regarded as the showpiece of formal mining in Amazonia. As a result of these pressures, the DNPM was detailed in March 1983 to produce a scheme for the mechanisation of mining in Serra Pelada. It suggested an investment of 25.5 million dollars, envisaging a monthly production of 770 kilos of gold (considerably below monthly production by garimpeiros in 1983 when Serra Pelada was at its peak), and projecting the labour force required as a mere 340 workers and supervisors.[10] By mid-1983 Brasília's naturally technocratic instincts were reasserting themselves, with the election safely out of the way, and Figueiredo, with characteristic inconsistency, acceded to them. In June 1983 he proposed handing Serra Pelada over to the CVRD on 15 November, transferring the garimpeiros there to 'garimpeiro reserves' in Cumarú and the Tapajós. With this renunciation of the two public promises he had made to the garimpeiros in Serra Pelada, the question of what was to happen to the garimpo became a fiercely debated national controversy.

Curió had been placed in an impossible position. He was instructed by Brasília to facilitate the closure of the garimpo, which would have meant the destruction of his electoral base and the instant loss of his credibility as a political leader in the Araguaia–Tocantins. In August he broke with the government, demanded that Serra Pelada be kept for the garimpeiros, and assumed the leadership of the campaign to keep it open. In September he introduced a bill in Congress to keep Serra Pelada in the hands of the garimpeiros for a further five years, proposing the garimpeiros should form themselves into a co-operative to run it. As a preliminary step he organised the richer donos into a professional association, set up a regional branch of the national garimpeiro union in Marabá, and, a delicious irony for an ex-major in the SNI, sent out telegrams appealing for support to the powerful metalworker unions of São Paulo, the electoral base of José Genoíno Neto, a congressman for São Paulo who had fought Curió in the Guerrilha, survived, and become a politician. On 1 October a convoy of garimpeiros left Serra Pelada to travel down to Brasília and lobby for Curió's bill. That same day, to the consternation of the DNPM, which protested it was not competent to fill the role Brasília was requiring of it, the Conselho de Segurança Nacional withdrew the SNI from the Coordenação and ordered the DNPM to take over the administration of the garimpo.

The campaign to keep Serra Pelada in the hands of the garimpeiros was highly sophisticated. The courts were used to the full, adverts were placed in the national press, congressmen and senators showered with letters and telegrams, and support sought from a wide variety of unions and professional associations. Such a coordinated use of the institutions of civil society would have been beyond the capacity of almost all garimpeiros, and points to the most significant fact about the campaign: it was led and organised by entrepreneurs – regional, internal, and external – who had been attracted to garimpagem by the rise in the price of gold since 1979, and who for the first time in the history of garimpagem were able to confront the formal mining sector and the state on its own terms – within the political and judicial apparatus which had previously been used to define the parameters of law and debate on the mineral question in Brazil. This was an unprecedented and critical change: with it, one can say that in political terms garimpagem came of age.

> The mass of peões didn't see it in these terms, but there are a lot of people from the liberal professions here [in Serra Pelada], over 200 doctors, lawyers, engineers, and businessmen. So we went to court, filed writs, lobbied Brasília. . .[11]

The debate was hotly contested on both sides. The formal mining sector realised from the start that Serra Pelada was a vital test case which raised fundamental questions about the relationship between garimpeiros and the formal mining sector, mining legislation, and the whole issue of how mining in Amazonia should proceed in the future. The Executive Secretary of IBRAM put the issue in these terms:

> What we stand for is the idea that the development of Brazil should be carried out in an orderly fashion, regulated by due process of law, and that in the case of mineral legislation the guiding principle must be economic rationality, and not social or political expediency. Where you have a climate where everybody respects the law or not according to whether they feel like it, or because they can pressurise Congress, something crucial disappears – security of investment. Investors cannot feel secure, because in mining what guarantees

investment is the security afforded by the permanence of basic legislation. It was this principle which the episode of Serra Pelada contravened. Contravened is too weak a word – it flattened it.

After Curió's bill was passed in a rare display of bipartisan unity in Congress and the Senate on 5 October 1983, IBRAM and the CVRD lobbied intensively for a presidential veto. IBRAM circulated legal opinions arguing that the bill was unconstitutional on the grounds that mineral rights in Serra Pelada had been held by the CVRD since 1974 and could not be handed over to garimpeiros: the CVRD argued that the investment needed in construction work to make Serra Pelada safe for garimpagem would in any case be greater than the investment the CVRD believed necessary to mechanise production once the garimpeiros had left. On 26 October Figueiredo, as had been expected, vetoed Curió's bill. The garimpeiro associations immediately obtained an injunction forbidding any attempt to remove the garimpeiros by force for ninety days. Meanwhile, Curió set about trying to muster the two-thirds majority needed in Congress and the Senate to overturn the veto. Finally, Figueiredo tacitly acknowledged the political damage the issue was causing the government at a particularly delicate stage of the transition to civilian rule by postponing closure of the garimpo to an unspecified date, attempting to placate the formal mining sector with a decree that became internationally notorious allowing mining in Amerindian reserves.

For a while the situation became calmer. Curió set up and registered a garimpeiro co-operative in January 1984: the directorate was from the beginning dominated by rich donos linked to Curió, and although all garimpeiros in Serra Pelada were nominally members, it was a mass organisation in name only. However, when the rainy season drew to an end in March 1984, pressure quickly built up to settle the legal status of the garimpo once and for all. This time, it became clear that feelings were running so high in the Araguaia–Tocantins that there was a danger Curió might not be able to keep the garimpeiros in check any longer. Curió, who knew more about federal nightmares of popular uprisings in Amazonia than most, astutely used the spectre of revolt to press his claims, presenting himself as the only person capable of preventing a bloodbath.

It is no exaggeration to say that for a few months in 1984 it really did seem that the situation would spiral out of control and that violent conflict was a distinct possibility. Marabá was a worrying place to be at that time; rumours were so rife that it was impossible to know what was really happening, and there was enormous tension in the city. Throughout March and May there were mass demonstrations and vigils in all the towns and cities of the region. Government personnel were withdrawn from Serra Pelada as a precaution, although the DNPM staff stayed at their posts, worried about work safety in the garimpo should they have left. The reports of the DNPM staff in Serra Pelada during this period paint a graphic picture of the heightened pitch of tension in the garimpo. DNPM markers fencing off unsafe areas were for the first time openly ignored. Geologist Carlos Neto reported that 'the garimpeiros are not satisfied with the lack of certainty about whether they will be able to stay and are waging a cold war with the state agencies. We in the DNPM are the ones feeling the most pressure because we are the only ones who must deal directly with them, expected to carry out a policing function unarmed and without protection.'[12] As a result, the DNPM director in Belém was forced to issue instructions that DNPM personnel in Serra Pelada should cease attempts to prevent garimpeiros from entering interdicted areas and to ensure that tailings were dumped in designated spots only. The crisis of conscience this provoked amongst the DNPM geologists, forced to acquiesce to practices they knew were potentially lethal, was considerable.

On 7 June 1984 it became clear that 'the escape valve had become a time bomb waiting to explode'.[13] Even Curió could not control the impatience of the garimpeiros any longer, and several thousand of them blocked the Belém–Brasília highway while colleagues in Serra Pelada cut the police telecommunications system. In a fulfillment of the worst nightmares of the CVRD and IBRAM, several hundred armed garimpeiros left for the CVRD settlement at Serra Norte in Carajás. At the first CVRD settlement on the road, Parauapebas, they disarmed the police, burnt down the CVRD buildings, headed back to Serra Pelada, and put roadblocks on all roads leading to the garimpo, effectively making hostages of the few DNPM employees and policemen still there. Curió was forced to leave Brasília and personally make the rounds of the roadblocks, persuading the garimpeiros to hold off for a few more days to allow him to negotiate a settlement. The garimpeiros agreed only with reluctance, and it was by then clear that the only way to re-establish federal authority in the region was military intervention on a greater scale even than the original military intervention in 1980. It would certainly meet violent resistance, and given the imminence of the end of the military regime the political preconditions for an operation of this type simply did not exist. In 1970

President Médici had yielded to pressure from the private sector and sent in troops to expel garimpeiros from part of Rondônia. On 11 June 1984 the wheel turned full circle when Figueiredo at last surrendered to the inevitable and signed Curió's bill into law, with the proviso that the CVRD be compensated to the tune of sixty million dollars, to be paid by an extra levy on gold sales. Curió returned to Serra Pelada in triumph, and in October the DNPM formally handed administration of the garimpo over to Curió's co-operative. It was an historic victory for garimpagem over the formal mining sector, and over the state itself.

The final irony in a tale full of twists and turns was that IBRAM and the CVRD, having lost, would be proven largely correct in their criticisms of garimpagem's capacity to work gold on such a scale and at such great depths. Since 1984 Serra Pelada has been in a steady decline, which shows some sign of becoming terminal. Despite spending several million dollars on contouring and other construction work, gold production at Serra Pelada has been constantly interrupted by landslides, garimpeiros have continued to get killed there at an alarming rate (nine in a single accident in November 1986), and production has plummeted to 3.5 tons in 1986 from the 1983 peak of 13.946 tons. By 1989, with garimpagem becoming increasingly difficult at the site, only a few thousand garimpeiros remained. On economic grounds it would clearly have been more rational to hand the garimpo over to the CVRD, as the formal mining sector had wished. Yet this only points to the success of the campaign to keep the garimpo open, which was to turn Serra Pelada into a political issue decided in the public arena, pushing purely economic considerations into the background.

1984 also marked the high water mark of Curió's influence. Since then it has declined: he had earned the undying enmity of Figueiredo, could not build bridges with his more centrist civilian successors because he was tainted by association with the SNI, and the Pará PMDB would not contemplate a rapprochement with the suppressor of the Guerrilha do Araguaia. With Serra Pelada no longer sealed off by a military cordon, opposition parties, strengthened by the capture of the Presidency by the PMDB in 1985, rapidly eroded his power base in Serra Pelada and Marabá, already weakened by the decline in garimpagem at Serra Pelada. In some ways he became a victim of his own success, since once it became clear in 1984 that the garimpo's future was finally assured, in political terms at least, Curió could no longer present himself as essential to the continuation of garimpagem at Serra Pelada. In November 1985 his candidate lost the election for prefeito of Marabá to the PMDB, and the *bancada do Curió* fell apart. In 1986 Curió brought what had been an astonishing political career to an end, for the time being at least, when he decided not to stand for re-election to Congress.

AFTER SERRA PELADA

It seemed for a time in the early 1980s that the federal takeover of Serra Pelada heralded a new pattern of government policy towards garimpagem. In November 1980 César Cals, the Minister of Mines and Energy in the Figueiredo administration, talked in a preface to the most comprehensive report the DNPM had yet produced on garimpos in Brazil of mounting similar actions in other areas of garimpagem. Interestingly, the terms in which these proposals were put made it quite clear that he saw garimpos primarily as potential threats to internal security, and not as a form of mineral production which could be brought under the wing of the relevant state agencies, as might have been expected. He wrote that 'the rapid action which took place in Serra Pelada, uniting technical and policing bodies, proved itself successful and constitutes a model which could be repeated in other tumultuous [sic] garimpos',[14] and, even more explicitly, 'the success of the state's actions in Serra Pelada indicate that the operation should be repeated in all the garimpos which bring together a great mass of people and become a public order problem'.[15]

It was because intervention was seen as at bottom a policing action rather than part of a mining policy that Serra Pelada did not, as the formal mining sector feared it might, become a model for a new relationship between garimpagem and the state. For IBRAM and the CVRD, Serra Pelada raised the spectre of competition from garimpeiros who were effectively being subsidised by the state. While garimpeiros were expected to work under the direction of the DNPM in Serra Pelada, and were compelled to alter certain work practices, they were provided with basic facilities in return, and the state even paid for the expensive contouring work essential to continued garimpagem at the site. In other words, as far as the formal mining sector was concerned, the state was institutionalising garimpagem. Any proposals about using Serra Pelada as a model for federal intervention in other parts of Amazonia could only cause them deep unease.

In fact they need not have worried. The Brazilian government has only mounted one operation since 1980 even vaguely similar to Serra Pelada, and once again it was a response to a perceived threat to public order and not a deliberate policy to consolidate garimpagem. This was the Cumarú episode, already referred to as a case study of a closed fofoca in Chapter 3. Although the reaction of the federal authorities was in many ways similar to Serra Pelada, and the political motive – the displacement of an oligarchy that was becoming an electoral liability – was identical, Cumarú in other respects bears little or no relation to Serra Pelada, and federal intervention there was modified by a very different regional context.

In the second half of 1980 a series of gold strikes were made to the west of the town of Redenção, about 250 kilometres south of Maraba, on the borders of the Gorotire reserve of the Kayapó tribe. Unlike Serra Pelada there was no single enormously rich strike, but several dozen garimpos established themselves both inside and outside Kayapó territory. There were conflicts between garimpeiros and local landowners, who tried to set up closed fofocas, and between garimpeiros and the Kayapó. The Kayapó, who have a reputation for fierceness and who several times had been in conflict with Brazilian settlers, showed commendable restraint in the circumstances. They did not kill a single garimpeiro, either expelling them or conceding them temporary permission to stay provided that they recognised Kayapó ownership of the land and paid a percentage of gold production to them.

In March 1981 the federal authorities took over the area as they had Serra Pelada, partly to pre-empt any possibility of a clash between the garimpeiros and the Kayapó and partly to resolve the vicious conflicts which were developing over closed fofocas outside the Gorotire reserve. As in Serra Pelada, military checkpoints were installed on the roads, work cards were issued without which the area could not be entered, in theory at least, and some basic facilities were installed, although on a smaller scale than in Serra Pelada. Once again, the federal takeover was generally welcomed in the region: the opening up of the closed fofocas was especially popular. Again the DNPM attempted to reform garimpo work practices as they had in Serra Pelada, but with much less success. Garimpagem in Cumarú is scattered over a wide area in several dozen garimpos. Serra Pelada could be kept under strict control because garimpagem was concentrated in a small area. In Cumarú there are DNPM and federal police posts on the roads and in the most important garimpos, but the federal presence is inevitably much more diffuse, and its control of garimpagem in the region rather more indirect and tenuous as a result.

The Kayapó both gained and lost from the garimpeiro incursions. They handled the garimpeiros with a great deal of sophistication. By exploiting the terror of Indians that many garimpeiros, over-reliant on lurid stereotypes, certainly feel, notably by a calculated display of force by several hundred Kayapó warriors in the garimpo of Maria Bonita in 1985, they were able to collect a ten per cent levy on gold production which enabled them to keep more effective control over their land, paying for the hire of light planes to patrol its boundaries and the contracting of Brazilian guards. On the other hand, garimpagem upstream soon turned the clear waters of the Rio Fresco brown, forcing FUNAI to pipe in clean water and interfering with fishing, an important food source for the Kayapó. The relationship between garimpeiros and the Kayapó, if occasionally tense, is at least not one of violent antagonism. Were it not for the 1981 intervention, and the presence of the federal police deterring any attempts to move against the Kayapó, this might not have been the case.

Cumarú has proved to be the only analogous operation to Serra Pelada that the Brazilian government has mounted up to the time of writing. While some form of federal intervention may occur in the future, notably in Roraima, where there have been clashes between garimpeiros, landowners, and the Yanomami, there is no reason to think Serra Pelada has become a model that will be repeated in any consistent way. Federal intervention in garimpagem has been an ad hoc response to crises, and is not part of a co-ordinated and consistent state policy towards garimpagem. Nevertheless, federal intervention in Serra Pelada, and to a lesser extent in Cumarú, did mark a new phase in the relationship of garimpagem to the state and to the formal mining sector. Serra Pelada has been a vivid case study of themes and tensions in those relationships, which must now be considered more generally.

8   Garimpagem, Formal Mining and the State

State regulation of gold mining in Brazil dates from a proclamation issued by the Portuguese crown in 1535, some 50 years before any minerals were actually extracted in the colony. The very word 'garimpeiro' was an indirect product of state action. In 1731, almost exactly 250 years before federal intervention in Serra Pelada, the Portuguese crown mounted a military operation to take over the diamond garimpos of Tijuco, Minas Gerais. Patrols sealed off the area, with orders to prevent the entry of anybody not carrying a royal permit. But it seems to have been just as difficult 250 years ago as it is today to keep garimpeiros away from a strike. The records soon began to mention the appearance of *garimpeiros*, who took their name from *grimpas*, the foothills and valleys of the highlands of Minas Gerais, where miners hid from the patrols and extracted diamonds clandestinely. It is not difficult to find other echoes of contemporary Amazonia in the eighteenth century. From the 1720s on a series of gold strikes were made around Cuiabá, in Mato Grosso, which for decades to come would be a major administrative headache for the Portuguese authorities. In 1789, for example, gold was discovered at a place called Sapateiro, to the north of Cuiabá, and a disorderly fofoca ensued. The reaction of the Governor in Cuiabá bore an eerie resemblance to events in the Araguaia–Tocantins nearly 200 years later:

> On the 7th of July the recent discovery of Sapateiro was divided up into *datas* [an archaic word for barrancos] which were distributed by lot. 400 people owning a total of 2,250 slaves competed in the lottery, together with just over 100 freed slaves who entered as individuals.[1]

The full history of mining and mineral legislation in Brazil during the colonial, imperial and early republican periods cannot be dealt with at any length here. However, before the relationship between the state and garimpagem in modern times is examined, it is important to note that although garimpagem on a large scale has existed in Brazil since the end of the seventeenth century, it was not until well into the twentieth century that it was legally defined as a type of mineral production and formal attempts were made by the Brazilian state to construct an institutional relationship with it. Obviously, there was contact between garimpeiros and the state in Brazil for centuries before garimpagem was legally codified. An important theme in the history of the great gold cycles in Minas Gerais and Mato Grosso in the seventeenth and eighteenth centuries was the attempts of the Portuguese colonial authorities to tax and regulate all mineral extraction. Consequently, one can already discern a split between slave-owning, state regulated mining and clandestine, non-regulated mining in the early eighteenth century. This embryonic division of the mining economy of Brazil into a formal and an informal sector was accentuated during the nineteenth century, when capitalist mining supplanted mineral production based on slave labour. The point is that before garimpagem was legally recognised and defined, it was by definition a clandestine activity. The relationship between it and the state was consequently one of persecution on the one hand and resistance or withdrawal on the other.

Until relatively recently garimpagem was not seen as a type of mineral production which could be distinguished from other types: it was simply clandestine mining not regulated by the state. It was not until the establishment of a capitalist mining sector, radically different in terms of both technology and social organisation, that the division between the formal and the informal mining sector became something more than merely a question of legal status. Once the capitalist mining sector had established itself, it was clearly necessary for the state to begin to differentiate between different forms of mineral production and to deal with each of them differently. This was a process which began in 1817, with the first legislation permitting the creation of mineral companies in Brazil and specifying the relationship they were to have with the state, and still continues today, with the current revision of the 1967 Código de Mineração. Ironically, garimpagem as a legal category was an indirect creation of the very capitalist mining sector with which it is now locked in combat throughout Amazonia.

In 1930 Getúlio Vargas, who was to dominate Brazilian politics until the 1950s, was swept to power by a popular uprising in the south of Brazil. Vargas was a nationalist and a populist, and the period between 1930 and 1945 was marked by what he would later call *nacionalismo desenvolvimentista*, literally developmentalist nationalism, a concerted attempt to develop Brazilian industry and national resources, and bring them under domestic control. Mineral extraction formed an important part of this strategy, and in the mining sector as elsewhere the Estado Novo, as Vargas' dictatorship called itself, was a time of radical changes that marked a decisive break with the past. When Vargas came to power, in judicial terms the relationship between garimpagem and the state did not even exist. Within five years garimpagem had been legally defined for the first time, and a public mineral agency set up through which it was to be articulated to the state. These two steps can be seen as inaugurating the modern period in state-garimpo relations. In the mining sector at least the Estado Novo was a golden age, a time when state policy towards garimpagem approached a level of sophistication and benevolence it has never since been able to match.

The *annus mirabilis* was 1934, when the DNPM, the Departamento Nacional da Produção Mineral, was created, and the first Código de Mineração in Brazilian history was drawn up. The Código is a comprehensive body of laws, periodically revised, regulating all aspects of mineral extraction in Brazil, including garimpagem. The dispositions regarding garimpagem were actually decreed a week before the full Código was released in *Decreto Lei* no. 24.193, incorporated without alterations in the Código proper, which defined garimpagem as 'the extraction of precious stones and minerals from rivers, creeks, and hillsides, using temporary installations and simple machinery'.[2]

The administrative machinery the 1934 Código set up was designed to regularise the clandestine nature of garimpagem by creating institutional links between garimpos, the state, and civil society. The preamble to the Decreto contains the first statement by any Brazilian government to admit the importance of the contribution of garimpeiros to national mineral production, and praise garimpagem's historical role as 'the agent of the colonisation of much of the interior of Brazil'. It required garimpeiros to register, free of charge, at government offices, and gave registered garimpeiros the right to prospect and mine wherever they pleased in public land. Remarkably, it even created zones reserved exclusively for garimpagem in the states of Pará, Maranhão, Bahia, and Mato Grosso, and encouraged garimpeiros to form themselves into unions, asserting that 'it is necessary for garimpeiros to move along the path of unionism and cooperativism, for the defence of their interests, for better work methods, and for technical improvement'.

The definition of garimpagem was extended and refined in another Decreto, no. 1.374, June 1939, which for the first and so far only time recognised the semi-mechanised nature of garimpagem. It said that 'garimpagem is characterised above all by the simplicity of its use of mineral deposits: that is to say, by the nature of the processes, apparatuses, and methods employed – bateias, rockers, sluices, and mechanical bateias. [It is also] characterised by the quantity of material which can be extracted and processed in twenty-four hours, for which an upper limit of fifty cubic metres shall be set.'[3] This last point is crucial: it would clearly cover many modern moínhos, for example, and it is all the more impressive to see such a sophisticated definition emerge at a time when mechanisation in garimpagem was still at a very early stage. This Decreto was incorporated into an expanded Código issued in 1940, and no subsequent legal definitions of garimpagem have even approached its level of sophistication.

Yet, despite the flurry of legislation affecting garimpagem, almost nothing changed on the ground. All the 1934 and 1940 Códigos did was to ratify what was already happening, and their importance is more as an indication of how the state was formulating garimpagem *to itself*. Very few garimpeiros were even aware of the legislative sea-change which had taken place, and even fewer ever bothered to register as garimpeiros.[4] A national union, the Sindicato Nacional dos Garimpeiros, was set up in 1935 but swiftly became more a reservoir of political sinecures than a serious labour organisation. It was (and still is) based in Rio de Janeiro, over a thousand kilometres away from the nearest garimpos. Much more important in terms of concrete effects on garimpagem was the creation of the DNPM by Decreto Lei no. 23.979 on 8 March 1934. Mining had previously been the responsibility of a section of the Ministry of Agriculture: with the creation of the DNPM, made responsible for overseeing the implementation of all aspects of mineral legislation, the Estado Novo was able to operate a far more systematic and extensive mineral policy. The relationship between the DNPM and garimpeiros has ever since been the central feature of the more general relationship between garimpagem and the Brazilian state, and since 1979 it has assumed greater importance than ever.

The role envisaged for the newly created DNPM in garimpos was threefold: to provide reliable information about the size, location and potential of existing garimpos, to establish a public monopoly of gold buying in as many garimpos as possible, and to give technical help to garimpeiros. The philosophy which lay behind the actions of the DNPM during the Estado Novo was openly interventionist, but noticeably more positively inclined towards garimpeiros than the interventionism that has been a feature of the DNPM in the 1980s. During the 1930s and 1940s, as more recently, it was felt within the DNPM that garimpeiros, through no fault of their own, were subjected to exploitative work regimes and needed the protection of the state, a view cogently summarised in 1944 by the then Director of the DNPM, A.J. Alves de Souza:

> The garimpeiro, being poor, is often dependent on third parties and thus contracts his services out via an intermediary, like a trader in a place near a garimpo, or the owner of the land where the garimpo is located. These intermediaries supply him with food and the instruments necessary for his work, and the abuses which this system can lead to are well known, with garimpeiros often being cheated by their suppliers at the end of the day. Garimpeiros, then, need to be protected against those who usually present themselves as their protectors, their patrões. But the protection of garimpeiros can be effective only if there is an organisation of the government which can not only assist the garimpeiro at work, advising and helping in loco, but also buy what the garimpeiros produce, at a fair price, in the larger garimpos.[5]

The people with the task of putting this ambitious policy into effect were small teams of geologists and mining engineers attached to the DNPM offices in Rio, Belém and Recife. Their work was made difficult from the start by chronic under-funding, which particularly handicapped work in Amazonia, where costs were highest. Nevertheless, what was lacking in resources was often partially made up for in dedication. Henrique Capper Alves de Souza was a case in point. In the late 1930s he headed a team which produced a series of monographs on garimpagem in southern Pará and Maranhão which have the distinction of being the first, and best, detailed expert accounts of garimpagem in eastern Amazonia.[6] In 1942 he was in Bahia, in the Serra de Jacobina, researching gold garimpagem. The monograph he produced ended with a passionate defence of the reforming ideals behind the policy of the Estado Novo towards garimpagem, and a vision of future state action that is more radical than any of the policy ideas coming out of the DNPM in the 1980s:

> The current government, understanding the importance of gold to our balance of payments and understanding, even more importantly, that the gold produced in garimpos represents not merely a valuable sum for the Treasury but an essential guarantee of work and income to thousands of poor men in the remotest corners of the country, has been giving open and effective support to garimpagem. A great

many objections have been voiced against this policy of committed support for the poor, the only people capable of making a life for themselves in the inhospitable interior. . .The government, in our view, should respect the garimpo and its customs – what one sees in the garimpos of the interior is a surprising order, thanks to the rapid establishment of garimpo traditions – and regard the garimpo as an important factor in the spontaneous growth of the economy of the interior. It should seek to avoid the establishment of private monopolies in areas where garimpagem is the typical form of mineral extraction. It should seek to improve the condition of these areas by opening up roads, and by choosing active and impartial public officials, who can act to improve public sanitation, and, through the enforcement by all means available of the labour laws, to protect the local working population.[7]

For about ten years, between approximately 1935 and 1945, state policy towards garimpagem was more enlightened than it has been before or since. Nevertheless, despite the relative sophistication of the mineral legislation and the commitment of many DNPM researchers, the achievements of the DNPM in garimpos were disappointing. The problem was, once again, insufficient funding. The idea that the DNPM should act as a state monopoly gold buyer, foreshadowing the role of the CEF in Serra Pelada and Cumarú in the 1980s, never got off the ground because the DNPM never had the money to implement the scheme. Lack of resources also made it difficult for the DNPM to provide the detailed information about garimpagem that was a prerequisite of effective state action. Although the quality of the monographs on garimpagem which the DNPM produced during this period was high, there were few of them. The only area which was covered at all extensively was the Gurupí in Maranhão: there were a couple of published reports on southern Pará, and Souza's outstanding report on gold garimpos in Bahia, but other areas of garimpagem at the time, such as Mato Grosso, Roraima, Rondônia and Amapá, were not covered at all.

As the human and financial resources available were so limited, the amount of technical help the DNPM could provide to garimpeiros was correspondingly small. Posts were set up in Maranhão and Bahia, and a guide to small machines that could be imported from Britain, Germany or the United States was produced for the few who could think of buying them,[8] but the overall impact of the DNPM in garimpos was far below what had been envisaged in 1934. The final straw was the increasing emphasis given by Vargas to the discovery of oil and natural gas, which during the 1940s led to the DNPM diverting almost all of its efforts away from minerals towards hydrocarbons. The fall in the price of gold after the Bretton Woods agreements, which led to a considerable reduction in garimpagem throughout Amazonia, finally killed off a government programme of intervention in garimpagem that had been dying on its feet for a number of years.

Relations between garimpagem and the state then entered a quiescent phase which was to last until the late 1960s. There was a brief flurry of activity in 1957, when President Kubitschek founded the Fundação de Assistência aos Garimpeiros. FAG was meant to be a state body responsible for technical assistance and social welfare projects in garimpos, but it was never funded adequately and soon became moribund, being dissolved in 1975. Direct contact between state personnel and garimpeiros would not really be resumed until 1972, in the Tapajós, and then only on a very small scale. Despite this lack of direct contact, crucial changes in mineral legislation did take place in the 1960s, precipitated by the military coup in 1964. Like the Estado Novo, the military regime put great stress on the importance of developing the mining sector, and decided that a revision of mining legislation was necessary to bring that about. There, however, the parallel with the Estado Novo ended. The new phase in state-garimpo relations which the military regime inaugurated was in every respect a regression from the 1930s and 1940s. The legal definition of garimpagem was reformulated in a way that would greatly exacerbate conflicts between the formal mining sector and garimpagem from the 1970s on, and even make much of the work of the state mineral agencies in the 1980s technically illegal.

The roots of the change were in the way the 1964 coup changed the relationship between the state and the private sector in Amazonia. Economic policy under the military was essentially technocratic, aiming to develop Amazonia through a combination of private sector investment, both Brazilian and foreign, and large state funded development projects. It was overtly hostile to non-capitalist modes of production, a hostility that was explicitly stated in the preamble to the revised and expanded Código de Mineração issued in 1967, replacing the 1940 Código. Where the 1934 Código had stressed the importance of garimpagem to the mineral sector and talked of its development along cooperativist lines, the 1964 Código was quite open about its prejudices:

The general dispositions regarding garimpagem are retained, it being necessary to avoid the possibility that the granting of prospecting licences should interrupt such work, but the general principle maintained is that organised mining under a regime of licences of mineral production is more advantageous to the collective interest than the disordered work of the garimpeiro, whose economic future is always uncertain, and almost always unsuccessful.[9]

The 1967 Código devotes Articles 107 to 113 to garimpagem. It defines it as characterised by 'simple and portable machinery' but, unlike the 1940 Código, insists that this means 'manual machinery' only and drops any reference to capacity completely (Article 107). This refusal to recognise garimpagem as semi-mechanised was one important change from the 1940 Código; the other was the introduction of a new criterion in the definition of garimpagem – the 'individual character' of the work:

Article 109. Garimpagem is characterised by:
i.   the rudimentary nature of mineral extraction.
ii.   the nature of the deposits worked [i.e. alluvial]
iii. the individual character of the work, which is always done on one's own account.[10]

In other words garimpagem was now defined as mineral extraction using manual methods on alluvial deposits only, and a garimpeiro as a placer miner working individually. The change was rammed home in Article 113. Whereas the 1934 and 1940 Códigos had set aside areas to be worked exclusively by garimpeiros, the 1967 Código did the opposite:

Article 113. For reasons of public order, or to prevent the dilapidation of a rich mineral deposit, the Minister of Mines and Energy shall, upon the advice of the Director of the DNPM, have the power to determine the closing of certain areas to garimpagem, or to prohibit garimpeiros from extracting given mineral substances.[11]

Thus the 1967 Código constructed a complete dichotomy between mechanised, capitalist mining and manual garimpagem, with no intermediate categories. Despite the existence of reports produced by the DNPM since the 1930s attesting to the semi-mechanised nature of garimpagem it came to be defined as an entirely manual activity, and

on top of that viewed as 'individual' work, which even in colonial times
had never been the case. It is no exaggeration to say that the consequences of the passing of the 1967 Código into law were disastrous.
With the state choosing to define garimpagem in a way which bore no
relation to past or present reality, garimpagem once again became a
clandestine activity in the eyes of the law. This in turn meant that
mining companies had a powerful legal instrument which they could
wield whenever a conflict developed with garimpeiros in Amazonia,
encouraging the resolution of disputes through confrontation rather
than negotiation, as might have been possible had the legislation borne
some relation to what was actually happening on the ground. It
institutionalised a doctrinaire hostility towards garimpagem at the top
of the state mineral agencies, which conflicted with the more prag-
matic attitudes of the DNPM staff who had to deal directly with
garimpeiros, who recognised from the start that this Código was not
compatible with their duty to give technical advice to garimpeiros
and try to increase production in established garimpos. Interpreted
literally, the Código would have obliged them to confiscate much of
the machinery used by garimpeiros rather than attempt to improve its
efficiency. As an ex-head of the DNPM residency in Santarém in the
Tapajós, and head of the DNPM Coordenação in Serra Pelada in 1984
explained

> Technically, garimpeiros are only allowed to use simple machinery.
> But we don't know what a simple machine is. A cobra fumando? A
> pump? A small motor? To be honest, where it deals with garimpagem
> the Código, which we are meant to uphold, doesn't correspond to
> reality. So in the Tapajós we never tried to prevent the entry of
> machinery. Even if we had tried, it would have been smuggled in just
> the same. You can't police thousands of square kilometers of jungle
> with an army, let alone a few geologists. So we just let garimpagem
> evolve naturally there.

During the 1980s these legal distortions would put the Brazilian
government in the embarrassing position of having to subvert its own
laws in order to implement policy in garimpos.

In the late 1960s it was not immediately clear that the effects of the
new laws would be so damaging. Garimpagem in Amazonia was going
through a quiet phase, and would only begin to pick up with the rise in
the price of gold that began in the mid 1970s. Even the first large scale
exercise of the powers to expel garimpeiros seemed to go off relatively
well. In 1970, after representations from private Brazilian mining

companies, the Minister of Mines and Energy decreed the prohibition of garimpagem of cassiterite in Rondônia, and the army was sent in to remove about 20 000 garimpeiros. Although cassiterite production in Rondônia dipped immediately afterwards, by the end of the decade it was considerably higher. It seemed to have been a clear case of mineral production being improved by the substitution of garimpo technology by the capital intensive methods of the formal mining sector. It was not until 1977 that the chickens would begin to come home to roost.

In that year the DNPM and the CPRM, the Companhia de Pesquisas de Recursos Minerais, a public sector prospecting company based in Manaus, set up the Projeto Garimpo. This was a research project responding to the expansion of gold garimpagem in the Tapajós and elsewhere with the climb in gold prices that began in 1974 and would explode in 1979. The DNPM's objectives were the same as they had been since the 1930s; build up reliable information about garimpagem in Amazonia, assess the potential for an increase in production, and provide technical help to achieve it. In 1979, with the start of the gold rush in earnest, the Projeto Garimpo was expanded and renamed PEGB – Projeto de Estudo dos Garimpos Brasileiros, the project for the study of Brazilian garimpos.

PEGB encapsulated the contradictions which now began to cripple government policy towards garimpagem. The series of reports which it produced on garimpagem in Amazonia took the form of a collection of detailed articles by field staff on garimpagem in certain areas, preceded by statements of policy by administrators in the higher echelons of the Ministry of Mines and Energy, the DNPM, PEGB and CPRM.[12] In the policy statements it was obvious that the technocratic hostility towards non-capitalist forms of mineral production which had been so evident in the late 1960s was still alive and kicking, seriously hampering the production of a coherent policy towards garimpagem. In the introduction to the first PEGB report in 1980, for example, the antipathy was clear: 'While one must recognise its importance, the garimpeiro is usually regarded as depredatory, because of a pattern of action which is individualistic, greedy, and undisciplined.'[13]

Occasionally, the objections cease to be economistic and garimpagem is stigmatised with a vehemence that is more clearly cultural in tone. This, in a characteristic reflection of the authoritarianism of the military years, leads to a perception of the gold rush as a potential social and political threat. This was true of a statement by Yvan Barreto de Carvalho, Director of the DNPM in the critical years from 1979 to 1985, made in 1983:

In garimpagem we are dealing with a sporadic and non-germinative activity, by which I mean it does not generate investments in the regions where it is practised. . . .the garimpos of today are an important factor in the occupation of the interior, and, because of the low cultural level of garimpeiro communities, largely formed by cheap labour without any social or judicial regulation, they may become fertile soil for the growth of demagogic ideas and can thus easily be transformed into major social problems.[14]

Statements like this stood in stark contrast to many of the articles which followed them. A few pages after Carvalho's introduction, for example, the definition of garimpagem in the 1967 Código was simply set aside by two senior CPRM geologists:

Not all of the garimpeiro activities described below fall within the definition used by the Código de Mineração. The majority of cases of flagrant inobservance of mineral legislation do not so much constitute a motive for punishment as illustrate the real state of affairs in garimpos in this country, and should serve as points of reference for the arguments in train concerning the reformulation of the laws governing mining.[15]

These inconsistencies in the debate about policy were fully reflected in the policies themselves, which invariably began with a false premise and then elaborated upon it. One of the objectives of PEGB was to promote a transition from the 'garimpeiro' to the *'pequeno minerador'*, literally 'the small mining business'. The idea was to encourage more prosperous garimpeiros to register themselves formally as small mining companies, and thus bring them under the wing of the legislation governing the formal mining sector. But if garimpeiros are defined as manual placer miners working individually, the idea of even the most prosperous of them becoming a small company is ludicrous. And in any case, the mechanisation of garimpagem that had been developing since the Estado Novo meant that 'the small mining business' already existed – there is no better description of a garimpo entrepreneur. Only somebody with nothing more concrete to go on than a knowledge of the Código could believe otherwise.

Another of the functions of PEGB was to delimit areas of garimpagem. The idea behind this was to lessen conflicts by physically separating mining companies and garimpagem through the creation of 'garimpeiro reserves', away from areas covered by prospecting and mining licences held by companies. From 1979 on there was a stream of ministerial and presidential decrees creating small 'areas reserved for garimpagem' throughout Amazonia. From the point of view of the government, they only made the situation worse. While they clarified the legal situation of garimpos in the areas covered by the 'reserves', they did not, predictably, prevent garimpeiros from entering all the areas outside the reserves which were meant to be the preserve of the mining companies. Once again it had mistakenly been assumed that de facto and de jure occupation in Amazonia were the same.

But it was the intervention in Serra Pelada, and the successful campaign to keep it a garimpo, which dramatised how comprehensively the military regime had managed to paint itself into a corner. IBRAM rightly lamented that the Curió bill which Figueiredo signed into law was unconstitutional – the CVRD, a *public* company, had a prospecting licence for the area – and Serra Pelada made it very clear to mineral companies that they could no longer count on the Brazilian government to apply the advantages they enjoyed over garimpagem in mining law. However, it would be a mistake to think that what happened at Serra Pelada was entirely due to the lobbying power of the new social and economic interests involved in garimpagem. Since 1979 another important factor had been at work, compelling the military regime to find a way around its own laws. In a cruel twist of fate, events forced a re-evaluation of technocratic antipathies to the point where, to the horror of the formal mining sector, a policy of direct state stimulation of garimpagem had to be considered.

The rise in world gold prices and the upsurge of garimpagem in Amazonia was not the only significant event in Brazil in 1979. It was also the year that saw the beginning of the worst economic crisis in Brazilian history. Structural weaknesses aggravated by the increasing burden of debt repayment plunged the Brazilian economy into an unprecedentedly deep recession marked by rapidly rising inflation and unemployment and a fiscal crisis which continues to the present day. From the salad days of the 'economic miracle' of the late 1960s and early 1970s, the military regime found itself presiding over an economy that was effectively bankrupt. Suddenly, the need to increase revenue became an overriding consideration for the government. And so, reluctantly swallowing its instincts, it was forced to ponder the possibilities afforded by the rapid increase in gold production in Amazonian garimpos, which since 1979 have accounted for somewhere around 90 per cent of Brazil's annual gold production.

For a regime in deep economic trouble, the Amazon gold rush was a tempting opportunity. If it could buy the gold produced in garimpos, it would effectively be exchanging worthless cruzeiros for gold. Economists within the government were not slow to see the possibilities. Even before the intervention at Serra Pelada, the CEF was already playing a much more active role in the domestic gold buying market. CEF posts were set up in all the main areas of garimpagem, the strict bureaucratic requirements on selling gold to the CEF were waived and its prices were adjusted daily to take account of variations in the price of gold on the London Metal Exchange and fluctuations in the dollar–cruzeiro exchange rate. The CEF even hired helicopters to send gold buying teams to visit the more remote garimpos, and in places like Itaituba, where private gold buyers had long been established, the CEF began a price war, trying to keep its prices slightly higher than those of the Zé Arara chain.[16] It was even suggested, in a detailed proposal published in a government journal, that the state should subsidise the prices paid by the CEF to keep them around ten per cent higher than the prices offered by private gold buyers.[17] Direct price subsidies seem only to have been official CEF policy in the Tapajós, because more gold is extracted there by garimpeiros than anywhere else, but at a level just two or three per cent above the market price.

At the same time influential voices within the formal mining community were arguing forcefully for an approximation between state and garimpo, partly on humanitarian grounds and partly because it was widely recognised that if the government really did want to increase gold production, it would have to deal with garimpeiros rather than with the few small gold mining companies who only produced a small fraction of gold output. Lyrio, for example, argued in a 1981 DOCEGEO report that 'the only way for the government to achieve its stated target of fifty tons of gold a year by 1985 is through direct help to garimpeiros, in the form of medical assistance and basic foodstuffs at subsidised prices'.[18] Clearly the expansion of state gold buying via the CEF and the provision of basic facilities in Serra Pelada and Cumarú did not sit easily either with the government's own legislation, which made garimpagem as it existed by 1979 unambiguously illegal, or its instinctive bias against non-capitalist forms of production.

The unease surfaced during a conference held in 1983 in Brasília by the Ministry of Mines and Energy about gold production in Brazil and government policy. The DNPM and PEGB published a joint document which gave a very clear exposition of the economic motives underlying the need for an increasing state involvement with garimpagem, but which also demonstrated how uncomfortable the state mineral bodies felt about the reception its policies were likely to receive in the formal mining sector:

> The potential which gold production has and could have in the relief of the current difficult social and economic climate is becoming widely recognised. We therefore recommend that measures should be taken to produce, in the short term, a substantial increase in gold production. . .with a target of annual production of fifty tons of gold from garimpos by 1985. . .which would involve an increase of at least 50,000 in the number of garimpeiros. . .Despite the fact that a very significant proportion of the increase in gold production over the past four years has come from garimpos, we should nevertheless stress that garimpagem should not be thought an ideal method of mineral extraction, because it is incapable of maintaining a steady and predictable level of production. On the other hand, it should also be remembered that garimpo production involves a lessening of the social tensions that arise from the increase in unemployment, because of its labour intensive nature. And it should not be forgotten that a very large proportion of the people involved in garimpagem come from regions continually afflicted by drought, such as certain areas of the Northeast.[19]

Summarising the position in the 1980s, the inescapable conclusion is that since the Estado Novo one cannot really talk of a consistent state policy towards garimpagem. Since 1967 the various state bodies involved in the mining sector have said different things at different times, or even different things at the same time, depending which echelon of the agencies is examined. State action has often borne little relation either to professed motives or to mining law. Since 1979 in particular, the pattern of events has been one of a sporadic and inconsistent state response that reacted to facts rather than attempted to shape them. Although certain elements in the state's response to the gold rush were effective, such as the expansion of the CEF's gold buying role and the initial stages of the intervention in Serra Pelada, taken on the whole government policy fell between two stools. Anxious not to antagonise the formal mining sector, with hostility towards garimpagem entrenched at the upper levels of the state bodies, and a legislative framework that hampered rather than helped, it was never likely that a full-blooded programme of stimulation of garimpagem by a subsidised gold price and large scale technical and social assistance would be implemented. On the other hand, driven by economic necessity and political imperatives, the state did set up limited programmes of research and technical help, did buy a great deal of gold, and did take certain areas under direct control when matters threatened to get out of hand. As ever, falling between two stools meant getting the worst of both worlds. After Serra Pelada the government definitively lost the confidence and trust of the formal mining sector. Yet it failed to compensate by winning the confidence and trust of garimpeiros. Having initially won them over in Serra Pelada, it then moved to close the garimpo down. In the majority of garimpos not under federal control or regularly visited by state personnel, the absence of even the most basic social facilities – especially medical – is deeply resented and has led to a feeling that the state, while prepared to buy the gold, is quite happy to neglect those who produce it.

One result of the palpable disarray has been a general recognition that something has to be done with the Código de Mineração. Since 1985 a commission of lawyers, politicians, and mining experts has been working under the aegis of the Ministry of Mines and Energy to produce a new Código, which will become law before the decade is out. The situation it now has to regulate in Amazonia is chaotic, especially from the point of view of the formal mining sector. It is morosely summarised by Lestra and Nardi, in a section of their book aimed at those who might be thinking of investing in Amazonian mining:

> What one sees at the moment is an almost complete absence of ground rules. Each situation is analysed separately, the solutions differ according to the demands of the moment, the prejudices of the technicians who study the problem, the number of garimpeiros, and the capacity for lobbying or direct physical mobilisation of the garimpeiros or the mineral companies concerned.[20]

Nevertheless, by the mid 1980s the Brazilian government was finally coming to recognise that garimpagem was important. It had been driven into doing so by a disparate bundle of motives – desperate financial need, political opportunism, the relief of social tension – and was burdened with a body of legislation about garimpagem that was misconceived from the start and finally became unworkable. It would, perhaps, have been unrealistic to expect even a minimally consistent state policy towards garimpagem to emerge from such a tangled mess of motives and objectives.

At this point, having sketched out this anarchic backdrop, we must look a little more closely at the relationship between garimpagem and the formal mining sector, which these days occupies so much of the foreground of the Amazonian stage.

GARIMPAGEM AND FORMAL SECTOR MINING

Capitalist mining began in Brazil in the 1820s in Minas Gerais. It did not grow organically: it was financed for the most part by British capital, and was implanted by German and British mining engineers.[21] The nineteenth century saw many attempts by mineral companies to mine gold in Amazonia, but almost all were very short lived. A high proportion were rather dubious operations, aimed not so much at gold extraction as at making a killing on European or North American stock exchanges by floating stock after priming a gullible market with exaggerated rumours of rich gold deposits in the region.[22] Then, as now, people could be enticed into believing almost anything about Amazonia, especially if it concerned mineral riches and remote jungles: the social psychology of investment in Amazonia has remained remarkably constant since the seventeenth century. The genuine gold operations had to contend with very high costs, a rudimentary transport network, and, not infrequently, with the hostility of local Brazilian interests resentful of foreign incursions. The history of capitalist gold mining in nineteenth century Maranhão described in Chapter 2 is similar in its essential details to the history of gold mining in nineteenth-century Mato Grosso, Bahia and Minas Gerais, the other states where gold mining companies operated during the last century.

The nineteenth century and the first decades of the twentieth century did nevertheless see several episodes which serve as a reminder that conflict between garimpagem and mineral companies in Amazonia is not a recent phenomenon. In Maranhão there were the disputes around Montes Aureos described in Chapter 2, and an invasion of a French mining company's site on Ilha do Inglês on the western coast in 1910.[23] Since 1885 there were periodic disputes between garimpeiros and mining companies in Amapá and French Guiana (where garimpeiros are known as *orpailleurs*) and there were conflicts over the rights to alluvial sites in Mato Grosso during the 1880s. But the growth in the frequency and intensity of clashes between mineral companies and garimpeiros during the modern period is historically unprecedented. From a patchwork of isolated disputes between gold mining companies and garimpeiros the struggle has become more generalised, as mining companies, both public and private, have had to grapple since 1979 with a resurgent garimpagem capable of damaging the interests of the formal mining sector as a whole.

To understand the relationship between garimpagem and mineral companies, a little background information on how the formal mining sector has developed and evolved in Amazonia is necessary. Mining in Amazonia received a great boost with the construction of the highway network, the fiscal incentives for investment in Amazonia set up by the military regime in the 1960s, and the expansion in geological mapping of the region since the 1950s. Mineral production, notably of iron, bauxite, cassiterite, manganese, nickel and gold, is now an important part of the economy of all the Amazonian states and Pará has become the leading mineral exporter in all Brazil. The formal mining sector itself has three elements: multinational companies, private Brazilian companies, and the wholly or partly publicly owned mining concerns, most importantly the CVRD. Although multinational penetration of Amazonia was a source of a great deal of polemic during the 1970s both inside and outside Brazil, that decade did see the start of a process of substitution of foreign capital by Brazilian investment which has gathered pace in the 1980s. It was symbolised by the sale of Jarí, an enormous estate on the north bank of the Amazon, by the American magnate Daniel Ludwig to a consortium of Brazilian companies, but its most important expression has been the establishment of the CVRD as Amazonia's leading mineral company in terms of volume of production, scale of operations and number of people employed.

This has meant that conflict between garimpeiros and mineral companies has largely been a domestic Brazilian affair. The 1970s were a difficult decade for mining multinationals in Amazonia. Recession and the high costs of mining in the region led to the withdrawal of some and the formation of partnerships with Brazilian companies by others. The 1970s also saw public companies, with the CVRD in the forefront, become very much more important in Amazonian mining than ever before. Although private mineral companies operating in Amazonia far outnumber public ones, even the largest (Andrade Gutierrez or Paranapanema, for example) cannot compete with the CVRD. Serra Pelada, the most important episode in relations between garimpagem and the formal mining sector in recent times, did not directly involve any private mining companies, although it did of course have extremely important consequences for them. Taking Amazonia as a whole, when one looks at relations between the formal mining sector and garimpagem the most important companies involved are public rather than private: the CVRD, DOCEGEO and the CPRM.

The many conflicts between mining companies and garimpeiros in Amazonia since the 1960s can be rooted squarely in the 1967 mineral legislation. The inadequacy of the law in relation to garimpagem is half of the problem: the other contributory factor is the legislation governing the granting of prospecting licences, *alvarás de pesquisa*, to mining companies. An alvará is very simple to obtain: a mining company requests a prospecting licence for a given area from the DNPM, supported merely by a plan of research saying what minerals are being sought, proof that the company in question is legally registered, and the paying of a fee to the Ministry of Mines and Energy.[24] The licence is initially granted for three years, but may be extended indefinitely at the discretion of the DNPM upon production of reports of research.[25] This smoothing of the path towards the granting of prospecting licences was clearly intended as a stimulus to mining in Amazonia and is part of the explanation for the expansion of mineral extraction there since the 1960s. Many of the alvarás granted were speculative: given that alvarás were so easy to obtain, and could be renewed with no fixed time limit merely on the basis of a skilfully written report – the mining companies knew very well that the underfunded DNPM was incapable of more than token verification – it clearly made sense to get hold of as many alvarás as possible and then sit on them, carrying out geological surveys at leisure, or even waiting for garimpeiros to find something and then expelling them on the grounds that they were trespassing on company land.

In other words, the legislation governing prospecting licences ensured that there would be perennial clashes between de facto occupation by garimpeiros and de jure occupation by mining companies. Theoretically it allowed mining companies to expel even long established garimpeiros from areas which had not been declared 'garimpeiro reserves' – precisely what happened in Rondônia in 1970 for example – and had the added advantage of not compelling the mining companies to do very much once the garimpeiros had been expelled. Garimpeiros, in the same way as smallholders, were made subject to a legal regime, of which they invariably had no knowledge, that systematically discriminated against them. Legally, their position was even worse than that of smallholders, who at least had the legal principle of *uti possidetis* conceded in the land laws, even though they rarely had the money or the necessary legal knowledge to register a land claim.

When one adds to this legislative tinder the sparks of the increasing technological sophistication of garimpagem, the rise in the price of gold, and the presence of hundreds of thousands of people to whom the opportunity of working or investing in garimpagem came as a godsend, the resulting conflagration is not difficult to imagine.

Rondônia in 1970 was the first large scale conflict; others followed between mining companies and cassiterite garimpeiros in Roraima in 1975, between gold garimpeiros and small mining companies in Nova Planeta, Novo Mundo and Alta Floresta in Mato Grosso from 1979 on, between gold garimpeiros and the CVRD in Serra das Andorinhas in Carajas in 1979, Serra Pelada in 1980 and Cumarú in 1981. These major flare-ups took place against a background of literally hundreds of other conflicts of greater or lesser intensity between garimpeiros and mining companies in all areas affected by the gold rush. Since 1979 the disputes have usually involved garimpeiros of gold: before 1979 they often involved cassiterite garimpeiros. Accusations and counter-accusations have flowed thick and fast, with each side accusing the other of being parasitic: mining companies have been denounced for sitting on alvarás and only asserting their claims after garimpeiros make strikes within 'their' areas, and have responded by saying that garimpeiros follow their prospecting teams and invade when they discover something. These are the two most common types of dispute, and many cases of both have occurred.

A new element since 1979 has been the appearance of organised 'invasion' by garimpeiros. A classic example of this type of conflict occurred in Roraima in 1985, in the Serra dos Surucucús. It was complicated by the fact that the Serra dos Surucucús, in the extreme north of Roraima on the border with Venezuela, is home for around 20 000 Yanomami Indians who have periodically been in conflict with cassiterite garimpeiros since the early 1970s.[26] The federal police, under pressure from FUNAI, expelled the garimpeiros in 1976. In 1984 a presidential decree gave mining companies the right to prospect in Indian lands, and several firms immediately put in applications for alverás. To forestall them, José Altino Machado, a regional garimpo entrepreneur based in Boa Vista, flew in dozens of garimpeiros through an old airstrip using his own planes in February 1985, hoping to present both FUNAI and the mining companies with a fait accompli. A furious FUNAI alerted the federal police and the garimpeiros were once again expelled. Had the attempted invasion not been on Indian lands it might well have succeeded.

In keeping with the chaotic state of mineral legislation and the lack of any consistent government policy on the regulation of garimpagem, no coherent pattern has yet emerged in the way these conflicts have been resolved. The outcome in each case has depended on the particular balance of forces involved; either lobbying capacity, or, depressingly frequently, armed force. Public companies have the option of calling in the federal police, while private companies might be able through political connections to mobilise the local military police in their favour: failing that they may hire private security firms or simply go out and hire gunmen – the distinction between the two is often blurred in Amazonia. Although mining companies do not always lose in a confrontation with garimpeiros – Nova Planeta in Mato Grosso being an example of a garimpo a mining company managed to close down for example – they are on the whole at a disadvantage, especially if one compares the current situation with the early 1970s. Unless a company can put a sufficient number of people into the field at a very early stage, the sheer scale of garimpagem in contemporary Amazonia means that they can become formidably well entrenched in a very short time. Many garimpeiros go armed as a matter of course, and they are quite capable of beating off an attempt to dislodge them. If a company does attempt violent expulsion, some form of state intervention may well follow. There is no longer any guarantee that state intervention will end up advancing the company's interests: local and regional political imperatives often prove more compelling for the government, as Serra Pelada demonstrated.

Since Serra Pelada signs of demoralisation have been appearing in the formal mining sector. In IBRAM's annual report for 1985, which described an audience with Aureliano Chaves, recently installed Minister for Mines and Energy in the new civilian government, there is the plaintive sentence, 'Reflecting the worries and preoccupations of our associated companies, IBRAM presented a document stressing the following recommendations; respect for the law and the re-establishment of a climate for investment in the Sector. . .'[27] This headed a list of eight policy recommendations, and showed that the fight against garimpagem had become a priority for IBRAM. With the 1985 transition to a more centrist civilian regime, it is now difficult to see how a mining company, public or private, could win a large scale dispute with garimpeiros: the political costs for the federal government would be too great.

Nevertheless, the formal mining sector has not reacted passively to the challenge posed by garimpagem. Since 1979 IBRAM, to which all the most important members of the formal mining sector are affiliated, has mounted a sustained attack on garimpagem in the technical mining press in Brazil, and lobbied intensively in Brasília and elsewhere against garimpagem and for the full application of the 1967 Código.

Garimpagem was attacked on three fronts; it was accused of being technologically inefficient, illegal, and exploitative. Perhaps because there certainly is an air of professional disdain for 'low technology' in geological circles in Brazil, most effort was expended on downgrading the technical capacity of garimpagem. In two extremely harsh technical critiques garimpagem was lambasted for technological crudity, a very inefficient rate of recovery of minerals, and for causing long term damage to deposits.[28] Much of this criticism was examined in Chapter 1: here, it need only be said that the effectiveness of the criticisms of recovery rates and 'rudimentary' technology were undermined by voices within the formal mining sector pointing out that the low cost and portability of garimpo technology made it very suitable for use in Amazonia,[29] and that rates of recovery after *repassagem* were actually quite respectable.[30]

However, the argument that garimpo technology made it very much more difficult for a mining company to work a deposit after garimpeiros had attacked it was rather more convincing. It was put in these terms by a DNPM geologist:

> The problem is that the garimpeiro specialises in getting out patches of rich material which are relatively near the surface. If you like, he takes the *filé mignon* and leaves the rest behind. Take Serra Pelada. All the rich accumulations of gold near the surface have gone. Now, even if the CVRD gets the deposit, the costs of working it will be higher because of the greater depths, and there is the further handicap that no mapping was made of where rich material occurred, which means it will be impossible for the CVRD to follow up anomalies.

This point of view is universally held – even garimpeiros concede it in conversation – but the fact that there is a convincing case for garimpagem making it technically more difficult for mineral companies to mine deposits is ultimately neither here nor there, given the social and political realities that now circumscribe the mineral debate in Brazil. In a sense the formal mining sector did not need to argue that garimpagem was technologically crude or inefficient: this was taken for granted by a majority of working geologists already, was absolutely believed at the top of the DNPM and the Ministry of Mines and Energy, and was universally accepted by politicians. The problem was that by the 1980s the debate had passed the point where technical arguments could make any impact: the arguments defending garimpagem were political in nature, and the government was acting out of expediency. Even if the technical arguments had been unanswerable, it would not have mattered.

The intrusion of social and political realities into the debates on mining policy marginalised IBRAM's arguments that garimpagem was illegal and exploitative in the same way.[31] The same seems to have been the case with the attempts of the formal mining sector to influence government policy more directly. IBRAM did not welcome the attempts to separate garimpos from mining companies by the creation of 'garimpeiro reserves', feeling that such a policy implicitly undermined the favouring of the mineral company over the garimpeiro enshrined in the 1967 Código:

> As for the delimitation of areas destined for the garimpo, through which the government is proposing to attend to the more obviously social and political aspects of the problem, the position of IBRAM is that this demarcation should be carried out with absolute respect for mineral rights conceded to mineral companies by the DNPM under the terms of the Código which regulates mining activities under law.[32]

Recently, the formal sector has been attempting to defend itself by influencing the reformulation of the Código de Mineração. In 1985 Aureliano Chaves created a commission, on which IBRAM representatives sit, to produce a draft Código for him to revise and send to Congress for ratification. In this forum IBRAM maintained, uniquely amongst all the actors involved in the redrawing of the legal definitions that have proved so unworkable, that the current legal definition of garimpagem was adequate.

What is the position of IBRAM on the ministerial committee about the articles relevant to garimpagem?

We in IBRAM continue to think that the definitions of garimpagem are good and do not obstruct the state policies which I mentioned [the creation of garimpo reserves]. But we are worried that the Código being revised at the moment will try to legislate the administration of social facts which are now in the process of emerging. We think that we should not lose sight of the fact that the Código should be as permanent a document as possible. It has to be concerned with constructing the basic principles for the development of mining in this country, complementing political action to deal with these emerging social facts.

The problem is that a prerequisite of such political action is a change in the legal definition of garimpagem to take account of current realities.

Relations between the formal mining sector and garimpagem have since 1979 sunk to a historically low point, yet the association representing formal mining interests in Brazil persists in believing that the 1967 Código should still structure the relationship it has with garimpagem. It is certainly true that it is unlikely to get another Código more favourable to its interests. Yet if the experience of the last decade in Amazonia means anything, it is that changes have to be made in the relationship between garimpagem and formal mining, and one of those changes must be a more realistic legal framework that will redress the systematic discrimination against garimpagem in the 1967 Código, by reformulating the legal definition of garimpagem so that it bears some relation to reality, by making prior discovery and working of a deposit the main criteria for determining who should have the right to work it, and by reforming the process of granting *alvarás de pesquisa* to ensure they are not used to speculate with the subsoil.

9 The Implications of the Gold Rush

The social and economic consequences that flow from the establishment of garimpagem in a particular region reverberate far beyond the garimpos themselves, but as good a place as any to begin is with the effect the gold rush has on a local economy when it touches an area. Many commentators have noted that garimpagem stimulates local economies, but the richly diverse range of stimuli has neither been described nor fully appreciated. Take the Gurupí in western Maranhão as an example.

It is a relatively small goldfield and easier to get to than most: buses from Belém or São Luís run along the BR-316 highway which bisects the region. To travel to the garimpos, one simply leaves the crowded buses at any one of a series of roadside towns between the settlements of Zé Doca and Gurupí: Santa Teresa, Puruá, Santa Helena, Maracassumé. Wherever one chooses to get off, several garimpeiros will leave the bus at the same time and head for one or other of a series of roadside bars, dormitories, eating houses and hotels. There they rest and prepare for the journey ahead. They stroll through the town, dropping in on gold buyers to talk about price movements, and catch up on the latest news and gossip on rádio peão. Some will be old hands who have made the journey dozens of times: they may be dropping in on a mechanic to see how repairs on a moínho are going, or catching a bus to the cities of Castanhal or Bacabal to buy new machinery from a licensed dealer. Other garimpeiros huddle with traders and shopkeepers, settling accounts, collecting sacks of rice and manioc flour, or trying to wheedle further credit. Some take the chance to have a checkup at a small and very basic clinic; others prefer to have the local chemist inject them with a 'vitamin cocktail', a concoction of vitamins made up at roughly a dollar a time 'to guard against disease'.

Some will be there for the first time, perhaps some smallholders travelling down from a village on the coast, or a group of young shop assistants and bank clerks from Santa Luzia, nervously keeping together. Shops stay open until late, displays heaped with all one needs for a stay in the garimpos: food, cooking utensils, medicines, radios and tape recorders, chemicals, showy watches, kerosene, tapes of *sertanejo* music, the Brazilian equivalent of country and western, butane gas cylinders, clothes. There is a brisk trade in diesel oil and petrol, with tankers from Belém and São Luís rumbling through several times a day. Tucked away discreetly behind a row of cashew and mango trees on the other side of the highway are a few large buildings with tile roofs which serve as both hotels and brothels.

There is a choice of ways to make the next stage of the journey. Those who have the money and want to go to one of the larger garimpos like Serrinha and Chega Tudo can get off at Maracassumé or Santa Helena and take a *teco-teco*, a small plane operated by one of the several air taxi firms. The less well off (and those whose research grants do not stretch to an airfare) take one of the several pick-up trucks and lorries that leave every couple of hours to the village of Geraldo, twenty kilometres inland along a good quality dirt road. The road comes to an end on the banks of the Maracassumé river, and each truck or lorry is immediately surrounded by children clamouring to carry luggage for a pittance, while canoes come out from the village on the other side of the river to ferry people across for a small fee. The village offers many of the same facilities as the roadside towns, but on a smaller scale: the bars and brothels are seedier, the shops have a smaller range of goods, the gold buyers do not have enough cash on hand to buy more than a few dozen grams of gold at a time. Even during the rainy season, when the tracks leading to the garimpos turn into quagmires, there is a constant flow of garimpeiros leaving and entering, with mule drivers loading up sacks of rice and jerrycans of diesel oil for their clients in the garimpos. Cantineiros periodically arrive to pick up consignments of goods from suppliers in the village and ferry them inland.

To get to the garimpos themselves, one either walks or hires a mule. To Cerqueiro it is eighteen kilometres, four or five hours of leisurely travel during the dry season when the going is good, at least twice that during the rains, much of it spent wading through mud which in its worst patches comes up to the chest. At a couple of points along the trail enterprising smallholders have set up stalls where weary travellers can buy soft drinks, fruit and manioc pancakes. Arriving at the garimpo hammocks are strung in huts that were built for a fee by local smallholders. A meal might be served by a woman from Geraldo working as a cook, using locally supplied charcoal to fire an oven – pork from a pig slaughtered and sold that morning by a smallholder, or armadillo hawked by a hunter, together with luxuries like tomatoes and okra grown specifically to sell in the garimpo by another small-holder. Perhaps a couple of young women are staying in a neighbouring hut: they move from garimpo to garimpo cooking and selling sexual services and are called *garimpeiras*. In the larger garimpos in the Gurupí women may come from as far afield as Belém or São Luís: in garimpos where the entry of women is prohibited, like Serra Pelada between 1980 and 1985, boys and transvestites supply the demand. Also spending the night might be a travelling photographer, who moves through garimpos taking portraits and developing them on the spot with bottles of chemicals he carries in a rucksack, or a gold buyer moving on to Montes Aureos in the morning.

In all garimpos there is a considerable floating population of non-garimpeiros supplying goods and services: cooks, male and female prostitutes, mechanics, mule drivers, gold buyers, police troopers, traders, pilots, doctors and dentists, entertainers, photographers and others. Before the gold rush arrived in the Gurupí in 1982 the level of economic activity was much lower and the local and regional economy nothing like as diverse as it has become under the galvanising influence of garimpagem. The gold mined and sold is only part of the economic system: its production depends on a local infrastructure which creates demands that a great number of people, living both locally and further afield, can turn to their advantage. This is as true for local smallholders as it is for small and large capitalists in the urban centres.

Before 1982 the Gurupí's economy was based mainly on smallholder agriculture and some hunting and fishing. The expansion of garimpagem has not meant that these activities were curtailed: on the contrary, it has stimulated them by providing a voracious local market for food-stuffs. By 1985 garimpeiros and non-garimpeiros, agriculture and gold extraction, stood in a relationship that was clearly symbiotic. Garimpeiros needed goods and services which non-garimpeiros could supply, and smallholders also had the additional option of working in the garimpo as their other commitments allowed, the flexibility of garimpo work regimes meaning that the two could easily be combined.

Moving further up the economic scale, the economic consequences of the growth of garimpagem ripple outwards. Large traders moved to the area, attracted by the increasing flow of garimpeiros, and based themselves in the towns along the BR-316. They in turn extended credit and supplies to smaller traders in villages like Geraldo or directly to cantineiros in garimpos. Fuel for machinery is shipped into the area by tanker lorries, and machinery itself arrives in the larger urban centres, sold by licensed dealers and representatives of the manufacturers in São Paulo and Rio Grande do Sul, where moínhos, pumps and motors are freighted north as soon as they come off the production lines. Some of the gold produced in the area was bought by the CEF at its post in Maracassumé, and must have ended up in bars in Fort Knox and Geneva. More found its way to countries like Uruguay, via São Paulo, and from there entered the international gold market.

But perhaps the most significant fact about the growth of garimpagem in the Gurupí, contrary to popular stereotype, was that the arrival of the gold rush marked a reduction in the level of violent conflict in the region. This is not to say that the gold rush was entirely pacific, of course: it was seen in the dispute between Luisão and Zé how gold mining can be an important strand in political conflicts that can easily slide into violent confrontations. But when one compares them with the vicious land conflicts which raged in the Gurupí during the 1970s, the gold years of the 1980s have been much more peaceful. It could be argued that this was because the smallholders had successfully beaten off the pressures on their land before the gold rush began there in 1982. But if they have beaten off the ranchers and speculators – and as the *guerrinha* showed, the enemies of the smallholders have neither gone away nor accepted defeat – the surge in garimpagem goes a long way towards explaining how they were able to do it. The gold rush strengthened them economically, by providing them with a market for foodstuffs, services, labour, and even the application of modest amounts of capital. Unlike ranching garimpagem uses little land and its growth in an area does not mean the automatic expulsion of small-holders. In the Gurupí, as elsewhere, it integrated them into a local economy that combined agriculture and extractivism, historically the classic pattern of development in the interior of the Amazon.

Furthermore, as the lands coveted by ranchers and landgrabbers became dotted with garimpos, it became ever more unlikely that they could be physically appropriated. If expelling scattered and lightly armed smallholders was difficult, expelling heavily armed garimpeiros who lived in large clumps hardly bore thinking about. The gold rush can stimulate land speculation in certain contexts, as we shall see shortly. But it is more common for garimpagem to constrain it by deterring potential land speculators from moving in. If smallholders happen to be struggling for control of an area, a gold discovery on the land in question will usually work in their favour, by attracting large numbers of people who will be equally hostile to the idea of appro-priation of the land by large capital, since garimpeiros stand to lose as much as smallholders if access to the land is restricted.

It might be argued that the Gurupí is not a typical area of garimpagem.

It is, for example, very different from the Tapajós, where the small-holder population is much smaller and more thinly spread. Yet the basic argument that the growth of garimpagem galvanises and diversifies local and regional economies holds good everywhere. The main difference between the Gurupí and other goldfields is that the Gurupí is smaller than most, and the changes in the regional economy have if anything been less intense than elsewhere. This is very obvious if the Gurupí is compared to Cumarú and Serra Pelada in southern Pará.

The difference in scale is plain in the city of Marabá, and to a lesser extent in Imperatriz, geographically in Maranhão but very much a part of the social and economic matrix of southern Pará. Marabá, along with Itaituba in the Tapajós, is the clearest example in Amazonia of a city that has been transformed by the gold rush. Catering for the tens of thousands of garimpeiros who use Marabá as a base or jumping off point has become central to the economy of the city. The volume of trading in gold, machinery, foodstuffs, fuel and other supplies dwarfs the Gurupí; it is big business, attracting entrepreneurs from all over Brazil.

The city itself is obviously booming. At the bus station and airport the movement of traffic is very heavy, and entire districts of the city have turned themselves over to catering for the gold rush trade. The number of flophouses and cheap hotels and bars, clustered especially thickly around the bus station, the luxury houses of the *bamburrados*, the scores of machine repair shops, the dealers displaying moínhos and high capacity motors, the taxis clogging the streets, the high level of male and female prostitution, the air taxi companies and road haulage firms, the trading posts and shops stuffed with supplies, the politicians chasing the garimpeiro vote – all testify to the way the gold rush has become central to the life of the city. There are a considerable number of state employees, bureaucrats and technicians, brought to the city by the gold rush and the federal intervention in Serra Pelada. They range from the police and army to CEF managers, DOCEGEO staff, DNPM technicians and geologists and CVRD personnel. In many areas the increasing involvement of the Brazilian state with garimpagem has meant that it now has more people on the ground and a more direct involvement with local affairs in Amazonia than was the case before 1979. The same is true, although on a lesser scale, for other towns and cities throughout Amazonia: Itaituba, Imperatriz, Santarém, Porto Velho, Alta Floresta, Redenção, Xinguará and Boa Vista, to name but a few.

Marabá is also a very good example of the way garimpagem changed the relationship between the various components of the extractive economy in Amazonia. As Chapter 7 explained, Marabá came into being because of the Brazil nut trade and is still one of the most important centres of the Brazil nut economy. Yet the relationship between garimpagem and castanha has changed completely. Although the two co-existed long before 1979, castanha was always by far the senior partner: it was the demands of the Brazil nut trade which did most to dictate the flow of population into the area and shape the social and political hierarchies of the region. Now the boot is very much on the other foot. The growth of first Serra Pelada and then Cumarú has meant that the Brazil nut industry has not been able to retain workers since the gold rush began, and the donos dos castanhais have permanently lost their economic and political hegemony in the region. Only the rubber industry, with *seringueiros* concentrated in Acre where garimpo activity has so far been minimal, has as yet been largely unaffected by the gold rush.

Finally, what of the garimpeiros themselves – what have the consequences been for the hundreds of thousands of people who are or have been participating directly in the gold rush?

The most obvious effect has been to reinforce the position of the two social groups who have suffered most in the development of Amazonia since 1964, rural smallholders and those at the bottom end of the urban economy. For them, the rise of garimpagem has been an unalloyed benefit. They may go to and return from garimpos whenever they please. They can easily combine garimpagem with other activities, and while the daily wage may not be large, the fact that food and accommodation is thrown in as well means that most of the money earned can be saved. It is one of the few reliable sources of income available to colonos and the urban poor, perhaps making the difference between continuing as a smallholder or being forced to move to the cities, or between getting by and going hungry in the favelas. And for some there is the chance to become a full time garimpeiro with real possibilities of upward mobility.

But it is not only the poor who have benefited. In order to understand the sheer scale of the Amazon gold rush, it is important to realise that the rise in the price of gold and the fact that there was a mass of underemployed people in Amazonia ready and willing to work in garimpos were not the only factors at work. Garimpagem also became an attractive alternative for entrepreneurs in the formal economy. It was not just a case of taking advantage of the new demands for goods and services, although many entrepreneurs did rush into activities like trade in foodstuffs, air transport, gold buying and road haulage. Direct investment in garimpos was equally important, but to see why one needs to understand the economic environment in Amazonia in the late 1970s and early 1980s. During this period Brazil's inflation rate climbed steadily until it had reached a monthly level of between fifteen and twenty percent in 1985, threatening to make Brazil a hyperinflationary economy like Argentina in the early 1980s and Bolivia in the late 1980s. This led, amongst other things, to an economic climate that rewarded speculation rather than investment. For small and medium entrepreneurs, without large amounts of capital, things became difficult. To many of them, garimpagem presented itself as an alternative kind of investment. Given the highly unstable economic climate, getting involved with the gold rush, with the possibility of large short term profits, was seen as less of a risk than it would have been had the gold rush begun in the early 1970s, for example.

A good example of the kind of entrepreneur who now began to invest in garimpagem is Francisco, a businessman in São Luís. Together with his brother he owns a small engineering firm and machine repair shop. In 1983 he decided to invest in the garimpo of Cachoeira, on the BR-316 highway just over the state border in Pará. He bought a moínho, a motor, and fuel and food to last several months, and contracted a work crew of garimpeiros. He himself was unable to spend more than the occasional weekend in Cachoeira, as his business commitments in São Luís occupied most of his time, and as often happens in the case of absentee external entrepreneurs he was swindled by the garimpeiros he contracted and within a year had lost all he had invested. Nevertheless, he had no regrets, and his explanation of the motives that drove him to invest in the gold rush, despite the risk, was revealing:

> The current economic climate in the country is extremely difficult for the entrepreneur. At times your capital works against you. Let me explain this better. If I stopped working today and realised all my assets, I'd have a considerable amount of capital which I could use to speculate in the financial markets. It wouldn't be producing anything, but it would give me a high rate of return. Today, to maintain my activities, I have costs. The government taxes me, inflation is a terrible problem, and I have to work extremely hard just to stay in the same place. In a way, the fact that I have capital works

against me, then. So I see this alternative, garimpagem, as something akin to a lottery. You might think it strange for an entrepreneur to be interested in lotteries, but when normal business activity itself becomes a lottery, perhaps you can understand why. . .

I spent a lot of money, but in compensation there was the possibility that I could get a large profit in the short term. I was always aware of the fact that I was playing in the dark, that it was basically a lottery, but I always thought, well, it might come off. Today I feel frustrated that it didn't, but I don't regret losing the investment that I made, because I knew that this was a likely outcome, that it either works out or it doesn't. I'm not angry about losing the money. I knew that losing money was one of the characteristics of this type of activity. I played and lost, but at least I went to see what it was like. . .

And I wasn't the only person among the business class in São Luís to take this attitude. I know three people from my immediate circle of acquaintances who have interests in Serra Pelada, and two others in Serrinha. Then there's Ferreira, the holder of the Coca Cola franchise, who has machinery in Cerqueiro. There's another who owns a telecommunications company, but he lost his money and pulled out as I did. I know a university professor who invested in Cachoeira, a car dealer, a supermarket owner, and a big chicken farmer. Many capitalists like them, like me, have become involved with garimpagem over the last few years.

Across Amazonia – and in some cases beyond it – entrepreneurs of all kinds are investing in garimpagem. Some of them are urban capitalists, some are from long established elite groups based on ranching, rubber and Brazil nuts, others are internal and regional entrepreneurs generated by the gold rush itself. As a result, an entrepreneurial elite based on gold garimpagem has come into being in many parts of Amazonia. In places like Marabá it has displaced older elites and achieved political dominance at the same time as the gold rush has transformed the regional economy. This is a recent development and there is little detailed work on elites in Amazonia, but the crystallisation of an elite based on gold garimpagem is very obvious in cities like Marabá and Itaituba, and also important in smaller centres like Redenção and Boa Vista. The existence of this elite has already had important consequences.

In the first place, it tends to precipitate conflicts with other elite groups. The picture here is rather complicated: it is not always a simple case of a new elite based on gold challenging and displacing an older one based on ranching, Brazil nuts or rubber. Miller has described the formation of an elite based on garimpagem in Itaituba, but showed that many garimpo entrepreneurs had a wide portfolio of economic interests, and could also have been classified as members of other elite groups.[1] It often makes little sense to draw a hard and fast distinction on the ground between elites based on garimpagem and other elite groups; in Marabá, for example, many entrepreneurs have interests in both Serra Pelada and the Brazil nut trade. Yet despite the complications and exceptions which must always attend the analysis of things political in Brazil, the recent political history of Marabá can only be seen as the displacement of a Brazil nut elite by a garimpagem elite, symbolised by the eclipse of the Mutran family and the rise of Curió. Things were much less neat on the ground than this simple explanation suggests, of course. *Donos dos castanhais* became involved in garimpagem as well, and it could be argued that the castanha oligarchy was doomed anyway – it could not have maintained its grip on power for very long, in the face of the transformations sparked off by the highway construction programme, Carajás, and the increasing federal presence in the Araguaia–Tocantins – and it just happened to be garimpagem that gave the final push to an elite already in terminal decline. Yet the fact remains that garimpagem and garimpeiros became the primary consideration in local politics in Marabá, and garimpagem has had a significant impact on elite composition and political preoccupations in cities and towns like Imperatriz, Santarém, Boa Vista, Porto Velho and Redenção, to name but a few. These are the largest urban centres in Amazonia, excluding Belém and Manaus, and the rise of the political and economic profile of garimpagem in these towns and cities is an important new development for the whole of the region.

It has, for example, put representatives into state and federal legislatures who were elected by garimpeiro votes, and who, if they want to be re-elected, must press for the construction of roads and provision of facilities which garimpeiros in their power base need. It also helps to be seen defending garimpagem itself against attacks from the state and the formal mining sector. Garimpeiros have never before had any kind of political representation: neither the federal authorities nor the mining companies have ever before had to deal with an organised 'garimpeiro lobby'. It should be stressed that these politicians with close links to garimpagem can be of considerable importance in regional and national politics: one thinks of how Curió became for a while the dominant political figure in southern Pará, for example, or how José Altino Machado threatens to become a major political force in Roraima. It means that in future state mining operations like the CVRD and DOCEGEO are likely to come under increasing political pressure to cede mineral concessions to garimpeiros, and in particular it poses questions about how long a civilian regime will be able to maintain the exclusion zone around the Carajás projects, especially given the further decline of Serra Pelada and the inevitable garimpeiro incursions into the Carajás area.

Another consequence of the gold rush has been an increase in the amount of venture capital available in Amazonia for both investment and speculation. The money generated by the mining and selling of such large amounts of gold has been spent in a variety of ways. Some is conspicuously consumed, some is invested in the 'ancillary sector' of garimpagem, like air transport and gold buying, some is invested in the formal economy, and some has been applied in what is rapidly becoming a traditional area for venture capital in Amazonia – land speculation.

Take the case of Marlon. Marlon was one of the first to bamburrar in Serra Pelada, and although the exact value of the bamburro is impossible to establish it certainly made him into a dollar millionaire. He used part of the money to buy large tracts of land in the Araguaia–Tocantins, violently expelling any smallholders who happened to be on them. He was almost certainly responsible for the massacre of eleven smallholders near Marabá in 1985, but his wealth allowed him to bribe his way out of trouble. He set up a couple of small cattle ranches, but most of the land he bought was deliberately kept empty, waiting for an opportune moment to sell. Nevertheless, Marlon's career was in some ways atypical. For garimpagem to feed into land speculation in any significant way, two preconditions have to be filled. Firstly, the amount of gold involved has to be large. Stealing land may not be difficult in certain circumstances, but it is difficult to do on the cheap: bribes have to be paid, gunmen hired, forgers contracted, and political sweeteners distributed, on top of the expenses of ensuring that smallholders do not return. In addition, the land has to be either free of smallholders, or occupied by smallholders not sufficiently well-organised to defend themselves effectively. There are only a few areas of Amazonia where these conditions apply, the vicinity of Marabá, long since dominated by large capital and land speculators, being one of them. It is a cause for concern that another area where these conditions do not yet obtain, but may well in the near future, is

Roraima in northern Amazonia, until the 1980s relatively untroubled by land conflicts.

Nevertheless, the fact remains that in contemporary Amazonia the gold rush has had important social benefits. This may seem surprising, given the hostile way in which mining companies and the Brazilian state invariably characterise garimpagem, the popular stereotype within Brazil of the garimpeiro as a violent and greedy marginal, and the way that both in Brazil and the international media the Amazon gold rush is portrayed as exploitative and socially degrading, the last resort of the poor and desperate trapped in 'jungle hellholes'.[2] These perspectives fail to take into account the important role the gold rush plays in the lives of many of the Amazonian poor. Far from being enslaved in garimpos, they work under labour regimes which are extremely flexible and give what in Brazilian terms is an extraordinary amount of autonomy and freedom of action – an autonomy which is central to the social organisation of garimpagem and the social identity of many garimpeiros, as we have seen. If garimpagem is seen as oppressive and exploitative, how do we account for the mass mobilisations of garimpeiros in defence of their right to work, in Serra Pelada and elsewhere? What other activity can the poor in Amazonia enter and leave as they choose, save most of the money they earn, and have reasonable chances of upward mobility if they decide to stay in it full-time? Given the fact that the recession in Brazil since the late 1970s has hit the poor in relatively less developed parts of the country like Amazonia particularly hard, the way the gold rush has galvanised and diversified regional economies throughout Amazonia since 1979 ought perhaps to be better appreciated.

Not all the consequences have been beneficial, of course. The fillip garimpagem has given to land speculation in certain areas has already been mentioned, and the next section of this chapter will deal with the effects of the gold rush on the Amazonian environment and Indian groups, which have been mixed to say the least. Nevertheless, hundreds of thousands of people living in the Brazilian Amazon would have been worse off if the gold rush had never happened. The level of rural-urban migration would have been higher, extractivist industries which have genuinely oppressive work regimes, like the Brazil nut industry, would have continued unchanged, and the level of misery amongst the urban poor would have been higher. Last, but not least, there would have been a much smaller Amazonian entrepreneurial elite to stand as some kind of counterbalance to the dominance within Amazonia of business elites from southern Brazil, who favour national over regional markets and interests, with consistently disastrous results for the people of Amazonia.

Finally, consider the nature of garimpagem as a social and economic system as it has developed since 1979. It is above all an informal economic system. State regulation and control is tenuous outside a few limited areas. Paper contracts, the legal regulation of business transactions – all these are foreign to the garimpo. The mass of the workforce is temporary: there is no external regulation of labour contracting or work conditions. There is no way the system can be thought of as capitalist, although it has become increasingly capitalised in recent years. Although it has thrown up a few entrepreneurs who operate on a scale similar to that of large companies in the formal economy, it is basically a system that is built around the small and medium operator. It uses cheap, simple and portable technology that is well adapted to Amazonian conditions. The value of the gold it produced annually by the late 1980s was well above a billion dollars, and in addition it supported a diverse mass of activities in its 'ancillary sector'.

In other words, gold garimpagem in Brazil is an informal sector activity, but in terms of the amount of capital it generates and the number of people it involves, it can stand comparison with major industries in the formal economy. Although in terms of social organisation it stands outside the formal economy, the relationship between the two is symbiotic. Much of the machinery used in garimpagem is manufactured industrially, and the gold rush has stimulated demand in various sectors of the formal economy. Many entrepreneurs in the formal economy invest in garimpagem as well. Capital generated by garimpagem ends up in the formal economy, and vice-versa.

In fact the one big loser in the gold rush has been the formal mining sector. Their mineral concessions are invaded, even very powerful companies like the CVRD have been forced to back down in confrontations with garimpeiros, and their lobbying power is now under challenge within the very political institutions which had given them such direct support in the halcyon days of the military regime. The most obvious victims of the gold rush are not 'men who swarm in purgatorial torment, laden like beasts and dying like them, a desperate and gold-crazed multitude', but large mining companies like the Companhia do Vale do Rio Doce and Rio Tinto Zinc.

INDIANS AND THE ENVIRONMENT

There is little detailed research available to assess the impact the gold rush has had on Amazonian Indian groups, and even less on the Amazonian environment: the latter in particular urgently requires the attention of researchers versed in the work practices of garimpos. The possible biological dangers of contact between garimpeiros and previously uncontacted Indian groups are well known, and in the past garimpeiros, in their frequently played role as the advance scouts of Brazilian society moving into the interior, have been responsible, albeit unwittingly, for the infection of Indian groups with diseases against which they had no resistance. But once the biological traumas of initial contact passed, several Indian groups were drawn into stable and longlasting relationships with garimpagem and garimpeiros. The Amarakaeri of the Madre de Dios in Peru have worked as garimpeiros off and on since at least the 1930s,[3] and the Mundurucú of the Tapajós have worked in garimpos for part of the year since the 1950s.[4] The intrusion of a gold rush into an indigenous economy represents a change, but it is not automatically a threat to its integrity. Gray's verdict on the relationship between the gold economy and the Amarakaeri, for example, was that:

> Contrary to what might be expected, the gold economy itself is not destructive to Amarakaeri society. The people are organised according to models and principles with which they have run their economy from time immemorial, and the added financial gains which gold provides the communities are a change but not a threat.[5]

Similarly, Burkhatter describes a long and comfortably established tradition of Mundurucú migration to garimpos around Jacareacanga in the Tapajós, where they work as diaristas, and also comes to the conclusion that the gold rush in no way represents a threat to Mundurucú cultural integrity. The way that the Kayapó have so far successfully come to an accommodation with the Cumarú garimpos was referred to in Chapter 7, and a 'Disappearing World' documentary film showed a graphic image of how gold rush money can actually work to reinforce cultural identity: video cameras bought and operated by the Kayapó being used to record dances and chants for posterity. Nevertheless, whenever the gold rush comes into contact with Indian groups there are potential dangers, and the Kayapó would be the first to say that the relationship between Indians and garimpagem can be problematic. These considerations are particularly relevant to the Yanomami, a large group of around 20 000 Indians living in Roraima and southern Venezuela, whose relationship with garimpeiros is currently in the process of being defined. The first potential problem is environmental degradation. Garimpos themselves do not take up large amounts of land as a rule, but the environmental consequences that flow from the establishment of a garimpo stretch far beyond the actual physical space it occupies. Garimpeiros do not need to occupy Indian lands to pollute water sources upon which Indian groups downstream depend for part of their food base with mercury and sewage, as happened in the case of the Rio Fresco that runs by the Kayapó settlement of Gorotire. But, most importantly, the growth of garimpagem in an area may set off a chain of social and economic pressures that could conceivably end with Indian groups being deprived of their land, especially as so many indigenous 'reserves' have still not been officially demarcated. There are some worrying signs that something along these lines might happen to the Yanomami.

It is not individual garimpeiros who are responsible for this. Most garimpeiros, especially those with an urban background, tend to be frightened of Indians. They think of Indians in terms of lurid and racist stereotypes, which may be unfortunate on one level but which has at least had the consequence of making garimpeiros believe that Indians are masters of silent jungle warfare who respond ferociously to encroachments on their land. The Kayapó for one have been very adept at manipulating these stereotypes for their own purposes, famously intimidating many times their number of garimpeiros in 1985, for example, with a parade of four hundred warriors in full regalia through the garimpo of Maria Bonita. Ordinary garimpeiros are thus very wary about entering Indian territory.

However, such inhibitions are not felt to the same degree in the urban centres and state capitals away from the garimpos. Politicians on the make seize on 'the opening up of the garimpos' as a votewinning populist cause, entrepreneurs begin to think about what could be done with the area if the Indians were removed from their lands, and mutterings begin about the unfairness of letting 'so few' Indians have control of so much land 'which they don't use'. This is exactly what has been happening in Boa Vista in Roraima since the early 1980s. Under the direction of politically ambitious entrepreneurs, most notably José Altino Machado, a coordinated campaign for the opening up of Yanomami lands has developed. This has already involved one organised invasion of the Serra dos Sururucús (see Chapter 7) and has pitted strong political and commercial interests in Boa Vista against the Yanomami, FUNAI and the federal police. The outcome is still in doubt and conflicts seem likely to continue for the foreseeable future.

The environmental consequences of the gold rush are also worrying. The most obvious environmental problem is the use of mercury, but there are others. Garimpos do not as a rule take up large amounts of land, and compared to activities like smallholder slash and burn farming, logging and ranching, the gold rush's contribution to the deforestation of Amazonia is insignificant. But where an area of forest immediately surrounds a garimpo, it is at some risk from gold mining through the run-off of silt and overburden, which chokes roots and undergrowth. Once-crystalline rivers turn brown as a result of the activity of garimpeiros upstream, threatening fish stocks and thus the food base of many riverine communities. Garimpos were advanced as the cause for the sudden appearance of large shoals of dead fish in Mato Grosso and Pará in 1985 and 1986, and although no proven link with the gold rush has yet been established, it seems by far the most likely culprit. The fact that some garimpos in Mato Grosso drain into the Pantanal, the enormous swamplands that are home to one of the world's most impressive collections of bird, animal and reptile species, is thus rather worrying.

But it is above all the massive and almost completely unregulated use of mercury in the Amazon gold rush that gives cause for concern. Garimpagem can only be described as profligate in its use of mercury, and this has direct implications both for garimpeiros and the environment they inhabit. Although it is possible to use all the technology deployed in garimpos without mercury, to do so without losing the greater part of gold extracted demands experience and skill, especially when working with fine grained gold. While work practices at Serra Pelada were under the control of the DNPM, mercury was prohibited and the DNPM technicians mounted an education drive, explaining the dangers to garimpeiros and making an effort to provide technical help and advice for garimpagem without mercury. But this was not extended to other areas of garimpagem, and it is still difficult to come across garimpeiros who do not use mercury from choice: in five months in the Gurupí, for example, only one such garimpeiro was discovered, and he was regarded as an eccentric by his peers. The use of mercury was regarded as so important to the running of a successful operation that several times during fieldwork donos were seen to stop work if they ran out, only resuming when they had managed to buy or borrow more. When pressed they agreed that garimpagem without mercury was theoretically possible, but argued it would result in a sharp drop in recovery rates and therefore mean a lot more work, since material would have to be passed through machinery several times more often to compensate. Even DNPM technicians concede this point, and are universally pessimistic about the chances of convincing garimpeiros to go over to mercury-free garimpagem.

Although most garimpeiros are aware that mercury is dangerous, they do not know quite how toxic it is, nor the possible consequences of releasing it into ecosystems – fish caught in rivers and streams near areas of intensive mercury use is eaten without a second thought – nor the health implications of the long term accumulation of mercury in human tissue. But there are worries in garimpos about the effects of mercury. Some garimpeiros believe long term exposure leads to sexual impotence, and in 1988 the wife of a cantineiro told me she believed a deformed stillbirth she suffered that year after a series of trouble-free pregnancies was due to the fact that she lived in a house where regular burning of mercury amalgam took place.

Quantifying how much mercury is escaping into the environment is as difficult as estimating the number of garimpeiros or the amount of gold produced by them. Almost all gold in garimpos passes through a stage where it is amalgamated with an equal volume of mercury, as explained in Chapter 1. If, as informed opinion within the DNPM suggests, garimpos in the late 1980s are producing something over a hundred metric tons of gold annually in the Brazilian Amazon, an equivalent amount escaped into the atmosphere in the form of vapour as it was burnt off. Mercury is almost always burnt off without the use of facemasks, and some is inevitably inhaled. Even worse, the gas cylinders used to power the torches which do the burning are often connected the rest of the time to gas rings used for cooking. As a result, not only is the mercury often burnt off where garimpeiros live, but in the very area used for the preparation of food.

But not all mercury used in garimpos ends up amalgamated with gold. Before it comes into contact with gold, it is placed in a box at the top of the caixa, behind riffles, and may also be added to bateias during despescagem. In the normal course of operations, some will escape. Spillages are usually minor, since mercury costs money and the margins most donos operate on are narrow enough to ensure they take some care over its use: also, if mercury is escaping, donos know that gold is also being lost. Nevertheless, the cumulative effects of mercury spillages could be serious, especially around garimpos which have been in continuous production since the late 1950s, like some parts of the Tapajós. Higher levels of mercury pollution are also to be expected in and around garimpos where gold production is high. When expectations are high, or when gold production in a barranco has leapt upward, donos raise the amount of mercury they use to correspond to the expected level of gold. This can mean that over a kilo of mercury is put in the box at the top of the caixa and spread behind riffles, and this makes spillages more likely.

There has been concern for some time about the environmental consequences of such elevated levels of mercury use in garimpos, but only in the late 1980s has serious work begun to establish the levels of mercury contamination in garimpos and amongst garimpeiros themselves. The DNPM has carried out small scale surveys based on blood and hair samples taken from garimpeiros in the Tapajós, but has not released the results. In looking at the levels of mercury in the environment, the DNPM is handicapped by a lack of expertise in environmental toxicology, and there is as yet no co-ordinated programme of testing in different areas of garimpagem. The early results of what testing has been carried out are disquieting; one study carried out three months after the end of the raft mining season on the river Madeira found levels of mercury several times over WHO safety limits in commonly consumed fish species, including sardines.[6]

One fact worth bearing in mind in the testing of levels of mercury is that different types of garimpeiro have differing levels of exposure to it. In the normal course of operations, workers handle mercury much less than donos. It tends to be the dono who puts mercury into machinery, the dono who checks it every now and then, the dono who adds it to the bateia during despescagem and then pans with it, and the dono who burns the mercury off at the end of the process. The only type of garimpeiro likely to have more intensive contact with mercury is a cantineiro, who will routinely burn off mercury several times a day from gold that is brought in to sell by garimpeiros: the gold is invariably burnt on the counter of the cantina, next to the precision scales. Any study of body levels of mercury ought to treat cantineiros separately from donos, who in turn should be distinguished from workers. In addition, different types of garimpo should be examined. It would be interesting to know the levels of mercury contamination around fofocas, as opposed to mature garimpos, for example, or to compare the levels of mercury contamination associated with manual techniques, moínhos, chupadeiras and balsas.

Until a co-ordinated and large scale programme of research is carried out in enough different areas of garimpagem, it is frustratingly difficult to assess the extent of what could be a serious environmental problem. In March 1989 President José Sarney, in response to widespread international concern about environmental destruction in the Amazon, issued a proclamation formally banning the use of mercury in garimpos. In the absence of a crackdown on the buying and selling of mercury this was purely a cosmetic gesture, but it would be misguided to think repression of the mercury trade would make much difference. The likely result would be to make mercury use clandestine rather than eradicate it. With overstretched DNPM and police forces, together with thousands of garimpos and hundreds of thousands of garimpeiros scattered across enormous and often inaccessible areas, the logistical problems involved in enforcing such a ban would be horrendous. Whatever measures are taken, it seems inevitable that large amounts of mercury will continue to be deposited in Amazonian ecosystems – and the bodies of garimpeiros – for some time to come.

CONCLUSION: LOOKING TO THE FUTURE

Extractive booms are nothing new in Amazonia. The pattern has been remarkably constant since the seventeenth century; the historical record appears as a sequence of boom periods only matched in their intensity by the depths of the recessions that followed. Why should the current Amazon gold rush, which began very recently if we keep a sense of historical perspective, be any different? A few decades from now, might it not seem a repeat of the rubber boom, one of those periods of feverish activity which punctuate Amazonian history every so often, only to ebb away almost without trace?

  The first point is that while this traditional view of Amazonian history as a series of extractive booms and busts does have some basis in fact, it should not be taken too far. Extractivism in Amazonia, whether of rubber, gold, Brazil nuts or anything else, does not actually disappear after a boom: it becomes part of the economic and social fabric of the region. When people talk of 'the end of the rubber boom', for example, it does not mean that rubber tappers disappeared from the Amazonian scene: they merely became less prominent as the scale of activity declined. Tappers and the rubber trade still play important roles in parts of northern and western Amazonia, especially in Acre; Brazil nuts are still gathered in the Araguaia–Tocantins. The same is true of garimpagem. Questions like 'is garimpagem here to stay?' are misconceived, as neither garimpagem nor garimpeiros have ever been away.

A thread running through this book has been that gold garimpagem did not just suddenly appear on the scene in the late 1970s: it has been entrenched in Amazonia for centuries, and its present form cannot be fully appreciated without some sense of these historical roots. Some of the technology used in modern garimpos was also used by *mocambeiros* when Brazil still had an Emperor, some was used in California in 1849, some is less than a decade old. The one thing that is certain about the future of garimpagem is that it will 'last' in one form or another.

Its immediate prospects can rarely have been healthier. Its technology has been refined over the past decade, and its capacity is greater than ever before. Shortage of labour will never be a problem, given the level of poverty and underemployment in both urban and rural Amazonia, and, indeed, in the rest of Brazil. Nor, unless there are some radical changes in the economic climate, will it suffer from a shortage of investment. In fact, as inflation climbs to unprecedented levels as the 1980s draw to a close, the gold rush is likely to become an increasingly attractive option to investors from the formal economy. It seems inconceivable at present that world gold prices could fall to the point where garimpagem would be uneconomic. The continuing improvement in communications in Amazonia will open up new vistas to it. And whatever happens in the future, the gold rush has already had permanent consequences in parts of Amazonia.

Miller, for example, came to the following conclusion about Itaituba, the city at the centre of the Tapajós goldfield, after talking of the fragility of previous extractive booms:

> There are some indications that the current boom may be somewhat different. The intrusion of national social and economic institutions into the area has been unprecedented. Certainly, if gold proves harder to find, there will be some degree of retrenchment, but the bureaucrats, the successful small farmers, the landowners and the merchants who serve them will probably remain.[7]

As this quote implies, one cannot really talk of the gold rush in isolation. In every area of gold extraction, garimpagem has set off a chain of economic, social and political reactions. Places like Itaituba and Marabá will become cities permanently marked by the gold rush, just as Belém and Manaus were permanently marked by the rubber boom. The real question to answer is not whether the gold rush will last, or whether it will have any long term consequences, but how it is likely to develop in the future.

We have seen how the gold rush has not been without social costs, but also not without important social benefits. As a social and economic system it has many virtues: flexibility, accessibility, well adapted technology, low costs, a long tradition, opportunities for advancement, and a strongly held ethic of autonomy and freedom of action, to name merely the most important.

These tend to be glossed over in the stereotypes of garimpagem, and the garimpeiro, that dominate coverage of the Amazon gold rush in the Brazilian and especially the international media. Gold miners are portrayed either as violent outlaws or as trapped victims, and these crude distortions have too often contaminated debates about the Amazon. They are neither, and to hundreds of thousands of garimpeiros the Amazon gold rush is not so much a problem as part of a solution. This may pose difficulties, but it is a fact.

Postscript

When I submitted the thesis on which this book is largely based in 1987, I felt compelled to make a statement about the conditions under which it had been written. Two years later the conditions under which much research in British universities is carried out have not changed and I see hardship – real material hardship, not mere mental suffering – becoming the norm for too many friends and colleagues doing postgraduate research. I see no reason to alter the words I wrote then and reproduce them here without apology, merely regretting that they do not adequately express the strength of my feelings.

When I began postgraduate work, in October 1983, the Economic and Social Research Council, rightly in my view, made it plain that it expected doctoral theses to be submitted within four years. With the submission of this thesis in September 1987 I fill my part of that social contract with the state. However, having set four years as the mark, my ESRC grant ran out after three years in October 1986, when I was in the middle of writing up. As a result, in the year since then I have worked variously as a barman, cashier, secretary and word processor operator. All of this work was casual, lowly paid and time-consuming, but without it I could not have made ends meet. Writing a thesis can be a strain at the best of times: writing a thesis while constantly worrying about money and having to spend so much time on casual work imposed physical and mental stresses which at times I found almost intolerable.

I think it quite wrong for a state body to say that four years is the acceptable limit for completion of a doctoral thesis and then end funding after only three years. The reason many theses take so long to complete is that researchers are forced to devote a significant proportion of their time and energy to earning the money which allows them to continue writing. I feel deep bitterness and anger that I was expected to write decently under these conditions. I feel especially bitter that this hardship was suffered in a rich industrial country with a government constantly proclaiming its commitment to education.

DAVID CLEARY
1989

231

Appendix

ITEMISED BUDGETS FOR THREE OPERATIONS

All prices are approximate, converted into US dollars from cruzeiros at rate of exchange for months expenditure made, after correcting for inflation. Cost of machinery used not included. Value of gold production calculated using gold price for month operation ended.

Barranco 1   Mechanised Dono- Cerqueiro

Operation began	January 1985
Operation ended	June 1985
Number of workers	6 (all diaristas)
Machinery used	moínho, 2 motors, pump.

Expenditure

Labour 1,050
Food... 385
Fuel 987
Flails for moínho 125
Tools (spades, pickaxes, crowbars, mallets,
    sledgehammers, sacks, bateias)... 166
Paid to muledriver in Geraldo.. 120
TOTAL **3,008**
Gold production ....351 grams
Value of gold production .... 3,062 dollars
All production to dono
PROFIT .... **54 dollars**

Barranco 2   Mechanised Dono- Cerqueiro

Operation began	January 1985
Operation ended	June 1985
Number of workers	6 (all diaristas)
Machinery used	2 moínhos, 3 motors, pump

Expenditure

Labour 1,050
Food 500
Fuel 1,750
Mercury..27.50
Mule driver.. 100
Flails for moínho 40

Tools 24
TOTAL **3,502.50**
Gold production .... 1,681 grams
Value of gold production...14,700 dollars
All production to dono
PROFIT ....**11,197.50 dollars**

Barranco 3   Mechanised Dono- Cerqueiro

Operations began	August 1985
Operation ended	December 1985
Number of workers	5 porcentistas + 2 diaristas taken on for 5 days each in October
Machinery used	moínho, 2 motors, pump, chupadeira (rebaixamento only)

Expenditure

Labour 25% of gold production
  + 7.50 paid to diaristas
Food 327
Fuel 216
Mule driver..87
Flails for moínho 15
Tools 14
Plastic sheeting 11
TOTAL **677.50**
Gold production ....133 grams
Value of production .... 1,330 dollars
Gold production divided: 25% to porcentistas, 5% to owner of barranco, 70% to dono.
PROFIT **263.50**

Notes

Variation in cost of flails extreme. Barranco 1 was hard rock, which wears flails out almost daily, while Barrancos 2 and 3 were alluvial. This also explains the higher outlay on tools in Barranco 1.

  The low fuel costs in Barranco 3 were a consequence of the mining strategy employed. The moínho was not used until the final part of the operation, when accumulated material was put through in one concentrated bout – this reduces wear and tear on machinery as well as fuel costs.

Notes and References

1 An Introduction to the Amazon Gold Rush

1. Anuário Mineral, MME–DNPM, 1987.
2. Figures from Guimarães *et al*, 1982. It should also be remembered that garimpagem in Brazil is not restricted to gold. It accounts for 70 per cent of Brazilian diamond production, 30 per cent of cassiterite production, the raw material of tin, half of columbite and tantalite production and all Brazilian mica. Detailed discussions of the level of gold production in garimpos are Lyrio, 1982 and MME–DNPM, 1983.
3. *Isto É*, 23 March 1987: Corrida ao Ouro.
4. DNPM–PEGB–CPRM, 1980c–1983c.
5. FAG, 1970, 1971, 1974.
6. DNPM, 1980, p. 1.
7. Guimarães *et al*, 1982.
8. See for example Paiva, 1935; Souza, 1935a, 1935b, 1942; Löfgren, 1936; Paiva, Souza and Abreu 1937 and Gomes, 1942.
9. For Guyana see Baird, 1982. There are photographs of the long tom in use during the Californian and Australian gold rushes that show it is identical to the contemporary Amazonian lontona. See Lavender, 1969, pp. 288–9 for California and Watkins, 1971 for Australia.
10. From the verb *sacudir*, to shake.
11. For example in Paiva, Souza and Abreu, 1937.
12. Garimpeiros are quite aware of this failing, but will still use cobras on fine-grained gold if they have no alternative. It is not done out of ignorance, as often assumed by the formal mining sector, but necessity.
13. Guimarães, 1936.
14. See for example Paiva, Souza and Abreu 1937; Calógeras, 1938; Souza, 1942; Gomes, 1942.
15. Phrase from MME–DNPM, 1983, Introduction. It was written by the then Director of the DNPM, Yvan de Carvalho.
16. MME–DNPM, 1984, p. 20.
17. Da Silva, 1982, pp. 86–7.
18. CPRM–Riofinex Ltd, 1975, p. 74.
19. MME–DNPM, 1983, pp. 63–6.
20. Guimarães *et al*, 1982, pp. 7–9.
21. Da Silva, 1982, p. 8.
22. A few writers from the formal mining sector recognise this: See for example Salomão, 1980 and Dall'Agnol, 1981.

2 Garimpagem in Maranhão

1. For example Gayozo, 1818; Marquês, 1970; Ferreira, 1885; Lisboa, 1935 and Paiva, Souza and Abreu, 1937.

2. Gayozo, 1818, pp. 108–9.
3. For example Boxer, 1962; Sweet, 1974.
4. Marquês, 1970, p. 367 (my emphasis).
5. Marquês, 1970, p. 620.
6. Ferreira, 1885, p. 67.
7. *O Publicador Maranhense*, no. 1502, 21 February 1854.
8. *O Estandarte*, 6 October 1853.
9. An extensive search in the Arquivo Público in São Luis failed to locate the report, though it is possible that it lies buried somewhere in a mass of unclassified nineteenth-century documents. The police reports from the districts of Santa Helena and Turiaçú, which more than any other source should contain information about the quilombos, begin in 1809 and were examined to 1870. Unfortunately, those reports not eaten by termites were written in ink on both sides of thin paper. Over time the ink has soaked through, rendering them illegible.
10. See Paiva, Souza and Abreu, 1937, pp. 7–10 for a fuller account of the Companhia Maranhense de Mineração.
11. Paiva, Souza and Abreu, 1937, p. 9.
12. Governo do Estado do Maranhão, 1870, pp. 198–207.
13. Governo do Estado do Maranhão, 1870, p. 206.
14. Literally, 'Saint Benedict from Heaven', a fascinating name for a quilombo to have. São Benedito is a black saint still widely revered in Maranhão, which has a large black population.
15. Viveiros, 1955, p. 3.
16. Dodt, 1981, p. 87.
17. Lisboa, 1935, p. 13.
18. Almeida, 1961, pp. 44–5.
19. The initial members of the DNPM team who in 1935 set up posts at Viseu, near the mouth of the Gurupí, and Pirocauá, were Glycon de Paiva, Henrique Capper Alves de Souza and Pedro Moura. Their work, and that of later DNPM scientists who came after them, is contained in: DNPM, 1935; Paiva, 1935; Souza 1935a, 1935b, 1936, 1937; Gomes, 1942 and the classic *Ouro e Bauxita na Guiana Maranhense* (Paiva, Souza and Abreu, 1937), the most detailed and valuable source on garimpagem during the period. The debt subsequent researchers of the region owe to them makes it fitting that their names and publications be recorded here.
20. Paiva, Souza and Abreu 1937: 14.
21. Souza, 1935b, pp. 2–3.
22. Paiva, Souza and Abreu, 1937, passim.
23. Gomes, 1942, p. 5.
24. For example Ferreira, 1885; Paiva, Souza and Abreu, 1937; Almeida, 1961.
25. Almeida, 1961, p. 76.
26. SUDEMA, 1971a, 1971b.
27. Lestra and Nardi, 1984, p. 29. Badin has since been overwhelmed by the influx of garimpeiros.
28. Lestra and Nardi, 1984, p. 30.

3 Fofoca: The Formation of Garimpos

1. MME–DNPM, 1984, p. 53–4.
2. They can be thought of as variants of what Schmink, talking of the appropriation of land in Amazonia by large capital before and after the arrival of migrant settlers, has called 'closed frontiers' (Schmink, 1982).

4 The Social Structure of the Gold Rush

1. Respondents were asked for a full occupational history. As was to be expected, given the high rates of rural-urban migration in eastern Amazonia, many people began their occupational lives as smallholders and went on later to urban occupations like construction work. Thus the high figure for 'smallholder agriculture' in Tables 4.6 and 4.7 is not fully reflected in the urban/rural background estimates.
2. Although 'bankrupted' is the nearest equivalent in English to *blefado*, it does not come close to conveying the multiple connotations and force the word has for garimpeiros. To *blefar* is not merely to be in financial difficulties but also to be ground down both physically and spiritually. It combines the notions of physical weakness, financial hardship, mental exhaustion and despair.
3. Similar parasitic strategies have been noted in informal sector antimony mining in Bolivia. See Godoy, 1985, p. 155.
4. See for example Santos, 1981; Salomão and Machado, 1985; Guerreiro, 1984; Kotscho, 1984 and Andrade, 1983. All of these authors are influential opinion formers who together have done much to define the parameters of the debates about mineral policy and mining in Brazil. Santos was one of the discoverers of the Carajás deposits and now heads the important DOCEGEO residency in Belém. Salomão is a prominent geologist and the most acute analyst and critic of garimpagem in the formal mining sector. Machado is a regional entrepreneur in Roraima, northern Amazonia, and Kotscho a nationally famous journalist. Guerreiro, besides being a geologist, was a state deputy and, later, federal congressman for Pará. Andrade is also a federal deputy for Pará whose electoral base includes Cumarú, and has consistently involved himself with garimpeiro-related issues.
5. For example by Andrade, 1983, pp. 88–113.
6. It was presented to the annual conference of the SBPC (Sociedade Brasileira para a Proteção da Ciência) in Belém in 1983 although, frustratingly, it was never published. I could not locate it in the DOCEGEO archive in Belém. It is directly quoted, with the figures given above, in Salomão and Machado, 1985, pp. 11–13.
7. Salomão and Machado, 1985, p. 12.
8. Although this was rare and contrary to the popular image of the rubber boom. See Weinstein, 1984 for an excellent overview of labour relations in the rubber boom.
9. With the rare exceptions of closed fofocas and garimpos – see previous chapter.
10. Again, with the exception of closed fofocas and garimpos.

5 Economic Life in the Garimpo

1. There are more complicated systems. Schmink (1987a, 1987b) reported that in the garimpo of Cuca, near Serra Pelada, some differentiation in percentage shares has occurred as a result of increasing specialisation in chupadeira working methods. *Jateiros* and *maroqueiros*, those who operate the high pressure hoses and the chupadeira nozzle respectively, earn 7 or 8 per cent.
2. The rice prices that year were especially good because the Gurupí had survived the floods that destroyed the harvest in other parts of Maranhão.
3. Von Eschwege, 1944, vol. 1, p. 163n.

6 Social Relations in the Garimpo

1. *'No garimpo, a lei é do mais forte'.*
2. *'Isso aqui é o fim do mundo, garimpo é fim do mundo'.*
3. *Mutirão* is a difficult word to translate. It essentially means a collective effort. Specifically, in urban areas it often refers to a type of development where the state provides building materials and the community mobilises to build its own houses. In rural areas mutirão often refers to institutionalised mutual help. If there is a major job that needs doing, such as preparing a field for burning, friends and relatives are invited to help in return for food and drink during and after – and the promise of reciprocal help in the future.
4. An important minority of garimpos, notably raft garimpagem in the Tapajós and along the river Madeira in Rondônia, have workforces that are exclusively porcentista. The absence of diaristas would entail changes in the relationship between workers and between workers and dono. The exact nature of these changes could only be properly clarified by fieldwork in a garimpo of this type, which I did not undertake.
5. See for example Ackermann, 1972; Salomão, 1980 and Schmink, 1985, to name but a few.
6. Mayor.

7 Serra Pelada: The Gold Rush on the National Stage

1. Hart, 1898, p. 186.
2. Katzer, 1902, pp. 139–40.
3. Rego, 1933; Lofgren, 1936; Shearer and de Souza, 1944.
4. CPRM, 1971, p. 9.
5. DNPM–PEGB–CPRM, 1980a, p. 3.
6. These changes, the rationale that lay behind them and the reaction of the garimpeiros, are documented in fascinating detail in the *Relatórios de Viagem: Area Serra Pelada* (the reports written by DNPM geologists after their tours of duty in Serra Pelada) and in the annual reports on DNPM activities in Serra Pelada; DNPM–PEGB–CPRM, 1980a–1984a.

These basic sources for the history of Serra Pelada are deposited in the DNPM archive in Belém.

7. Two such incidents occurred between 25 September and 5 October 1981, for example, described by geologist Alberto Rogério da Silva in *Relatório de Viagem: Area Serra Pelada*, 24 September 1981–6 October 1981.

8. The worst single accident took place on 19 July 1983, when a landslide killed 19 garimpeiros. The DNPM geologists on duty in Serra Pelada at the time complained bitterly that the accident would never have happened were it not for the fact that pressures to close the garimpo led to garimpeiros ignoring DNPM prohibitions, and resulted in the postponement of earthmoving work which would have made the area safe. See the *Relatório de Viagem* for 7 July 1983–27 July 1983, 19 July 1983–28 July 1983 and 1 August 1983–17 August 1983.

9. Production figures from DNPM–PEGB–CPRM, 1984a.

10. DNPM, 1983, pp. 6–10.

11. A dono quoted in Kotscho, 1984, p. 57.

12. *Relatório de Viagem* for 25 January 1984–17 March 1984.

13. Phrase from Kotscho, 1984.

14. DNPM, 1980, p. 15.

15. DNPM, 1980, p. 26.

8 Garimpagem, Formal Mining and the State

1. Leverger, 1949, p. 289.

2. Decreto Lei cited verbatim in Martins, 1984, pp. 211–4.

3. Martins, 1984, p. 213.

4. The only exceptions were the garimpeiro co-operatives producing wolfamite, tantalite and sheelite in the Northeastern states of Paraiba and Rio Grande do Norte, which were registered with the state and organised according to the corporatist labour laws of the Estado Novo during this period. But these garimpos had already become stable mining villages by the 1930s, socially and technologically very distinct from Amazonian garimpos.

5. Statement reproduced verbatim in Rio newspaper *A Noite*, photocopy in DOCEGEO archive, Belém.

6. See Chapter 2 for an account of the work of the DNPM in Maranhão during the 1930s and 1940s, together with references.

7. Souza, 1942, pp. 44–5.

8. Guimarães, 1936.

9. MME–DNPM, 1984, p. 20.

10. MME–DNPM, 1984, p. 100.

11. MME–DNPM, 1984, p. 101. This power was invoked almost immediately. *Portaria* (directive) no. 494 prohibited garimpagem of gold along the border with Bolivia in 1968.

12. DNPM, 1980; MME–DNPM–PEGB, 1982; DNPM–PEGB, 1983; MME–DNPM, 1983.

13. DNPM, 1980, p. 1.

14. MME–DNPM, 1983, Introduction.
15. MME–DNPM, 1983, p. 6.
16. DNPM–PEGB–CPRM, 1980c–1983c.
17. Batista, 1981, p. 182.
18. Lyrio, 1981, p. 2. See also Sarmento, 1976 for an even earlier argument that Brasília should stimulate gold garimpagem.
19. DNPM–PEGB, 1983, pp. 1–3.
20. Lestra and Nardi, 1984, p. 351.
21. See Eakin, 1985 on this point. Much technological expertise was also British. The first deep shaft mines in Brazil were designed and largely built by Cornish tin miners and mining engineers – the legendary Gongo Soco gold mine in Minas Gerais being the most famous example. See Gardner, 1975, pp. 210–25.
22. Some such fly-by-night operations are described by Von Eschwege, 1944:v.1, pp. 78–82, in Minas Gerais, Filho, 1926, pp. 14–19, in Mato Grosso and Calógeras, 1938, pp. 25–63 in Bahia.
23. Paiva, Souza and Abreu, 1937, p. 15.
24. MME–DNPM, 1984, pp. 27–8, Articles 16 and 17.
25. MME–DNPM, 1984, p. 31, Article 22.
26. It was to Sururucús that many of the cassiterite garimpeiros expelled from Rondônia in 1970 retreated.
27. IBRAM, 1985, p. 3.
28. Willig, 1979; IBRAM, 1983.
29. Dall'Agnol, 1981.
30. Guimarães *et al*, 1982.
31. Thus arguments that the gold rush was exploitative came from both the left – for example Santos, 1981; Salomão, 1983; Guerreiro, 1984 – and the right – for example Willig, 1979; IBRAM, 1983 and Viana, 1984.
32. IBRAM, 1983, p. 37.

9 The Implications of the Gold Rush

1. Miller, 1979; 1985.
2. Phrase from 'In the Hellhole' cover story on Serra Pelada, *Sunday Times Magazine*, 17 May 1987.
3. Gray, 1986.
4. Burkhatter, 1982.
5. Gray, 1986, p. 39.
6. Martinelli *et al*, 1988.
7. Miller, 1985, p. 170.

Bibliography

F. Ackermann, 'O Ouro na Amazônia', DNPM (Belém: 1972)

R. Almeida, 'A Região Noroeste do Maranhão', *Revista da Geografia e História do Maranhão*, no. 6, pp. 31–82 (1961)

A. Andrade, *O Povo é a Maior de Todas as Autoridades*, Câmara dos Deputados – Centro de Documentação e Informação (Brasília, 1983)

W. Baird, *Guyana Gold: The Story of Wellesley A. Baird, Guyana's Greatest Miner* (Washington: Three Continents Press, 1982)

P. Batista, 'A Política de Preços para o Ouro', *Revista Brasileira de Mercado de Capitais*, v. 17, no. 20, pp. 175–84 (1981)

C. Boxer, *The Golden Age of Brazil 1695–1750* (Berkeley: University of California Press, 1962)

S. Burkhatter, 'Amazon Gold Rush: Markets and the Mundurucú Indians', unpublished Ph.D. thesis (New York: Columbia University, 1982).

P. Calógeras, *As Minas do Brasil e sua Legislação* (São Paulo: Companhia Editora Nacional, 1938)

CPRM, 'Projeto Marabá: Relatório Progressivo 1' (Belém: 1971)

CPRM–Riofinex Ltd. 'The Tapajós Project: Final Report' (CPRM Manaus: 1975)

W. Culver and C. Greaves (eds) *Miners and Mining in the Americas* (Manchester: Manchester University Press, 1985)

R. Dall'Agnol, 'Tecnologias de Exploração Mineral no Brasil', Núcleo de Altos Estudos Amazônicos, Universidade Federal do Pará (Belém: 1981)

DNPM, 'Notas Preliminares sobre o Comércio do Ouro no Pará e no Maranhão' (Rio de Janeiro: 1985)

DNPM, 'Garimpagem no Brasil' (Goiânia: 1980)

DNPM, 'Projeto Ouro Serra Pelada – 1983' (Belém: 1983)

DNPM–PEGB–CPRM, Relatórios de Viagem, Area Serra Pelada (Belém: 1980a–1984a)

DNPM–PEGB–CPRM, Area Serra Pelada: Relatórios Anuais (Belém: 1980b–1984b)

DNPM–PEGB–CPRM, Sub-Projeto Ouro de Tapajós: Relatórios Anuais (Belém 1980c–1983c)

DNPM–PEGB–CPRM, Area Cumarú: Relatórios Anuais (Belém: 1982d–1983d)

G. Dodt, 'Descrição dos rios Parnaíba e Gurupí em 1873' (São Paulo: Editora da Universidade de São Paulo, 1981)

M. Eakin, 'The Role of British Capital in the Development of Brazilian Gold Mining', in Culver and Greaves (ed.) op. cit., pp. 10–29

W. von Eschwege, *Pluto Brasiliensis* (2 vols) (São Paulo: Companhia Editora Nacional, 1944)

FAG, Relatórios do Exercício Ministério de Trabalho e Previdência Social (Brasília: 1970, 1971, 1974)

F. Ferreira, *Diccionário Geográphico das Minas do Brasil*, (Rio de Janeiro: Imprensa Nacional, 1885)

V. Filho, 'Subsídios para o Histórico da Mineração em Mato Grosso', *Revista do Instituto Histórico e Geográfico de Mato Grosso*, v. 15, pp. 3–25 (Cuiabá: 1926)

J. Gardner, *Viagem ao Interior do Brasil* (Belo Horizonte: Livraria Itatiaia Editora, 1975)

R. Gayozo, *Compêndio Histórico-Político dos Princípios da Lavoura no Maranhão* (Paris: P-N Rougeron Impressor, 1818)

R. Godoy, 'Entrepreneurial Risk Management in Peasant Mining: the Bolivian Experience', in Culver and Greaves (ed.) op. cit., pp. 136–161

E. Gomes, Ouro na Localidade de Guarimanzal, Município de Carutapera, Maranhão, DNPM (Rio de Janeiro: 1942)

Governo do Estado do Maranhão, *Colecção das Leis, Decretos e Resoluções da Província do Maranhão 1855–1870* (São Luís: Typografia Ferreira, 1870)

A. Gray, 'And After the Gold Rush? Human Rights and Self-Development Among the Amarakaeri of Southeastern Peru', International Working Group in Anthropology Doc. No. 55 (Copenhagen: 1986)

G. Guerreiro, 'Garimpagem de Ouro na Amazônia: Reflexos Econômicos, Sociais e Políticos' (1984), in Rocha (ed.) op. cit. pp. 87–106

D. Guimarães, 'Informações sobre Aparelhos e Dispositivos para a Extração de Ouro de Aluvião', DNPM, Avulso no. 1 (Rio de Janeiro: 1936)

G. Guimarães, L. Guimarães, and J. Brandão, 'Garimpos Brasileiros: Da História aos Fatos Atuais' in MME–DNPM 1982, PEGB – Palestras, Brasília.

C. Hart, 'O Rio Tocantins', *Boletim do Museu Paraense Emílio Goeldi*, v.2 pp. 181–91 (Belém: 1898)

J. Hemming (ed.) *Change in the Amazon Basin Vol. 2: The Frontier After a Decade of Colonisation* (Manchester: Manchester University Press, 1985)

IBRAM, 'Garimpo versus Empresa de Mineração', *Minérios: Extração e Processamento*, v. 6, no. 78, pp. 23–25

IBRAM, Relatório Anual (Brasília: 1985)

Katzer, F. 'Relatório Resumido sobre os Resultados Geológicos Práticos da Viagem de Exploração ao Rio Tapajós em novembro de 1897', *Boletim do Museu Paraense Emílio Goeldi*, v. 3, pp. 135–65 (Belém: 1902)

R. Kotscho, *Serra Pelada: Uma Ferida Aberta na Selva* (São Paulo: Editora Brasiliense, 1984)

D. Lavender, *The American West* (Harmondsworth: Penguin Books, 1969)

A. Lestra and J. Nardi, *O Ouro da Amazônia Oriental: O Mito e a Realidade* (Belém: Grafisa Editora, 1984)

A. Leverger, 'Apontamentos Cronológicos da Província da Mato Grosso', *Revista do Instituto Histórico e Geográphico Brasileiro*, v. 205, pp. 208–385 (Rio de Janeiro: 1949)

M. Lisboa, 'O Rio Gurupy e suas Minas de Ouro', Serviço de Fomento da Produção Mineral Boletim no. 7, DNPM (Rio de Janeiro: 1935)

A. Löfgren, 'Reconhecimento Geológico nos rios Tocantins e Araguaia', Ministério de Agricultura-Serviço Geológico e Mineralógico Boletim no. 80, DNPM (Rio de Janeiro: 1936)

J. Lyrio, 'Estimativas da Produção Brasileira de Ouro' DOCEGEO (Belém: 1981)

C. Marquês, *Dicionário Histórico-Geográfico da Província do Maranhão*

(São Luís: Governo do Estado do Maranhão, 1970 – commemorative reprinting of 1870 first edition)

A. Martins, 'Breve História dos Garimpos de Ouro no Brasil' (1984) in Rocha (ed.) op. cit. pp. 177–215

L. Martinelli, J. Ferreira, B. Forsberg and L. Victoria, 'Mercury Contamination in the Brazilian Amazon: A Gold Rush Consequence', *Ambio*, v. 17, no. 4, pp. 252–4 (1988)

MME, Ouro-Bases para uma Nova Política (Brasília: 1982)

MME–DNPM, *Projeto de Estudo dos Garimpos Brasileiros – Palestras e Trabalhos* (Brasília: 1982)

MME–DNPM, *Garimpos do Brasil* (Brasília: 1983)

MME–DNPM, *Anuário Mineral Brasileiro* (Brasília: 1983, 1987)

MME–DNPM, *Código de Mineração e Legislação Correlativa: Edição Revisada* (Brasília: 1984)

D. Miller, 'Transamazon Town: Transformation of a Brazilian Riverine Community', Ph.D. thesis, University of Florida-Gainesville (1979)

D. Miller, 'Replacement of Traditional Elites: An Amazon Case Study', in Hemming (ed.) op. cit., pp. 158–71 (1985)

G. Paiva, 'Trabalhos Efectuados sobre os Recursos Minerais da Região Gurupí-Turiaçú', DNPM (Rio de Janeiro: 1935)

G. Paiva, H. Souza and S. Abreu, 'Ouro e Bauxita na Guiana Maranhense', DNPM Boletim no. 13 (Rio de Janeiro: 1937)

L. Rego, 'Notas sobre a Geologia do Estado do Maranhão', *Revista do Museu Paulista*, v. 21, pp. 1–30 (1937)

G. Rocha, (ed.) *Em Busca do Ouro: Garimpos e Garimpeiros no Brasil*, (São Paulo: Editora Marco Zero, 1984)

E. Salomão, 'Garimpos do Ouro do Médio Tapajós', DOCEGEO (Belém: 1980)

E. Salomão, 'Garimpos: O Começo do Fim de um Conceito', *Ciências da Terra*, no. 8, pp. 38–9 (1983)

E. Salomão, 'O Ofício e a Condição de Garimpar', in Rocha (ed.) op. cit. pp. 35–86 (1984)

E. Salomão and J. Machado, 'Depoimento á Comissão das Minas e Energia do Congresso Nacional, 21.8.85', Departamento de Taquigrafia, Congresso Nacional (Brasília: 1985)

B. Santos, *Amazônia: Potencial Mineral e Perspectivas de Desenvolvimento* (São Paulo: Editora da Universidade de São Paulo, 1981)

C. Sarmento, 'Desenvolvimento da Mineração de Ouro', *Mineração e Metalurgia*, v. 40, no. 379, pp. 29–38 (1976)

M. Schmink, 'Land Conflicts in Amazonia', *American Ethnologist*, v. 9, no. 2, pp. 341–357 (1982)

M. Schmink, 'Social Change in the Garimpo', in Hemming (ed.) op. cit., pp. 185–200 (1985)

M. Schmink, 'Social Conflict in the Garimpo', Center for Latin American Studies, University of Florida – Gainesville (ms.) (1987a)

M. Schmink, 'Ourilândia and Cuca: The New Eldorado', Center for Latin American Studies, University of Florida – Gainesville (ms.) (1987b)

H. Shearer and H. Souza, 'Araguaia – Recursos Minerais', DNPM Boletim no. 61 (Rio de Janeiro: 1944)

A. Silva, 'Considerações sobre as Mineralizações Auríferas da Região do Tapajós', in MME–DNPM (1982) op. cit. *PEGB-Palestras e Trabalhos*.

H. Souza, 'Sobre o Distrito Aurífero de Alto Maracassumé – Médio Gurupí – Montes Aureos', DNPM (Rio de Janeiro: 1935a)

H. Souza, 'Faiscação no Estado do Maranhão', DNPM (Rio de Janeiro: 1935b)

H. Souza, 'Relatório sobre Algumas Jazidas de Ouro no Maranhão', DNPM (Rio de Janeiro: 1936)

H. Souza, 'Algumas Conclusões do Trabalho de Prospecção das Bacias Auríferas dos Rios Piriá, Gurupy, Maracassumé e Outros', DNPM (Rio de Janeiro: 1937)

H. Souza, 'Ouro na Serra de Jacobina, Bahia', DNPM (Rio de Janeiro: 1942)

D. Stone, *Gold Diggers and Gold Digging: A Photographic Study of Gold in Australia 1854–1920* (Melbourne: Lansdowne Press, 1974)

SUDEMA (Superintendência do Desenvolvimento do Maranhão) 'Projeto Ouro: Aurizona, Ilha de Pirocauá – Relatório de Viagem', São Luís (1971a)

SUDEMA 'Projeto Ouro: Município de Turiaçú – Relatório de Viagem', São Luís (1971b)

D. Sweet, 'A Rich Realm of Nature Destroyed: The Middle Amazon Valley 1640–1750', Ph.D. thesis, University of Wisconsin (1974)

P. Viana, 'Como Conciliar os Garimpos e a Mineração', *Minérios: Extração e Processamento*, no. 92, pp. 25–28 (1984)

J. Viveiros, 'A Revolta dos Pretos', *Cidade de Pinheiro* 28 August 1955, no. 1676 (1955)

B. Weinstein, *The Amazon Rubber Boom 1850–1920* (Stanford: Stanford University Press, 1983)

C. Willig, 'O Garimpo e as Empresas de Mineração', *Mineração e Metalurgia*, v. 42, no. 409, pp. 36–42 (1979)

Index